The House of Life

BOOKS BY PAUL BROOKS

ROADLESS AREA

THE PURSUIT OF WILDERNESS

THE HOUSE OF LIFE

SPEAKING FOR NATURE

TWO PARK STREET

The House of Life

RACHEL CARSON
AT WORK

WITH

SELECTIONS FROM HER WRITINGS

PUBLISHED AND UNPUBLISHED

BY

PAUL BROOKS

Illustrated

HOUGHTON MIFFLIN COMPANY BOSTON

For information about permission to reproduce selections from
this book, write to Permissions, Houghton Mifflin Company,
2 Park Street, Boston, Massachusetts 02108.

ISBN 0–395–13517–6
ISBN 0–395–51742–7 (pbk.)

Library of Congress Catalog Card Number: 72–173777

Printed in the United States of America

D 10 9 8 7 6 5 4 3 2 1

The author gratefully acknowledges permission to reprint selections from
the published works of Rachel Carson, as follows:

"Undersea," originally published in *The Atlantic Monthly*, September
1937. Copyright 1937 by Rachel L. Carson; copyright © renewed 1965 by
Roger Christie.

Under the Sea-Wind. Copyright 1941 by Rachel L. Carson; copyright ©
renewed 1969 by Roger Christie. Reprinted by permission of Oxford University Press, Inc.

The Sea Around Us. Copyright © 1950, 1951, 1961 by Rachel L. Carson. Reprinted by permission of Oxford University Press, Inc.

The Edge of the Sea. Copyright © 1955 by Rachel L. Carson. Reprinted by permission of Houghton Mifflin Company.

"Our Ever-Changing Shore," originally published in *Holiday*, July 1958.
Copyright © 1958 by Rachel Carson.

Silent Spring. Copyright © 1962 by Rachel L. Carson. Reprinted by permission of Houghton Mifflin Company.

The Sense of Wonder. Copyright © 1956 by Rachel L. Carson. Reprinted by permission of Harper and Row.

Grateful acknowledgment is also made to Harcourt Brace Jovanovich,
Inc. for permission to quote from "The Dry Salvages" in *Four Quartets*,
copyright, 1943, by T. S. Eliot.

~~~~~~~~

The river is within us, the sea is all about us;
The sea is the land's edge also, the granite
Into which it reaches, the beaches where it tosses
Its hints of earlier and other creation:
The starfish, the horseshoe crab, the whale's backbone;
The pool where it offers to our curiosity
The more delicate algae and the sea anemone.
. . . .
. . . The sea has many voices . . .
. . . .
The distant rote in the granite teeth . . .
. . . .
And under the oppression of the silent fog
The tolling bell
Measures time not our time, rung by the unhurried
Ground swell . . .
. . . .
When time stops and time is never ending;
And the ground swell, that is and was from the beginning,
Clangs
The bell.

> T. S. Eliot, from "The Dry Salvages,"
> *Four Quartets*

ACKNOWLEDGMENTS

THE SUGGESTION for this book was made to me by Marie Rodell, Rachel Carson's literary agent, close friend, and trustee of her literary estate. Mrs. Rodell's knowledge and support have been indispensable.

Though Miss Carson's letters and other writings are the main source of the narrative, I have supplemented them with reminiscences of those who knew her before the year 1950, when my own friendship with her began. Shirley Briggs, her constant companion during their years together in the U.S. Fish and Wildlife Service, generously provided me not only with anecdotes of those days but with notes made at the time; for the picture of Rachel in postwar Washington, I am largely indebted to her. Bob Hines and Dorothy Algire, both close friends and professional colleagues, were kind enough to read the manuscript and add their comments. Others helpful for this period were Ira N. Gabrielson, then chief of the Fish and Wildlife Service, Mrs. Herbert Zim, then on the staff of Simon and Schuster, and Louis J. Halle, who has provided an eloquent pen portrait of Rachel at this time in her life.

Clarence Cottam, Rachel Carson's staunch supporter throughout her career, kindly gave me permission to quote from his correspondence and checked my account of the events in which he took such an important part.

I wish to thank Edith Oliver of *The New Yorker* for sharing her memories of Rachel and for reading the manuscript; Mrs. Curtis Bok for giving permission to quote from Judge Bok's correspondence; Marjorie Spock and Mary Richards for material on the Long Island lawsuit, in which they were the prime movers; Frank Graham for sharing notes made during the writing of *Since Silent Spring*; Paul Knight for allowing me to print passages from his unpublished account of the *Silent Spring* controversy; William H. Drury, Jr., for expert advice in my treatment of the pesticides problem and the fundamental issues involved therein.

Rachel's lifelong friend and admirer, Edwin Way Teale, provided insights such as one might expect only from a fellow writer of wisdom and humor.

For providing facts about various aspects of Rachel Carson's career, I wish to thank Philip Sterling, Ruth Swisshelm, Ann Cottrell Free, Lillian Moore, Nada Kramar, Dr. Wilhelm C. Hueper, Dr. Morton S. Biskind, Harold S. Peters, Mrs. Thomas Duff, Dr. Duncan Howlett.

Rachel's devoted niece, Mrs. Virginia King, who grew up in the Carson household, was kind enough to read the manuscript, as was Mrs. Jeanne Davis, who became so much more than a secretary during the final years.

By allowing me to read and quote from her many and always intimate letters from Rachel Carson, Dorothy Freeman Rand has given this book a dimension that it would otherwise have lacked. I am most grateful for her trust and confidence.

As always, my wife's editorial judgment has been essential at every stage in the project.

Finally, my thanks to Mary Kelly, who typed the manuscript and kept innumerable papers under control.

PREFACE

RACHEL CARSON was a very private person. When after some fifteen years as a relatively obscure government employee, she suddenly found herself famous, she became "acutely aware of the public's prying curiosity about an author's life." As those who knew her best agree, the last thing she would have wanted published after her death would be a book designed to satisfy that curiosity. I have not attempted to write a personal biography. Her professional life, however, is another matter. Anyone interested in how good books are written — particularly in that difficult and ever more crucial area of scientific interpretation for the general reader — should find it an enlightening experience to watch Rachel Carson at work. So should anyone concerned with the origins of the environmental revolution which is now sweeping our country and the world.

The present volume has a twofold purpose: to present a selection of Rachel Carson's best writing, both published and unpublished, and to show — whenever possible in her own words — how she achieved what she did. Material from her personal papers will illustrate the meticulous research, the courage in the face of adversity and opposition, the poet's gift for language which, taken together, made her books such an effective union of science and literature.

These books were five in number: *Under the Sea-Wind*, 1941; *The Sea Around Us*, 1951; *The Edge of the Sea*, 1955; *Silent Spring*, 1962; and *The Sense of Wonder*, 1965.*

Rachel Carson also wrote a number of newspaper and magazine articles, in addition to her professional publications for the U.S. Fish and Wildlife Service, where she was employed from 1935 to 1952. Many of these come under the head of journalism; some are of more permanent value. From the latter, and from a number of speeches that she delivered in her later years, I have chosen whatever seems to be of lasting interest, or to be immediately relevant to the development of her career. (A complete bibliography of published work will be found at the back of the book.) Some early unpublished sketches have also been included.

Selections from Rachel Carson's letters, largely unpublished, form the basis of the connecting narrative. Much of her correspondence deals of course with routine publishing matters or consists of replies to the deluge of mail that descended on her when she became a best-selling author. Yet here and there is a letter, or perhaps just a paragraph or two, that reveals more about her attitude toward her life and work than any formal statement. From her personal correspondence, I have (as she would have wished) chosen sparingly, printing only such passages as bear directly or indirectly on her writing.

The relative amount of space given to passages from the books compared to biographical narrative varies with the nature of the material. I have included generous selections from the first — and initially unsuccessful — book, *Under the Sea-Wind*; for despite the fact that the re-issue was a best seller, it remains her least known major work. On the other hand, the actual events of her life during these early years are not of great public concern. By contrast, *Silent Spring* was written long after she had become a public figure. Owing to the nature of the subject, the controversial issues involved, and the handicaps faced by the author,

* Published posthumously; written as a magazine article in 1956.

the story of its creation and its impact is almost inseparable from the book itself, and deserves to be told at some length.

Though Rachel Carson's last book, *Silent Spring*, may have changed the course of history, she was not at heart a crusader; once in a lifetime, she remarked, was enough. I have sought here to stress her achievements as an author rather than as a prophet. Yet fully to appreciate her work one should remember that, in her intense feeling for man's relationship to the living world around him, she was ahead of her time. When she began writing, the term "environment" had few of the connotations it has today. Conservation was not yet a political force. To the public at large the word "ecology" — derived from the Greek for "habitation" — was unknown, as was the concept it stood for. This concept, however, is central to everything that Rachel Carson wrote. Few of us have dwelt with such awareness and understanding in the house of life.

Seventeen years after the first publication of *The House of Life*, at this time of unprecedented environmental concern, we find in the career and achievements of Rachel Carson two heartening facts: the vital role that literature can play in interpreting the natural world, and the enduring ability of one dedicated individual to make an impact on society. The first is illustrated by her three great books dealing with the sea, the second by the extraordinary power of her last and most influential book, *Silent Spring*.

In 1972, when this biography appeared, *Silent Spring* was just ten years old. It had already done much to change prevailing attitudes toward our natural surroundings. "A few thousand words from her," declared one editorial writer about Rachel Carson, "and the world took a new direction." One of the nation's most effective environmentalists, Supreme Court Justice William O. Douglas, predicted that *Silent Spring* would become "the most important chronicle of this century for the human race." Time will tell. But there is no question that it did much to spark the environmental movement, to convince us that our own welfare is dependent on the health of the environment as a whole. It led to the creation of new agencies in the federal government to oversee the use of agricultural poisons; it also led to much needed legislation to ensure that these regulations were enforced. Yet if Rachel Carson were alive today — she died a year and a half after *Silent Spring* was published — she would be the first to realize how much remains to be done. Controls are still inadequate. Greater quantities of pesticides are being produced now than when she wrote, and there has been a huge growth in the use of toxic petrochemicals. Even the notorious DDT, banned for use in the United States, can still be legally manufactured for export (an interesting moral decision), and is finding its way back on produce imported from other countries.

One could write volumes about the inadequacy of the government's regulations, and about its failure to implement those that do exist. But there is a positive side to the picture. Thanks to Rachel Carson, thanks to the countless numbers who have thought and felt as she did, we are aware as never before of what the human race is doing to the planet as a whole. This is not a local or national issue; it is worldwide, as she well knew. But when she suggested that the pesticides we were using so freely might spread to the uttermost parts of the earth, she was ridiculed by her detractors; such an assumption, they claimed, was obviously nonsense and proved that her work was unscientific. Later they learned differently, when traces of these poisons were found in the Antarctic ice!

During the half century since Rachel Carson started writing for publication, there has been a dramatic change in the way most of us think about the natural world. We have come to recognize what the scientists — particularly those we now know as ecologists — have been telling us all along. The furious controversy that immediately followed the publication of *Silent Spring* has slowly subsided as the facts that she set forth so eloquently have been proven abundantly true. Not even her bitterest opponents can any longer call her a "hysterical woman." If anything, she understated the case. Although spokesmen for the chemical industry have continued to denigrate her findings, the involvement of the general public in the battle to save the environment is far greater than ever before. In the words of Shirley Briggs, head of the Rachel Carson Council: "Into the fray have come the many ordinary people, neither scientists nor industrialists, who see both their own lives and the future of their children at stake."

The specific changes that have been made as a result of *Silent Spring* are obvious. Less easy to document, but even more fundamental, is our growing sense of responsibility for the welfare of a world that we now have the power to save or to destroy. Rachel Carson's concerns are more relevant today than they were when she wrote her epoch-making book. Though her immediate subject was the poisoning of our environment with lethal chemicals, the implications of what she was saying are boundless. What she did in *Silent Spring*, what so infuriated and frightened her detractors, was to question the basic irresponsibility of an industrial, technological society toward the natural world. That was her heresy. That is why her work endures.

CONTENTS

ILLUSTRATIONS

The House of Life

CHAPTER 1

THE WRITER AND HIS SUBJECT

WRITING is a lonely occupation at best," said Rachel Carson in accepting the Achievement Award of the American Association of University Women. "Of course there are stimulating and even happy associations with friends and colleagues, but during the actual work of creation the writer cuts himself off from all others and confronts his subject alone. He moves into a realm where he has never been before — perhaps where no one has ever been. It is a lonely place, and even a little frightening . . .

"No writer can stand still. He continues to create or he perishes. Each task completed carries its own obligation to go on to something new."

In her own writing, Rachel Carson was at once a daring adventurer and a meticulous craftsman: the stonemason who never lost sight of the cathedral. A modest person, she was bold enough to choose as the subject for her first major work nothing less than the sea itself. How she dealt with it is suggested in a letter she wrote five years after publication of *The Sea Around Us.* "The writer must never attempt to impose himself upon his subject. He must not try to mold it according to what he believes his readers or editors want to read. His initial task is to come to know his subject intimately, to understand its every aspect, to let it fill his mind. Then at some turning point the subject takes command and the true act of creation begins . . . The discipline of the writer is to learn to be still and listen to what his subject has to tell him." The establishment of the proper relationship between author and subject, she felt, was where "the real agony of writing is experienced. At best, one can achieve it only sometimes, and in those moments one knows that something important has happened."

Rachel Carson never published any formal statement about the writer's art. But here and there in her correspondence one finds such comments. Particularly revealing, in respect to her own life and work, is her reply to a fan letter from a college girl with whom she obviously felt a special rapport — a girl who had found her only real childhood happiness in her love of nature, and who was hoping to combine a writing and a scientific career: "Yes, I think we do have a great many things in common . . . You recognize clearly the field that is your own, and in which you have the magic combination of factual knowledge and deeply felt emotional response. And you are aware, too, of how your understanding may be clarified and deepened through further study, as in geology and archeology. In all this I think you are more clear-sighted than I was at your age . . . I think there is little danger that advanced scientific work will turn you into a dull writer; instead, it should feed and nourish those qualities that shine so clearly in your writing now." Again and again in various contexts one finds the comment that writing is a lonely business. "And I think you are wise enough to understand that being 'a little lonely' is not a bad thing. A writer's occupation is one of the loneliest in the world, even if the loneliness is only an inner solitude and isolation, for that he must have at times if he is to be truly creative. And so I believe only the person who knows and is not afraid of loneliness should aspire to be a writer. But there are also rewards that are rich and peculiarly satisfying — as, for example, a letter such as yours . . .

"Given the initial talent . . . writing is largely a matter of application and hard work, of writing and rewriting endlessly until you are satisfied that you have said what you want to say as clearly and simply as possible. For me, that usually means many, many revisions. If you write what you yourself sincerely think and feel and are interested in, the chances are very high that you will interest other people as well."

As she pointed out in her speech accepting the National Book Award,* there is no such thing as a separate literature of science, since after all the aim of science is to discover and illuminate the truth, which is also the aim of all true literature. She was opposed to "scientific books for young people, in which the author feels he has to write down to a supposed level of comprehension. I feel that if the author has something to say, and says it clearly, an intelligent reader of almost any age will understand him." While maintaining the highest professional standards, she wrote for the general public, and she avoided technical jargon. "My relation to technical scientific writing has been that of one who understands the language but does not use it." She was quite properly furious (though always polite) with editors who undertook to rewrite selections from her work. "It is my firm position, and one that I have stated before, that I will not knowingly permit any editor of any anthology to take liberties with my text." Or as she wrote with amazing restraint to the director of a university "reading laboratory" who had watered down a passage from The Sea Around Us for eighth grade use: "I have, I confess, rather strong and definite prejudice against altering an author's words when excerpts from his writings are reprinted. A quotation, in my probably old-fashioned view, should be a quotation."

In her use of words, as in most aspects of her life, Rachel Carson was a perfectionist. She did not write easily. "I wonder why it is so much easier and so much more pleasant to write a letter

* For the text of this speech, see page 127.

than to do something that is going to be bound between the pages of a book," she wrote to her friend Judge Curtis Bok. "When I read your books I knew that you must suffer as much over your writing as I. Those exquisitely turned phrases, the thoughts that seem to flow with such ease, are achieved only at the cost of prolonged anguish, as I know too well!"

On a "very good day," she might do fifteen hundred words; the average was nearer five hundred. "I am a slow writer, enjoying the stimulating pursuit of research far more than the drudgery of turning out manuscript." From her own painful experience, she was prepared to give one bit of definite advice to a friend who was considering a book project. "Don't set up an impossible time schedule." This inevitably led to a sense of failure, a need for excuses, a feeling of having let people down. "The important thing is to get under way, to see it growing and developing in its own way, at its own pace, but always going on. Never mind how long it takes, or what anyone else expects."

Her first drafts were generally in longhand; she would revise and revise until she was satisfied with the result, which always had to pass the final test of being read aloud to her, as she listened "for passages where disharmonies of sound might distract attention from the thought." When she read E. B. White's piece on Will Strunk in *The New Yorker*, she wrote to him: "I was delighted to find you saying that you 'write by ear, always with difficulty, and seldom with any exact notion of what is taking place under the hood.' This describes my method, or lack of one, precisely." She may have lacked method, but she was impatient with poor editing and sloppy syntax. She concluded one book review: "Often it is difficult to hear what the author is saying because of the tumult of verbs at war with their subjects, and of 'sentences' that are only a confused tangle of phrases lacking sometimes a subject, sometimes a predicate. E. B. White once remarked that 'English usage is sometimes sheer luck, like getting across a street.' The trouble is that witnessing so many traffic accidents makes the reader apprehensive, and unable to keep his mind on the subject."

Like most writers, she required seclusion and freedom from distractions. "My best hours for writing are late at night, and whenever I could get an uninterrupted period of time for working on *The Sea* I would work most of each night and sleep in the mornings. There was usually a volume of Thoreau's Journal or of Richard Jefferies' nature essays beside my bed, and I would relax my mind by reading a few pages before turning out the light. As might be expected, such great sea books as Tomlinson's *The Sea and the Jungle,** Beston's *Outermost House,* and *Moby Dick* are all favorite volumes."

Rachel Carson's choice of reading seems to have been closely related to her own professional career. She particularly admired the English writer, Henry Williamson, author of *Tarka the Otter* and *Salar the Salmon.* "So you, too, love Henry Williamson!" she wrote to a friend and fellow author who had praised *Under the Sea-Wind.* "He has influenced my writing more than anyone else, and to have you link my book with his is the greatest tribute you could possibly pay it." Her other great enthusiasm among living writers was closer to home. "I wonder whether you know Henry Beston's *Outermost House!* I have a feeling you would love it. That, and the two Williamson books, are the volumes I would most certainly grab for the proverbial sojourn on a desert island. The Beston work is the story of a year the author spent living alone in a little house on an isolated Cape Cod beach. It is written with great simplicity and beauty, and with a feeling for the great rhythms of nature." Reviewing reprint editions of *Tarka the Otter* and *The Outermost House,* she recalled her dis-

---

* "Last night," she wrote to a friend in 1957, "I read a lot in Tomlinson — wishing all the while that you were here and we could read it sentence by sentence and talk about it. I seem to get some new meaning or significance each time I read him." On another occasion, referring to a description of a sunset in *The Sea and the Jungle,* she wrote: "The whole passage is really sublime." Again: "Do you know Tomlinson's *The Lost Wood?* Written a generation ago, but applicable to so much of modern life."

covery of both volumes "in a far corner of the Pratt Library in Baltimore years ago. Since then I have read and reread them more times than I can count; they are among the books that I have loved best and that have influenced me most." Her comment on Williamson's achievement in *Tarka* reflects her own goal in writing her first book, *Under the Sea-Wind*: "He enters into the life of the otter, sees with its eyes, follows and portrays the moving drama of its everyday life." *The Outermost House* had first been published the year before Rachel Carson graduated from college. As she later wrote to the author (see page 161), it was a book she returned to again and again with renewed enjoyment. The feeling was clearly reciprocated, since Beston's review of *Under the Sea-Wind*, was particularly sympathetic and perceptive.

Though she was a great admirer of popular poems that expressed "the eternal fascination and the irresistible call of the sea," such as John Masefield's *Sea Fever* and *Roadways*, her choices were not always the obvious ones. "It is interesting to find that the same yearning pervades one of the earliest works of English literature, a wonderful old poem called *The Seafarer* that dates probably from the 8th Century. Its unknown author evidently had known the terrors of shipwreck on lonely shores, where

> *I heard only*
> *The roar of the sea, ice-cold waves, and the song of the swan;*
> *For pastime the gannets' cry served me; the kittiwakes chatter*
> *For laughter of men.*

But in spite of this bitter knowledge, he feels 'always a longing, a yearning uneasiness,' to wander again 'over the tide, o'er the home of the whale.' "

In the writings of Joseph Conrad, she felt that his awareness of the sea occurred in its purest form in one of his less known works, *The Mirror of the Sea*. "The great waves and the converse of wind and water over the wide spaces of ocean have never been more magnificently described." Another source of inspiration (unlikely to be found in English literature courses) was the highly practical yet intrinsically romantic publications of the Government Printing Office, the "Coast Pilots and Sailing Directions" for the guidance of mariners. "The directions for the least known, least traveled coasts always seem to me the most rewarding reading, along with those for particularly dangerous waters. The Alaska Pilot and the directions for Norway, the Shetlands and Orkneys, and some of the arctic and sub-arctic islands have delighted me especially. In fact, I can think of few better vehicles for arm-chair traveling. Many of the descriptions of dangerous reefs and forbidding shores might almost have come out of Conrad. There is the sense of the sea's power and its capacity for doing the unexpected. And there is always the reminder of how little we know, and of the mystery that is eternally the sea's."

Rachel Carson herself never needed that reminder. The more she learned of the natural world, the greater became her "sense of wonder." As a writer she used words to reveal the poetry — which is to say the essential truth and meaning — at the core of any scientific fact. She sought the knowledge that is essential to appreciate the extent of the unknown. She never worried lest the scientific discipline in which she was trained would dull her pen; *mutatis mutandis*, she was not ashamed of her emotional response to the forces of nature. When a friend confessed to being deeply moved by the "heart-stopping sight" of a flight of wildfowl above the spruces on the Maine coast, she replied: "Don't ever dream I wondered at your tears. I've had the same response too often — perhaps always when alone. (I suppose there is a certain inhibition in the presence of anyone else . . .) The experience I relate in *Under the Sea-Wind* about the young mullet pouring through that tide race to the sea is one that comes to mind . . . I didn't tell it as a personal experience, but it was — I stood knee-deep in that racing water and at times could scarcely see those darting, silver bits of life for my tears."

Though she had the broad view of the ecologist who studies the infinitely complex web of relationships between living things and their environment, she did not concern herself exclusively with the great impersonal forces of nature. She felt a spiritual as well as physical closeness to the individual creatures about whom she wrote: a sense of identification that is an essential element in her literary style. (One thinks of Henry Thoreau, who felt wiser in all respects for knowing that there was a minnow in the brook: "Methinks I have need even of his sympathy, and to be his fellow in a degree.") If I myself had to choose a single revealing moment during a long friendship with her, it would be shortly after dusk one July evening at her Maine cottage, while she was working on *The Edge of the Sea.* We had spent an hour after supper examining minute sea creatures under her brightly lit binocular microscope: tube worms, rhythmically projecting and withdrawing their pink, fanlike tentacles in search of invisible food; tiny snails on fronds of seaweed; flowerlike hydroids; green sponges whose ancestry goes back to the earliest record of life on earth. At last we were finished. Then, pail and flashlight in hand, she stepped carefully over the kelp-covered rocks to return the living creatures to their home. This, I think, is what Albert Schweitzer (to whom *Silent Spring* is dedicated) meant by "reverence for life." In one form or another it lies behind everything that Rachel Carson wrote.

Though the Fish and Wildlife Service, for which she worked for so many years, was closely associated with the hunting fraternity, Rachel Carson had little sympathy with blood sports. When she detected in the writing of others what she considered a "glorification of cruelty," she was moved to cold anger. ". . . until we have courage to recognize cruelty for what it is — whether its victim is human or animal — we cannot expect things to be much better in the world. There can be no double standard. We cannot have peace among men whose hearts find delight in killing any living creature. By every act that glorifies or even tolerates such moronic delight in killing, we set back the progress of humanity."

Though she would probably have recoiled at the term "nun of nature" that has sometimes been applied to her, her attitude toward the natural world was that of a deeply religious person. When an elderly fundamentalist accused her of ignoring God and the Bible in writing *The Sea Around Us*, she took the trouble to reply to him at length. "It is true that I accept the theory of evolution as the most logical one that has ever been put forward to explain the development of living creatures on this earth. As far as I am concerned, however, there is absolutely no conflict between a belief in evolution and a belief in God as the creator. Believing as I do in evolution, I merely believe that is the method by which God created, and is still creating, life on earth. And it is a method so marvelously conceived that to study it in detail is to increase — and certainly never to diminish — one's reverence and awe both for the Creator and the process." (She put the matter more succinctly on another occasion, when her mother reminded her that the Bible tells us God created the world. Yes, Rachel replied, and General Motors created her Oldsmobile, but *how* is the question.)

With the coming of the atomic age, Rachel felt that certain deep convictions she had cherished since childhood were being threatened. This realization had a direct effect on her writing career. Following the success of *The Sea Around Us* and *The Edge of the Sea*, she had hoped to write a book on the origins of Life and the relation of Life to the physical environment. But, as she herself recognized, she was mentally blocked by an unwillingness to accept some of the implications of the scientific revolution that had occurred during the previous decade. "Some of the thoughts that came were so unattractive to me that I rejected them completely, for the old ideas die hard, especially when they

are emotionally as well as intellectually dear to one. It was pleasant to believe, for example, that much of Nature was forever beyond the tampering reach of man: he might level the forests and
dam the streams, but the clouds and the rain and the wind were
God's . . . It was comforting to suppose that the stream of life
would flow on through time in whatever course that God had
appointed for it — without interference by one of the drops of
the stream, man. And to suppose that, however the physical environment might mold Life, that Life could never assume the
power to change drastically — or even destroy — the physical
world.

"These beliefs have almost been part of me for as long as I
have thought about such things. To have them even vaguely
threatened was so shocking that, as I have said, I shut my mind
— refused to acknowledge what I couldn't help seeing. But that
does no good, and I have now opened my eyes and my mind. I
may not like what I see, but it does no good to ignore it, and it's
worse than useless to go repeating the old 'eternal verities' that
are no more eternal than the hills of the poets. So it seems time
someone wrote of Life in the light of the truth as it now appears
to us."

The book was never written. But the sense of outrage at
man's heedless tampering with nature, the unwelcome awareness
that it was now possible literally to destroy the physical world,
undoubtedly played a part in Rachel Carson's ultimate decision
to write Silent Spring. It also gave to that epoch-making work a
moral conviction which intensified the impact of its scientific
facts.

If the world she believed in had changed, so had she. The
woman who reacted with monumental calm and apparent indifference to both the abuse and the praise that followed publication of Silent Spring was obviously a long distance from the
shy girl who had gone to work for the Bureau of Fisheries twenty-
six years earlier. Though her colleagues in that government office

remember her as professionally imperturbable, and though from the start she had confidence in the quality of her own work, it was the dramatic success of *The Sea Around Us* that forced her to accept the role of a public figure. This did not come easily. But once overboard, she knew she had to swim. Speaking engagements and the glare of publicity gradually lost their terror. She enjoyed the honors and awards, the tributes that poured in from all over the world, and not least the money — for by this time family obligations and illnesses had driven her deeply into debt. (Like many successful writers, she had no difficulty in developing a business sense; her correspondence shows that she soon became aware of what her work was worth in the literary marketplace.) During all the excitement over *The Sea Around Us,* her agent recalls, she lost twenty pounds; by the time *Silent Spring* came along, she was used to being a celebrity and took it all in her stride.

Yet never did she take her success — or the response of her readers — for granted. She would drive to her cottage in Maine with a carload of fan mail, determined to answer as many letters personally as her time and strength allowed. A request for help or advice always got her attention, whether from another professional writer checking some technical point or from a ninety-year-old lady who described herself as "an ardent amateur follower of beaches" seeking a peaceful spot remote from sunbathers. Particularly touching is the voluminous correspondence with a blind girl of literary ambitions, hospitalized with what turned out to be an incurable disease. She had written the author after listening to *The Edge of the Sea* on Talking Books.

"I hope you can realize the very deep and lasting pleasure your letter gave me," Rachel Carson replied. "In my writing I have always tried not to lean on illustrations (of which most of my books have had few) but to create in words an image that would register clearly on the eyes of the mind. You make me feel I may have succeeded." Later, when they had become very intimate by mail, the girl sent her a manuscript to criticize. Rachel Carson wrote: "I especially loved the part where you reconstructed your surroundings merely from sounds. I have always believed the sense of sound was greatly neglected. (For that matter, most of our senses are!) I have always liked just to be still and listen, sometimes deliberately shutting my eyes to exclude what I might see . . ." She cited a passage in one of her booklets on the wildlife refuges* and went on to suggest that description through sounds could be "a whole chapter in a book you write some day. Think about it now."

Those who met Rachel Carson only after she had become famous may have difficulty in envisaging the young editor whose humor and sense of fun enlivened the long hours of government routine; who ruefully remarked that she would have to stop taking part in office hoaxes now that she was in the public eye. But no one who knew her — and particularly who had explored a beach or tide pool with her — could fail to sense a youthful enthusiasm, a sense of adventure that, to the end of her life, turned the humblest trip into a voyage of discovery.

The final phase of Rachel Carson's life was at once the saddest and the most splendid. Her last book, *Silent Spring,* is obviously the product of immense labor and talent. Less apparent is the fact that it represents an act — a series of acts — of amazing moral courage. First, there was the hard decision to give up all else and tackle the grim subject of pesticides. There was the foreknowledge that she would be personally attacked and ridiculed. But transcending all this, known to virtually no one at the time or since, was the lonely battle against a whole "catalogue of illnesses" (as she later put it) which in retrospect make the completion of the book seem almost a miracle. She knew the importance of what she was doing. In fighting against the poisoning of

* See *Mattamuskeet,* page 106.

the earth, she was standing up for everything she most valued. Somewhere she found the strength for this final effort. Not only that, but she managed to make this book about death a celebration of life.

As she neared completion of the manuscript of *Silent Spring*, Rachel Carson wrote to a close friend: "No, I myself never thought the ugly facts would dominate, and I hope they don't. The beauty of the living world I was trying to save has always been uppermost in my mind — that, and anger at the senseless, brutish things that were being done. I have felt bound by a solemn obligation to do what I could — if I didn't at least try I could never again be happy in nature. But now I can believe I have at least helped a little. It would be unrealistic to believe one book could bring a complete change."

It may have been unrealistic, but history has proved it true.

CHAPTER 2

TWO CURRENTS MEET

IN HER DEMEANOR, as in her writing, Rachel Carson had what a friend termed "a classic quality." Whatever the circumstances, she always seemed to have the situation, and herself, under firm control. Her quiet manner, her subdued voice and curiously uninflected speech, gave an impression of reserve. As she said of herself, she had "no small talk." Her conversation was to the point. When she spoke in public, it was from a prepared text, never off the cuff; her delivery was always calm and matter-of-fact.

This public image of a very withdrawn person must be set against the private view of her family and her closest associates. With them she could be gay and unbend. Her niece Virginia Williams (Mrs. L. L. King), who was a member of the Carson household from early childhood until her marriage, recalls that "Rachel was more like an older sister; she was a lot of fun, and certainly made a happy home for us. She was also someone we could turn to in time of trouble, and she never failed us."

Yet it has been shrewdly said that, with the exception of her mother and her intimate friend and Maine neighbor, Dorothy Freeman, Rachel Carson never gave herself completely to anyone — she had something for each. One finds a possible explanation in her own comment about her relationship with her family and her friends: "The few who understood the creative problem were not people to whom I felt emotionally close; those who loved the non-writer part of me did not, by some strange paradox, understand the writer at all!"

When *The Sea Around Us* was published — without her picture on the jacket — Rachel and her office mates in Washington were amused at the image of the author that it conjured up in many readers' minds: an Amazonian figure, or a sort of female Neptune. She was in fact rather slight, and never very robust. On occasion she had a physical timidity which contrasted with her extraordinary moral courage. But when at work, at her desk or in the field, nothing could stop her. Her colleague Bob Hines, who made the drawings for *The Edge of the Sea*, remembers her wading for hours on end in the icy, barnacle-covered tide pools of the Maine coast, indifferent to the cold, examining her discoveries with a hand lens while her body became numb to the point where she had to be carried ashore.

This tableau of the author in middle age is somehow symbolic; it leads one's eye back to the haunts of her childhood, where she developed her lifelong passion for nature many miles from the sea.

∞∞∞

Rachel Carson was not inclined to talk about herself. But when she became a celebrity, she was quite willing to answer the inevitable questions about her early life, and how she came to settle on her eventual career. The youngest of three children, she was born on May 27, 1907, in Springdale, Pennsylvania, in the lower Allegheny valley.* Her father, Robert Warden Carson, who came from Pittsburgh, had in 1900 bought sixty-five acres on the outskirts of town. Though it was not an active farm, it had cows

* She was christened Rachel Louise Carson, and her early work is signed Rachel L. Carson. Later she dropped the initial.

and horses and chickens and — more important to Rachel — woods and fields to explore. From her earliest days she was encouraged by her mother to become aware of the beauty and the mystery of the natural world. "I can remember no time when I wasn't interested in the out-of-doors and the whole world of nature," she said many years later. "Those interests, I know, I inherited from my mother and have always shared with her. I was rather a solitary child and spent a great deal of time in woods and beside streams, learning the birds and the insects and flowers." She frequently missed school, perhaps because of her mother's extreme solicitude for her health; but she was a bright child, and with her mother's tutoring easily kept up with her classwork, though her childhood friendships doubtless suffered. Mrs. Carson, née Maria McLean, was the daughter of a Presbyterian minister. She was both musical and bookish; a graduate of the Female Seminary in Washington, Pennsylvania, she had a brief career as a schoolteacher before marrying Robert Carson in 1894. She was thirty-seven years old when her second daughter was born.

Rachel herself always loved books, and from earliest childhood she assumed that she was going to be a writer. "I have no idea why. There were no writers in the family. I read a great deal almost from infancy [her mother read out loud to her from the age of two], and I suppose I must have realized someone wrote the books and thought it would be fun to make up stories, too." Her first success came at the age of ten, when she sent a story to the "League" in that famous publication for children, *St. Nicholas* magazine. It won the Silver Badge. "I doubt that any royalty check of recent years has given me as great joy as the notice of that award." She continued to contribute stories and essays. "Perhaps that early experience of seeing my work in print played its part in fostering my childhood dream of becoming a writer." She liked to say that she became a professional at the age of eleven, when an essay about *St. Nicholas*, written for her grammar school English class, was bought by the magazine's advertising department, which paid her three dollars and some cents, at the rate of a penny a word.

Not given to easy friendships, imbued by her mother with intellectual ambition and a sense of her own worth rather than desire for social success, Rachel was noticed at school more by her teachers than by her classmates. But she was respected, and she went her own way. Beside her photograph in her high school yearbook are the following lines:

> *Rachel's like the mid-day sun*
> *Always very bright*
> *Never stops her studying*
> *'Til she gets it right.*

Her dedication to writing continued through high school, and when she entered Pennsylvania College for Women (now Chatham College), with an annual scholarship of one hundred dollars toward her tuition, she became a member of Omega, the literary club, and joined the staff of the college paper. She also assumed that the way to become a writer was to major in English. She was fortunate in having a dedicated teacher who recognized her talent, Professor Grace Croff, whom she referred to many years later as "a wonderful woman who gave my course in English composition and really exerted quite an influence on my life." But by the end of her second year a required course in biology had so fascinated her that she began to wonder whether she didn't want to become a scientist rather than a writer. "I thought I had to be one or the other; it never occurred to me, or apparently to anyone else, that I could combine the two careers." Not till the middle of her junior year did she finally switch to a major in zoology — a decision taken so late in her college course that it meant spending most of her remaining college days in the laboratories. Again she found an exciting teacher, a young woman named Mary Scott Skinker, who became a close personal friend.

In her senior year, Rachel was elected president of the under-graduate science club. At the time she believed that she had abandoned her dream of a literary career; only later did she real-ize that, on the contrary, she had discovered what she wanted to write about. The merging of these two powerful currents — the imagination and insight of a creative writer with a scientist's pas-sion for fact — goes far to explain the blend of beauty and au-thority that was to make her books unique.

There was a long period, however, when she did no writing at all. After graduating magna cum laude from college in 1928, she went on to get an M.A.* in zoology at Johns Hopkins University where she studied genetics under H. S. Jennings and Raymond Pearl.

She taught zoology at Johns Hopkins Summer School and in the winter at the University of Maryland. Most important for her future career were the summers studying at the Woods Hole Marine Biological Laboratory in Massachusetts. Here were sown the seeds of *The Sea Around Us.* Yet the inspiration for that book goes even farther back — back to a childhood yearning for the sea she knew only in books, back to a memorable moment as a college undergraduate: "Years ago on a night when rain and wind beat against the windows of my college dormitory room, a line from *Locksley Hall* burned itself into my mind —

For the mighty wind arises, roaring seaward, and I go.

I can still remember my intense emotional response as that line spoke to something within me, seeming to tell me that my own path led to the sea — which then I had never seen — and that my own destiny was somehow linked with the sea.

* After publication of *Silent Spring*, certain spokesmen for the pesticide industry claimed that Rachel Carson was not a trained biologist. For them should be re-served a special corner in the Library of Hell, equipped with a barnacle-covered bench and a whale-oil lamp, by whose light they would be compelled to read out loud from her master's thesis: "The Development of the Pronephros During the Embryonic and Early Larval Life of the Catfish (*Inctalurus Punctatus*)."

"And so . . . it has been when finally I became its biographer, the sea brought me recognition and what the world calls success."

∽∾∽

Judging from the large and varied collection of rejection slips preserved in her files, Rachel Carson first sought publication as a poet. Beginning not later than her senior year in college, and probably before (most of the form rejections are undated), she submitted verse to *Poetry, The Atlantic Monthly, Good Housekeeping, Woman's Home Companion, The Saturday Evening Post, Century Magazine, American Magazine, The Delineator, The Youth's Companion* and several other periodicals which — like many on this list — live only in fading memory. She was persistent, but apparently wholly unsuccessful. Her first regular professional publication was of a more prosaic sort. In the mid nineteen-thirties she started writing a series of feature articles on fisheries and related themes for the Baltimore Sunday *Sun*. These continued for over five years and made use of material with which she was to become increasingly familiar in the course of her government work. They also served as trial runs for parts of her first book, *Under the Sea-Wind,* to be published in 1941. For example, a short front-page article in the Sunday *Sun* magazine for October 9, 1938 (for which she was paid ten dollars), is entitled "Chesapeake Eels Seek the Sargasso Sea." A few passages are virtually identical with those in chapter 13 of *Under the Sea-Wind,* "Journey to the Sea."

At approximately the same time that she began writing occasional articles for the Sunday *Sun,* Rachel Carson found herself faced with the problem of finding some regular employment. On July 6, 1935, while she was still teaching part time at the University of Maryland and Johns Hopkins Summer School, her father died suddenly. There was little money to support her mother and herself. These were depression years, and jobs were scarce. Fortunately for her, the Bureau of Fisheries in Washington had recently undertaken a series of broadcasts entitled "Romance Under the Waters" (referred to by the staff as "Seven-Minute Fish Tales") and wanted to hire someone on a part-time basis who knew marine biology and could also write. "I happened in one morning," she recalled later, "when the chief of the biology division [Elmer Higgins] was feeling rather desperate — I think at that point he was having to write the scripts himself. He talked to me a few minutes and then said: 'I've never seen a written word of yours, but I'm going to take a sporting chance.' That little job, which eventually led to a permanent appointment as a biologist, was in its way, a turning point."

The following year, Rachel's married sister, Marian Williams, died at the age of forty, leaving two girls of grammar school age, Marjorie and Virginia, to be brought up by Rachel and her mother. In the circumstances, Rachel needed a permanent appointment and an assured salary. The opportunity arose when she learned that a civil service examination was being given for the position of "junior aquatic biologist." She was the only woman competing for the job, and she won the top score. On August 17, 1936, she officially joined the Bureau at a salary of two thousand dollars a year. At Higgins's request, she was assigned to his office. As a lover of the outdoors she found her quarters somewhat confining. The Bureau's offices were on the first floor of the Commerce Building, the only windows facing on the interior court. A colleague remembers her remarking one day, as she peered up trying to get a glimpse of the sky: "It's like working in the bottom of a well." Later she was to have a more spacious office in the Interior Building.

The broadcasts ran for a year; when they were finished, she was asked "to produce something of a general sort about the sea. I set to work, but somehow the material rather took charge of the situation and turned into something that was, perhaps, unusual as a broadcast for the Commissioner of Fisheries. My chief read it and handed it back with a twinkle in his eye. 'I don't think it will do,' he said. 'Better try again. But send this one to the *Atlantic*.' Eventually I did, and the *Atlantic* accepted it. Since then I have told my chief of those days that he was really my first literary agent."

CHAPTER 3

"Undersea"

From *The Atlantic Monthly*, September 1937

WHO HAS known the ocean? Neither you nor I, with our earth-bound senses, know the foam and surge of the tide that beats over the crab hiding under the seaweed of his tide-pool home; or the lilt of the long, slow swells of midocean, where shoals of wandering fish prey and are preyed upon, and the dolphin breaks the waves to breathe the upper atmosphere. Nor can we know the vicissitudes of life on the ocean floor, where the sunlight, filtering through a hundred feet of water, makes but a fleeting, bluish twilight, in which dwell sponge and mollusk and starfish and coral, where swarms of diminutive fish twinkle through the dusk like a silver rain of meteors, and eels lie in wait among the rocks. Even less is it given to man to descend those six incomprehensible miles into the recesses of the abyss, where reign utter silence and unvarying cold and eternal night.

To sense this world of waters known to the creatures of the sea we must shed our human perceptions of length and breadth and time and place, and enter vicariously into a universe of all-pervading water. For to the sea's children nothing is so important as the fluidity of their world. It is water that they breathe; water that brings them food; water through which they see, by filtered sunshine from which first the red rays, then the greens, and finally the purples have been strained; water through which they sense vibrations equivalent to sound. And indeed it is nothing more or less than sea water, in all its varying conditions of temperature, saltiness, and pressure, that forms the invisible barriers that confine each marine type within a special zone of life — one to the shore line, another to some submarine chasm on the far slopes of the continental shelf, and yet another, perhaps, to an imperceptibly defined stratum at mid-depths of ocean.

There are comparatively few living things whose shifting pattern of life embraces both land and sea. Such are the creatures of the tide pools among the rocks and of the mud flats sloping away from dune and beach grass to the water's edge. Between low water and the flotsam and jetsam of the high-tide mark, land and sea wage a never-ending conflict for possession.

As on land the coming of night brings a change over the face of field and forest, sending some wild things into the safe retreat of their burrows and bringing others forth to prowl and forage, so at ebb tide the creatures of the waters largely disappear from sight, and in their place come marauders from the land to search the tide pools and to probe the sands for the silent, waiting fauna of the shore.

Twice between succeeding dawns, as the waters abandon pursuit of the beckoning moon and fall back, foot by foot, periwinkle and starfish and crab are cast upon the mercy of the sands. Every heap of brine-drenched seaweed, every pool forgotten by the retreating sea in recess of sand or rock, offers sanctuary from sun and biting sand.

In the tide pools, seas in miniature, sponges of the simpler kinds encrust the rocks, each hungrily drawing in through its myriad mouths the nutriment-laden water. Starfishes and sea anemones are common dwellers in such rock-girt pools. Shell-less cousins of the snail, the naked sea slugs are spots of brilliant rose and bronze, spreading arborescent gills to the waters, while the tube worms, architects of the tide pools, fashion their conical dwellings of sand grains, cemented one against another in glistening mosaic.

On the sands the clams burrow down in search of coolness and moisture, and oysters close their all-excluding shells and wait for the return of the water. Crabs crowd into damp rock caverns, where periwinkles cling to the walls. Colonies of gnomelike shrimps find refuge under dripping strands of brown, leathery weed heaped on the beach.

Hard upon the retreating sea press invaders from the land. Shore birds patter along the beach by day, and legions of the ghost crab shuffle across the damp sands by night. Chief, perhaps, among the plunderers is man, probing the soft mud flats and dipping his nets into the shallow waters.

At last comes a tentative ripple, then another, and finally the full, surging sweep of the incoming tide. The folk of the pools awake — clams stir in the mud. Barnacles open their shells and begin a rhythmic sifting of the waters. One by one, brilliant-hued flowers blossom in the shallow water as tube worms extend cautious tentacles.

The ocean is a place of paradoxes. It is the home of the great white shark, two-thousand-pound killer of the seas, and of the hundred-foot blue whale, the largest animal that ever lived. It is also the home of living things so small that your two hands might scoop up as many of them as there are stars in the Milky Way. And it is because of the flowering of astronomical numbers of these diminutive plants, known as diatoms, that the surface waters of the ocean are in reality boundless pastures. Every marine animal, from the smallest to the sharks and whales, is ultimately dependent for its food upon these microscopic entities of the vegetable life of the ocean. Within their fragile walls, the sea performs a vital alchemy that utilizes the sterile chemical elements dissolved in the water and welds them with the torch of sunlight into the stuff of life. Only through this little-understood synthesis of proteins, fats, and carbohydrates by myriad plant "producers" is the mineral wealth of the sea made available to the animal "consumers" that browse as they float with the currents. Drifting endlessly, midway between the sea of air above and the depths of the abyss below, these strange creatures and the marine inflorescence that sustains them are called "plankton" — the wanderers.

Many of the fishes, as well as the bottom-dwelling mollusks and worms and starfish, begin life as temporary members of this roving company, for the ocean cradles their young in its surface waters. The sea is not a solicitous foster mother. The delicate eggs and fragile larvae are buffeted by storms raging across the open ocean and preyed upon by diminutive monsters, the hungry glass-worms and comb jellies of the plankton.

These ocean pastures are also the domain of vast shoals of adult fishes: herring, anchovy, menhaden, and mackerel, feeding upon the animals of the plankton and in their turn preyed upon; for here the dogfish hunt in packs, and the ravenous bluefish, like roving buccaneers, take their booty where they find it.

Dropping downward a scant hundred feet to the white sand beneath, an undersea traveler would discover a land where the noonday sun is swathed in twilight blues and purples, and where the blackness of midnight is eerily aglow with the cold phosphorescence of living things. Dwelling among the crepuscular shadows of the ocean floor are creatures whose terrestrial counterparts are drab and commonplace, but which are themselves invested with delicate beauty by the sea. Crystal cones form the shells of pteropods or winged snails that drift downward from the surface to these dim regions by day; and the translucent spires of lovely *Ianthina* are tinged with Tyrian purple.

Other creatures of the sea's bottom may be fantastic rather than beautiful. Spine-studded urchins, like rotund hedgehogs of the sea, tumble over the sands, where mollusks lie with slightly opened shells, busily straining the water for debris. Life flows on monotonously for these passive sifters of the currents, who move little or not at all from year to year. Among the rock ledges, eels and cunners forage greedily, while the lobster feels his way with nimble wariness through the perpetual twilight.

Farther out on the continental shelf, the ocean floor is scarred with deep ravines, perhaps the valleys of drowned rivers, and dotted with undersea plateaus. Hosts of fish graze on these submerged islands, which are richly carpeted with sluggish or sessile forms of life. Chief among the ground fish are haddock, cods, flounders and their mightier relative, the halibut. From these and shallower waters man, the predator, exacts a yearly tribute of nearly thirty billion pounds of fish.

If the underwater traveler might continue to explore the ocean floor, he would traverse miles of level prairie lands; he would ascend the sloping sides of hills; and he would skirt deep and ragged crevasses yawning suddenly at his feet. Through the gathering darkness, he would come at last to the edge of the continental shelf. The ceiling of the ocean would lie a hundred fathoms above him, and his feet would rest upon the brink of a slope that drops precipitously another mile, and then descends more gently into an inky void that is the abyss.

What human mind can visualize conditions in the uttermost depths of the ocean? Increasing with every foot of depth, enormous pressures reach, three thousand fathoms down, the inconceivable magnitude of three tons to every square inch of surface. In these silent deeps a glacial cold prevails, a bleak iciness which never varies, summer or winter, years melting into centuries, and centuries into ages of geologic time. There, too, darkness reigns — the blackness of primeval night in which the ocean came into being, unbroken, through eons of succeeding time, by the gray light of dawn.

It is easy to understand why early students of the ocean believed these regions were devoid of life, but strange creatures have now been dredged from the depths to bear mute and fragmentary testimony concerning life in the abyss.

The "monsters" of the deep sea are small, voracious fishes with gaping, tooth-studded jaws, some with sensitive feelers serving the function of eyes, others bearing luminous torches or lures to search out or entice their living prey. Through the night of the abyss, the flickering lights of these foragers move to and fro. Many of the sessile bottom dwellers glow with a strange radiance suffusing the entire body, while other swimming creatures may have tiny, glittering lights picked out in rows and patterns. The deep-sea prawn and the abyssal cuttlefish eject a luminous cloud, and under cover of this pillar of fire escape from their enemies.

Monotones of red and brown and lusterless black are the prevailing colors in the deep sea, allowing the wearers to reflect the minimum of the phosphorescent gleams, and to blend into the safe obscurity of the surrounding gloom.

On the muddy bottom of the abyss, treacherous oozes threaten to engulf small scavengers as they busily sift the debris for food. Crabs and prawns pick their way over the yielding mud on stiltlike legs; sea spiders creep over sponges raised on delicate stalks above the slime.

Because the last vestige of plant life was left behind in the shallow zone penetrated by the rays of the sun, the inhabitants of these depths contrast strangely with the self-supporting assemblage of the surface waters. Preying one upon another, the abyssal creatures are ultimately dependent upon the slow rain of dead plants and animals from above. Every living thing of the ocean, plant and animal alike, returns to the water at the end of its own life span the materials that had been temporarily assembled to form its body. So there descends into the depths a gentle, never-ending rain of the disintegrating particles of what once were living creatures of the sunlit surface waters, or of those twilight regions beneath.

Here in the sea mingle elements which, in their long and amazing history, have lent life and strength and beauty to a be-

wildering variety of living creatures. Ions of calcium, now free in
the water, were borrowed years ago from the sea to form part of
the protective armor of a mollusk, returned to the main reservoir
when their temporary owner had ceased to have need of them,
and later incorporated into the delicate statuary of a coral reef.
Here are atoms of silica, once imprisoned in a layer of flint in
subterranean darkness; later, within the fragile shell of a diatom,
tossed by waves and warmed by the sun; and again entering into
the exquisite structure of a radiolarian shell, that miracle of
ephemeral beauty that might be the work of a fairy glass-blower
with a snowflake as his pattern.

Except for precipitous slopes and regions swept bare by submarine currents, the ocean floor is covered with primeval oozes in
which there have been accumulating for eons deposits of varied
origin; earth-born materials freighted seaward by rivers or worn
from the shores of continents by the ceaseless grinding of waves;
volcanic dust transported long distances by wind, floating lightly
on the surface and eventually sinking into the depths to mingle
with the products of no less mighty eruptions of submarine volcanoes; spherules of iron and nickel from interstellar space; and
substances of organic origin — the silicious skeletons of Radiolaria and the frustules of diatoms, the limey remains of algae and
corals, and the shells of minute Foraminifera and delicate pelagic
snails.

While the bottoms near the shore are covered with detritus
from the land, the remains of the floating and swimming creatures of the sea prevail in the deep waters of the open ocean.
Beneath tropical seas, in depths of 1000 to 1500 fathoms, calcareous oozes cover nearly a third of the ocean floor; while the
colder waters of the temperate and polar regions release to the
underlying bottom the silicious remains of diatoms and Radiolaria. In the red clay that carpets the great deeps at 3000 fathoms
or more, such delicate skeletons are extremely rare. Among the
few organic remains not dissolved before they reach these cold

and silent depths are the ear bones of whales and the teeth of sharks.

Thus we see the parts of the plan fall into place: the water receiving from earth and air the simple materials, storing them up until the gathering energy of the spring sun wakens the sleeping plants to a burst of dynamic activity, hungry swarms of planktonic animals growing and multiplying upon the abundant plants, and themselves falling prey to the shoals of fish; all, in the end, to be redissolved into their component substances when the inexorable laws of the sea demand it. Individual elements are lost to view, only to reappear again and again in different incarnations in a kind of material immortality. Kindred forces to those which, in some period inconceivably remote, gave birth to that primeval bit of protoplasm tossing on the ancient seas, continue their mighty and incomprehensible work. Against this cosmic background the life span of a particular plant or animal appears, not as a drama complete in itself, but only as a brief interlude in a panorama of endless change.

CHAPTER 4

FIRSTBORN

W HEN A WRITER has become famous, there is never any lack
of persons who, in retrospect, are willing to accept the honor of
having "discovered" a new talent. In the case of Rachel Carson,
the credit for having turned her toward the writing of books is
clearly shared by two prominent figures in the literary world:
Quincy Howe, a distinguished journalist and publisher, and Hendrik Willem van Loon, author of that famous best seller of the
twenties, *The Story of Mankind*. From that first *Atlantic
Monthly* essay Rachel Carson later recalled, "everything else followed. Quincy Howe, then editor for Simon and Schuster, wrote
to ask why I didn't do a book. So did Hendrik Willem van Loon.
My mail had never contained anything so exciting as his first
letter." After a lapse of twenty-five years, the incident was still
vivid in her memory. In 1962 Hendrik van Loon's son Gerard
Willem, gathering material for a biography of his father, wrote
to ask what she could remember about their relationship. "In
September 1937," she replied, "*The Atlantic* published a brief
essay of mine called 'Undersea.' This was my first appearance
in a national magazine. Shortly after its publication Quincy
Howe, then editor of Simon and Schuster, wrote to inquire
whether I had any idea of writing a book — if so, Simon and

Schuster would like to discuss it. Of course I replied at once, saying that although such an idea had not occurred to me I would like to talk about it.*

"Within a week or so a remarkable letter turned up in the mail, its envelope adorned with a bright green seascape from which a blue whale and perhaps a shark or two looked forth. It was of course a letter from your father. He had called Quincy Howe after reading my *Atlantic* essay and told him he must get in touch with its author. Mr. Howe replied that he had already done so and provided my address. Although the first step had been taken by Mr. Howe, the two independently discussed the article. Your father in his first letter urged me to come to Old Greenwich so that he might arrange a meeting with Simon and Schuster. I did spend a memorable two days with the van Loons, during which time Mr. and Mrs. Howe came to dinner. I think I visited in the publisher's offices the following day and then went home to start work on the book [*Under the Sea-Wind*] which everyone seemed to think I should write. This must have happened during the early months of 1938. I am a slow writer and the book was not published until the fall of 1941. In the meantime I had had frequent advice and encouragement from your remarkable father.

"At our first meeting he told me why he had been so interested in the *Atlantic* article. In his various crossings of the ocean he had been so impressed by its apparent lifeless aspect — 'Not a snout nor a spout did I see,' he said to me — yet he knew that under the surface there was life in enormous numbers and variety and he felt an intense curiosity to know more about it. When he

* On July 30, 1951, just before publication of *The Sea Around Us*, Quincy Howe wrote to Miss Carson: "I have been meaning for weeks to write and tell you how much I enjoyed the excerpts from your new book in *The New Yorker* and how pleased I was at the Book-of-the-Month Club Selection. I was proud to find my name mentioned once or twice among your earlier discoverers, but as you and I both know the real credit goes to dear Hendrik van Loon. How he would have purred over your success and what credit he would have taken for it — and deserved . . ." As the record shows Quincy Howe was taking less credit than he himself deserved — a rather uncommon stance in the publishing world.

read the *Atlantic* essay he felt he had found someone who could tell him what he wanted to know. I suspect that the book I wrote for Simon and Schuster, *Under the Sea-Wind,* was only a partial answer. Probably the book he really had in mind was *The Sea Around Us,* published in 1951. I do not remember the year of your father's death but I believe it was before this. Certainly, however, his influence is reflected in that book as well as in the first."

There is little in the record about the actual writing of this first book. Apparently she kept the project very much to herself. A friend and colleague, who was working in the Fisheries Laboratory at Woods Hole during the summer of 1940, knew that she was working on a book, but that was all. "I was getting more and more curious but knew nothing more until the book was published. We were very surprised and tremendously excited."

The foreword in the original edition (which was omitted in the 1952 reprint) gives some idea of the author's objective and her method.

Under the Sea-Wind was written to make the sea and its life as vivid a reality for those who may read the book as it has become for me during the past decade.

It was written, moreover, out of the deep conviction that the life of the sea is worth knowing. To stand at the edge of the sea, to sense the ebb and the flow of the tides, to feel the breath of a mist moving over a great salt marsh, to watch the flight of shore birds that have swept up and down the surf lines of the continents for untold thousands of years, to see the running of the old eels and the young shad to the sea, is to have knowledge of things that are as nearly eternal as any earthly life can be. These things were before ever man stood on the shore of the ocean and looked out upon it with wonder; they continue year in, year out, through the centuries and the ages, while man's kingdoms rise and fall.

In planning the book I was confronted at the very outset with the problem of a central character. It soon became evident that there was no single animal — bird, fish, mammal, or any of the sea's lesser creatures — that could live in all the various parts of the sea I proposed to describe. That problem was instantly solved, however, when I realized that the sea itself must be the central character whether I wished it or not, for the sense of the sea, holding the power of life and death over every one of its creatures from the smallest to the largest, would inevitably pervade every page.

In a letter to a friend enclosing some manuscript pages of the original longhand draft, Rachel Carson recalls her first experience in meeting a book publisher's deadline. "In those concluding months of work on the book (fall of 1940) I often wrote late at night, in a large bedroom that occupied the entire second floor of our house on Flower Avenue. My constant companions during those otherwise solitary sessions were two precious Persian cats, Buzzie and Kito. Buzzie in particular used to sleep on my writing table, on the litter of notes and manuscript sheets. On two of these pages I had made sketches, first of his little head drooping with sleepiness, then of him after he had settled down comfortably for a nap.*

"The notation 'October — November — December' on p. 3 obviously was a reminder to myself of how much time remained

* Rachel Carson had a lifelong passion for cats. She would sometimes talk or write about them as if they were human beings, and she obviously felt that their companionship was important to her work. While she was writing *The Edge of the Sea*, she replied to a letter from the Cat Welfare Association:

"I have always found that a cat has a truly great capacity for friendship. He asks only that we respect his personal rights and his individuality; in return, he gives his devotion, understanding, and companionship. Cats are extremely sensitive to the joys and sorrows of their human friends, they share our interests.

"For almost 20 years we had in our home a wonderful family of Persians — the mother and her three children. They lived to the ages of 11, 8, 13 and 16 respectively. Buzzie and Kito helped me write *Under the Sea-Wind*, taking turns lying on the manuscript beside my typewriter far into the nights. Tippy did the same for *The Sea Around Us* more recently. Now they are all gone. A little all-gray kitten named Muffin came into our home last September at the age of six weeks. He has now become a full-fledged associate with me on the book I'm now writing — a guide to the seashore. Since the middle of March he has travelled about 2000 miles with my mother and me." For one of her sketches of Buzzie, see illustrations following page 142.

until the completed manuscript was due in the hands of the publisher — Dec. 31, 1940. It was delivered on time."

Under the Sea-Wind, in the author's words, is "a series of descriptive narratives unfolding successively the life of the shore,
the open sea, and the sea bottom." Her approach is reminiscent
of Henry Williamson. As the principal actors on each stage, she
chose shore birds in the first instance, mackerel in the second, and
eels in the third. "To get the feeling of what it is like to be a
creature of the sea requires the active exercise of the imagination
and the temporary abandonment of many human concepts and
human yardsticks. For example, time measured by the clock or
the calendar means nothing if you are a shore bird or a fish, but
the succession of light and darkness and the ebb and flow of the
tides mean the difference between the time to eat and the time
to fast, between the time an enemy can find you easily and the
time you are relatively safe. We cannot get the full flavor of
marine life — cannot project ourselves vicariously into it — unless we make these adjustments in our thinking.

"On the other hand, we must not depart too far from analogy
with human conduct if a fish, shrimp, comb jelly, or bird is to
seem real to us — as real a living creature as he actually is. For
these reasons I have deliberately used certain expressions which
would be objected to in formal scientific writing. I have spoken
of a fish 'fearing' his enemies, for example, not because I suppose
a fish experiences fear in the same way that we do, but because I
think he *behaves as though he were frightened*. With the fish,
the response is primarily physical; with us, primarily psychological. Yet if the behavior of the fish is to be understandable to us,
we must describe it in the words that most properly belong to
human psychological states.

"In choosing names for the animals I have followed the plan
of using, whenever possible, the scientific name for the genus to
which each belongs. Where that name is too formidable I have
substituted something descriptive of the appearance of the crea-

ture, or, in the case of some of the Arctic animals, have used the Eskimo names."

Looking back in later years over her literary career, Rachel Carson expressed a particular affection for *Under the Sea-Wind*. Though she felt that it had faults, she recognized that no writer ever quite recaptures the freshness of his first book. And there is another reason perhaps for its special quality. To achieve creativeness, she once wrote to her friend Curtis Bok, "I need to lose myself completely in what I am writing. On the other hand there are the ever-increasing demands of personal life: the need to give one's self to family, friends, professional obligations. The creativeness, I'm afraid, can be utterly lost if one allows those demands the upper hand . . . I came nearest to achieving that complete losing of myself in writing the *Sea-Wind*."

Judge Bok, himself a distinguished author, shared her feeling for her firstborn: "I think the *Sea-Wind* will always be my favorite — a quiet and special harbor where one stores up strength and peace before riding the wonders of Oceanus outside."

CHAPTER 5

FROM *UNDER THE SEA-WIND*

"Flood Tide"

In Book One ("Edge of the Sea") I have re-created the life of a
stretch of North Carolina sea coast — a place of rolling sand
dunes where the sea oats grow, of wide, salty marshes, of quiet
sounds, and wild ocean beach. I begin with the spring, when the
black skimmers are returning from the south, shad are running
in from the sea to the rivers, and the great spring migration of
the shore birds is at its height. . . .*

THE ISLAND lay in shadows only a little deeper than those that
were swiftly stealing across the sound from the east. On its western shore the wet sand of the narrow beach caught the same reflection of palely gleaming sky that laid a bright path across the
water from island beach to horizon. Both water and sand were
the color of steel overlaid with the sheen of silver, so that it was
hard to say where water ended and land began.

Although it was a small island, so small that a gull might have
flown across it with a score of wing beats, night had already come
to its northern and eastern end. Here the marsh grasses waded

---

* Headings used with the extracts are taken from the foreword to the original
edition of *Under the Sea-Wind.*

boldly out into dark water, and shadows lay thick among the low-growing cedars and yaupons.

With the dusk a strange bird came to the island from its nesting grounds on the outer banks. Its wings were pure black, and from tip to tip their spread was more than the length of a man's arm. It flew steadily and without haste across the sound, its progress as measured and as meaningful as that of the shadows which little by little were dulling the bright water path. The bird was called Rynchops, the black skimmer.

As he neared the shore of the island the skimmer drifted closer to the water, bringing his dark form into strong silhouette against the gray sheet, like the shadow of a great bird that passed unseen above. Yet so quietly did he approach that the sound of his wings, if sound there were, was lost in the whisper song of the water turning over the shells on the wet sand.

At the last spring tide, when the thin shell of the new moon brought the water lapping among the sea oats that fringed the dunes of the banks, Rynchops and his kin had arrived on the outer barrier strip of sand between sound and sea. They had journeyed northward from the coast of Yucatán where they had wintered. Under the warm June sun they would lay their eggs and hatch their buff-colored chicks on the sandy islands of the sound and on the outer beaches. But at first they were weary after the long flight and they rested by day on sand bars when the tide was out or roamed over the sound and its bordering marshes by night.

Before the moon had come to the full, Rynchops had remembered the island. It lay across a quiet sound from which the banks shouldered away the South Atlantic rollers. To the north the island was separated from the mainland by a deep gutter where the ebbing tides raced strongly. On the south side the beach sloped gently, so that at slack water the fishermen could wade out half a mile before the water came above their armpits as they raked scallops or hauled their long seines. In these shallows young fishes swarmed, feeding on the small game of the waters, and shrimp swam with backward flipping of their tails. The rich life of the shallows brought the skimmers nightly from their nesting grounds on the banks, to take their food from the water as they moved with winnowing flight above it.

About sunset the tide had been out. Now it was rising, covering the afternoon resting places of the skimmers, moving through the inlet, and flowing up into the marshes. Through most of the night the skimmers would feed, gliding on slender wings above the water in search of the small fishes that had moved in with the tide to the shelter of grassy shallows. Because they fed on the rising tide, the skimmers were called flood gulls.

On the south beach of the island, where water no deeper than a man's hand ran over gently ribbed bottom, Rynchops began to wheel and quarter over the shallows. He flew with a curious, lilting motion, lifting his wings high after the downstroke. His head was bent sharply so that the long lower bill, shaped like a scissor blade, might cut the water.

The blade or cutwater plowed a miniature furrow over the placid sheet of the sound, setting up wavelets of its own and sending vibrations thudding down through the water to rebound from the sandy bottom. The wave messages were received by the blennies and killifish that were roving the shallows on the alert for food. In the fish world many things are told by sound waves. Sometimes the vibrations tell of food animals like small shrimps or oar-footed crustaceans moving in swarms overhead. And so at the passing of the skimmer the small fishes came nosing at the surface, curious and hungry. Rynchops, wheeling about, returned along the way he had come and snapped up three of the fishes by the rapid opening and closing of his short upper bill.

Ah-h-h-h, called the black skimmer. *Ha-a-a-a! H-a-a-a-a! H-a-a-a-a!* His voice was harsh and barking. It carried far across the water, and from the marshes there came back, like echoes, the answering cries of other skimmers.

While the water was reclaiming inch after inch of sandy shore, Rynchops moved back and forth over the south beach of the island, luring the fishes to rise along his path and seizing them on his return. After he had taken enough minnows to appease his hunger he wheeled up from the water with half a dozen flapping wing beats and circled the island. As he soared above the marshy eastern end schools of killifish moved beneath him through the forests of sea hay, but they were safe from the skimmer, whose wingspread was too great to allow him to fly among the clumps of grass.

Rynchops swerved out around the dock that had been built by the fisherman who lived on the island, crossed the gutter, and swept far over the salt marshes, taking joy in flight and soaring motion. There he joined a flock of other skimmers and together they moved over the marshes in long lines and columns, some-times appearing as dark shadows on the night sky; sometimes as spectral birds when, wheeling swallowlike in air, they showed white breasts and gleaming underparts. As they flew they raised their voices in the weird night chorus of the skimmers, a strange medley of notes high-pitched and low, now soft as the cooing of a mourning dove, and again harsh as the cawing of a crow; the whole chorus rising and falling, swelling and throbbing, dying away in the still air like the far-off baying of a pack of hounds.

The flood gulls circled the island and crossed and recrossed the flats to the southward. All through the hours of the rising tide, they would hunt in flocks over the quiet waters of the sound. The skimmers loved nights of darkness and tonight thick clouds lay between the water and the moon's light.

On the beach the water was moving with soft tinkling sounds among the windrows of jingle shells and young scallop shells. It ran swiftly under heaps of sea lettuce to rouse sand fleas that had taken refuge there when the tide ebbed that afternoon. The beach hoppers floated out on the backwash of each wavelet and moved in the returning water, swimming on their backs, legs uppermost. In the water they were comparatively safe from their enemies the ghost crabs, who roamed the night beaches on swift and silent feet.

In the waters bordering the island many creatures besides the skimmers were abroad that night, foraging in the shallows. As the darkness grew and the incoming tide lapped higher and higher among the marsh grasses, two diamondback terrapins slipped into the water to join the moving forms of others of their kind. These were females, who had just finished laying their eggs above the high-tide line. They had dug nests in the soft sand, working with hind feet until they scooped out jug-shaped holes not quite so deep as their own bodies were long. Then they had deposited their eggs, one five, the other eight. These they had carefully covered with sand, crawling back and forth to conceal the location of the nest. There were other nests in the sand, but none more than two weeks old, for May is the beginning of the nesting season among the diamondbacks.

As Rynchops followed the killifish in toward the shelter of the marsh he saw the terrapins swimming in the shallow water where the tide was moving swiftly. The terrapins nibbled at the marsh grasses and picked off small coiled snails that had crept up the flat blades. Sometimes they swam down to take crabs off the bottom. One of the two terrapins passed between two slender uprights like stakes thrust into the sand. They were the legs of the solitary great blue heron who flew every night from his rookery three miles away to fish from the island.

The heron stood motionless, his neck curved back on his shoulders, his bill poised to spear fish as they darted past his legs. As the terrapin moved out into deeper water she startled a young mullet and sent it racing toward the beach in confusion and panic. The sharp-eyed heron saw the movement and with a quick dart seized the fish crosswise in his bill. He tossed it into the air, caught it head first, and swallowed it. It was the first fish other than small fry that he had caught that night.

The tide was almost halfway to the confused litter of sea wrack, bits of sticks, dried claws of crabs, and broken shell fragments that marked high-water level. Above the tide line there were faint stirrings in the sand where the terrapins had lately begun to lay their eggs. The season's young would not hatch until August, but many young of the year before still were buried in the sand, not yet roused from the torpor of hibernation. During the winter the young terrapins had lived on the remnant of yolk left from embryonic life. Many had died, for the winter had been long and the frosts had bitten deep into the sands. Those that survived were weak and emaciated, their bodies so shrunken within the shells that they were smaller than when they had hatched. Now they were moving feebly in the sands where the old terrapins were laying the eggs of a new generation of young.

About the time the tide was midway to the flood, a wave of motion stroked the tops of the grasses above the terrapin egg bed, as though a breeze passed, but there was little wind that night. The grasses above the sand bed parted. A rat, crafty with the cunning of years and filled with the lust for blood, had come down to the water along a path which his feet and his thick tail had worn to a smooth track through the grass. The rat lived with his mate and others of his kind under an old shed where the fisherman kept his nets, faring well on the eggs of the many birds that nested on the island, and on the young birds.

As the rat looked out from the fringe of grass bordering the terrapin nests the heron sprang from the water a stone's throw away with a strong flapping of his wings and flew across the island to the north shore. He had seen two fishermen in a small boat coming around the western tip of the island. The fishermen had been gigging flounders, spearing them on the bottom in shallow water by the light of a torch which flared at the bow. A yellow splotch of light moved over the dark water in advance of the boat and sent trembling streamers across the wavelets that rippled shoreward from the boat's passing. Twin points of green fire glowed in the grass above the sand bed. They remained stationary until the boat had passed on around the south shore and had headed toward the town docks. Only then did the rat glide down from the path onto the sand.

The scent of terrapin and of terrapin eggs, fresh laid, was heavy in the air. Snuffling and squeaking in excitement, the rat began to dig and in a few minutes had uncovered an egg, had pierced the shell, and sucked out the yolk. He then uncovered two other eggs and might have eaten them if he had not heard a movement in a nearby clump of marsh grass — the scrambling of a young terrapin struggling to escape the water that was seeping up around its tussock of tangled roots and mud. A dark form moved across the sand and through the rivulet of water. The rat seized the baby terrapin and carried it in his teeth through the marsh grasses to a hummock of higher ground. Engrossed in gnawing away the thin shell of the terrapin, he did not notice how the tide was creeping up about him and running deeper around the hummock. It was thus that the blue heron, wading back around the shore of the island, came upon the rat and speared him.

∞∞∞

There were few sounds that night except those of the water and the water birds. The wind was asleep. From the direction of the inlet there came the sound of breakers on the barrier beach, but the distant voice of the sea was hushed almost to a sigh, a sort of rhythmic exhalation as though the sea, too, were asleep outside the gates of the sound.

It would have taken the sharpest of ears to catch the sound of a hermit crab dragging his shell house along the beach just above the water line: the elfin shuffle of his feet on the sand, the sharp grit as he dragged his own shell across another; or to have discerned the spattering tinkle of the tiny droplets that fell when a shrimp, being pursued by a school of fish, leaped clear of the water. But these were the unheard voices of the island night, of the water and the water's edge.

The sounds of the land were few. There was a thin insect tremolo, the spring prelude to the incessant chiton fiddles that later in the season would salute the night. There was the murmur of sleeping birds in the cedars — jackdaws and mockingbirds — who now and again roused enough to twitter drowsily one to another. About midnight a mockingbird sang for almost a quarter of an hour, imitating all the bird songs he had heard that day and adding trills, chuckles, and whistles all his own. Then he, too, subsided and left the night again to the water and its sounds.

There were many fish moving in through the deep water of the channel that night. They were full-bellied fish, soft-finned and covered with large silvery scales. It was a run of spawning shad, fresh from the sea. For days the shad had lain outside the line of breakers beyond the inlet. Tonight with the rising tide they had moved in past the clanging buoy that guided fishermen returning from the outer grounds, had passed through the inlet, and were crossing the sound by way of the channel.

As the night grew darker and the tides pressed farther into the marshes and moved higher into the estuary of the river, the silvery fish quickened their movements, feeling their way along the streams of less saline water that served them as paths to the river. The estuary was broad and sluggish, little more than an arm of the sound. Its shores were ragged with salt marsh, and far up along the winding course of the river the pulsating tides and the bitter tang of the water spoke of the sea.

Some of the migrating shad were three years old and were returning to spawn for the first time. A few were a year older and were making their second trip to the spawning grounds up the river. These were wise in the ways of the river and of the strange crisscross shadows it sometimes contained.

By the younger shad the river was only dimly remembered, if by the word "memory" we may call the heightened response of the senses as the delicate gills and the sensitive lateral lines perceived the lessening saltiness of the water and the changing rhythms and vibrations of the inshore waters. Three years before they had left the river, dropping downstream to the estuary as young fish scarcely as long as a man's finger, moving out to sea with the coming of autumn's chill. The river forgotten, they roamed widely in the sea, feeding on shrimps and amphipods. So far and so deviously did they travel that no man could trace their movements. Perhaps they wintered in deep, warm water far below the surface, resting in the dim twilight of the continent's edge, making an occasional timid journey out over the rim beyond which lay only the blackness and stillness of the deep sea. Perhaps in summer they roved the open ocean, feeding on the rich life of the surface, packing layers of white muscle and sweet fat beneath their shining armor of scales.

The shad roamed the sea paths known and followed only by fish while the earth moved three times through the cycle of the zodiac. In the third year, as the waters of the sea warmed slowly to the southward-moving sun, the shad yielded to the promptings of race instinct and returned to their birthplaces to spawn.

Most of the fish coming in now were females, heavy with unshed roe. It was late in the season and the largest runs had gone before. The bucks, who came into the river first, were already on the spawning grounds, as were many of the roe shad. Some of the early-run fish had pressed upstream as far as a hundred miles to where the river had its formless beginnings in dark cypress swamps.

Each of the roe fish would shed in a season more than a hundred thousand eggs. From these perhaps only one or two young would survive the perils of river and sea and return in time to spawn, for by such ruthless selection the species are kept in check.

"Winter Storm"

WINTER STILL GRIPPED the northland when the sanderlings arrived on the shores of a bay shaped like a leaping porpoise, on the edge of the frozen tundras of the barren grounds. They were among the first to arrive of all the migrant shore birds. Snow lay on the hills and drifted deep in the stream valleys. The ice was yet unbroken in the bay, and on the ocean shore it was piled in green and jagged heaps that moved, straining and groaning, with the tides.

But the lengthening days filled with sun had already begun to melt the snow on the south slopes of the hills, and on the ridges the wind had helped wear the snow blanket thin. There the brown of earth and the silver gray of reindeer moss showed through, and now for the first time that season the sharp-hoofed caribou could feed without pawing away the snow. At noon the white owls beating across the tundra beheld their own reflections in many small pools among the rocks, but by midafternoon the water mirrors were clouded with frost.

Already the rusty feathers were showing about the necks of the willow ptarmigans and brown hairs had appeared on the white coats of the foxes and weasels. Snow buntings hopped about in flocks that grew day by day, and the buds on the willows swelled and showed the first awakening of color under the sunshine.

There was little food for the migrant birds — lovers of warm sun and green, tossing surf. The sanderlings gathered miserably under a few dwarf willows that were sheltered from the north-west winds by a glacial moraine. There they lived on the first green buds of the saxifrage and awaited the coming of thaws to release the rich animal food of the Arctic spring.

But winter was yet to die. The second sun after the sander-lings' return to the Arctic burned dimly in the murky air. The clouds thickened and rolled between the tundra and the sun, and by midday the sky was heavy with unfallen snow. Wind came in over the open sea and over the ice packs, carrying a bitter air that turned to mist as it moved, swirling, over the warmer plains.

Uhvinguk, the lemming mouse who yesterday had sunned himself with many of his fellows on the bare rocks, ran into the burrows, winding tunnels in the deep, hard drifts, and to the grass-lined chambers where the lemmings dwelt in warmth even in midwinter. In the twilight of that day a white fox paused above the lemming burrow and stood with lifted paw. In the silence his sharp ears caught the sound of small feet along the runways below. Many times that spring the fox had dug down through the snow into these burrows and seized as many lem-mings as he could eat. Now he whined sharply and pawed a little at the snow. He was not hungry, having killed and eaten a ptar-migan an hour before when he had come upon it, in a willow thicket, snipping off twigs; so today he only listened, perhaps to reassure himself that the weasels had not raided the lemming colony since his last visit. Then he turned and ran on silent feet along the path made by many foxes, not even pausing to glance at the sanderlings huddled in the lee of the moraine, and passed over the hill to the distant ridge where a colony of thirty small white foxes had their burrows.

Late that night, about the time the sun must have been set-ting somewhere behind the thick cloud banks, the first snow fell. Soon the wind rose and poured across the tundra like a flood of icy water that penetrated the thickest feathers and the warmest fur. As the wind came down shrieking from the sea, the mists fled before it across the barrens, but the snow clouds were thicker and whiter than the mists had been.

Silverbar, the young hen sanderling, had not seen snow since she had left the Arctic nearly ten months before to follow the sun southward toward the limit of its orbit, to the grasslands of the Argentine and the shores of Patagonia. Almost her whole existence had been of sun and wide white beaches and rippling green pampas. Now, crouched under the dwarf willows, she could not see Blackfoot through the swirling whiteness, although she could have reached his side with a quick run of twenty paces. The sanderlings faced into the blizzard, as shore birds everywhere face into the wind. They huddled close together, wing to wing, and the warmth of their bodies kept the tender feet from freezing as they crouched on them.

If the snow had not drifted so, that night and all the next day, the loss of life would have been less. But the stream valleys filled up, inch by inch, throughout the night, and against the ridges the white softness piled deeper. Little by little, from the ice-strewn sea edge across miles of tundra, even far south to the fringe of the forests, the undulating hills and the ice-scoured valleys were flattening out, and a strange world, terrifying in its level whiteness, was building up. In the purple twilight of the second day the fall slackened, and the night was loud with the crying of the wind, but with no other voice, for no wild thing dared show itself.

The snow death had taken many lives. It had visited the nest of two snowy owls in a ravine that cut a deep scar in the hillside, near the willow copse that sheltered the sanderlings. The hen had been brooding the six eggs for more than a week. During the first night of wild storm the snow had drifted deep about her, leaving a round depression like a stream-bed pothole in which she sat. All through the night the owl remained on the nest, warming the eggs with her great body that was almost furry in its plumage. By morning the snow was filling in around the feather-shod talons and creeping up around her sides. The cold was numbing, even through the feathers. At noon, with flakes like cotton shreds still flying in the sky, only the owl's head and shoulders were free of the snow. Several times that day a great form, white and silent as the snowflakes, had drifted over the ridge and hovered above the place where the nest was. Now Ookpik, the cock owl, called to his mate with low, throaty cries. Numb and heavy-winged with cold, the hen roused and shook herself. It took many minutes to free herself from the snow and to climb, half fluttering, half stumbling, out of the nest, deep-walled with white. Ookpik clucked to her and made the sounds of a cock owl bringing a lemming or a baby ptarmigan to the nest, but neither owl had had food since the blizzard began. The hen tried to fly but her heavy body flopped awkwardly in the snow for stiffness. When at last the slow circulation had crept back into her muscles, she rose into the air and the two owls floated over the place where the sanderlings crouched and out across the tundra.

As the snow fell on the still-warm eggs and the hard, bitter cold of the night gripped them, the life fires of the tiny embryos burned low. The crimson streams ran slower in the vessels that carried the racing blood from the food yolks to the embryos. After a time there slackened and finally ceased the furious activity of cells that grew and divided, grew again and divided to make owl bone and muscle and sinew. The pulsating red sacs under the great oversized heads hesitated, beat spasmodically, and were stilled. The six little owls-to-be were dead in the snow, and by their death, perhaps, hundreds of unborn lemmings and ptarmigans and Arctic hares had the greater chance of escaping death from the feathered ones that strike from the sky.

Farther up the ravine, several willow ptarmigans had been buried in a drift, where they had bedded for the night. The ptarmigans had flown over the ridge on the evening of the storm, dropping into the soft drifts so that never a print of their feet — clad in feathered snowshoes — was left to guide the foxes to their resting place. This was a rule of the game of life and death which the weak play with the strong. But tonight there was no need to observe the rules, for the snow would have obliterated all footprints and would have outwitted the keenest enemy — even as it drifted, by slow degrees, so deeply over the sleeping ptarmigans that they could not dig themselves out.

Five of the sanderling flock had died of the cold, and snow buntings by the score were stumbling and fluttering over the snow crust, too weak to stand when they tried to alight.

Now, with the passing of the storm, hunger was abroad on the great barrens. Most of the willows, food of the ptarmigans, were buried under snow. The dried heads of last year's weeds, which released their seeds to the snow buntings and the longspurs, wore glittering sheaths of ice. The lemmings, food of the foxes and the owls, were safe in their runways, and nowhere in this silent world was there food for shore birds that live on the shellfish and insects and other creatures of the water's edge. Now many hunters, both furred and feathered, were abroad during the night, the short, gray night of the Arctic spring. And when night wore into day the hunters still padded over the snow or beat on strong wings across the tundra, for the night's kill had not satisfied their hunger.

Among the hunters was Ookpik, the snowy owl. The coldest months of every winter, the icebound months, Ookpik spent hundreds of miles south of the barren grounds, where it was easier to find the little gray lemming mice that were his favorite food. During the storm nothing living had showed itself to Ookpik as he sailed over the plains and along the ridges that overlooked the sea, but today many small creatures moved over the tundra.

Along the east bank of the stream a flock of ptarmigans had found a few twigs of willow showing above the snow, part of a shrubby growth that had been as high as the antlers of a barren-grounds caribou until the snow had covered it. Now the ptarmigans could easily reach the topmost branches, and they nipped off the twigs in their bills, content with this food until the tender new buds of spring should be put forth. The flock still wore the white plumage of winter except for one or two of the cocks whose few brown feathers told of approaching summer and the mating season. When a ptarmigan in winter dress feeds on the snow fields, all of color about him is the black of bill and roving eye, and of the under tail feathers when he flies. Even his ancient enemies, the foxes and the owls, are deceived from a distance; but they, too, wear the Arctic's protective colorings.

Now Ookpik, as he came up the stream valley, saw among the willows the moving balls of shining black that were the ptarmigans' eyes. The white foe moved nearer, blending into the pale sky; the white prey moved, unfrightened, over the snow. There was a soft *whoosh* of wings — a scattering of feathers — and on the snow a red stain spread, red as a new-laid ptarmigan egg before the shell pigments have dried. Ookpik bore the ptarmigan in his talons over the ridge to the higher ground that was his lookout, where his mate awaited him. The two owls tore apart the warm flesh with their beaks, swallowing also the bones and feathers as was their custom, to cast them up later in neat pellets.

The gnawing pang of hunger was a sensation new to Silverbar. A week before, with the others of the sanderling flock, she had filled her stomach with shellfish gathered on the wide tidal flats of Hudson Bay. Days before that they had gorged on beach fleas on the coasts of New England, and on Hippa crabs on the sunny beaches of the south. In all the eight-thousand-mile journey northward from Patagonia there had been no lack of food.

The older sanderlings, patient in the acceptance of hardship, waited until the ebb tide, when they led Silverbar and the other year-old birds of the flock to the edge of the harbor ice. The beach was piled with irregular masses of ice and frozen spray, but the last tide had shifted the broken floe and on retreating had left a bare patch of mud flat. Already several hundred shore birds had gathered — all the early migrants from miles around who had escaped death in the snow. They were clustered so thickly that there was scarcely space for the sanderlings to alight, and every square inch of surface had been probed or dug by the bills of the waders. By deep probing in the stiff mud Silverbar found several shells coiled like snails, but they were empty. With Blackfoot and two of the yearling sanderlings, she flew up the beach for a mile, but snow carpeted the ground and the harbor ice and there was no food.

As the sanderlings hunted fruitlessly among the ice chunks, Tullugak the raven flew overhead and passed up the shore on deliberate wings.

Cr-r-r-uck! Cr-r-r-uck! he croaked hoarsely.

Tullugak had been patrolling the beach and the nearby tundra for miles, on the lookout for food. All the known carcasses which the ravens had resorted to for months had been covered by snow or carried away by the shifting of the bay ice. Now he had located the remains of a caribou which the wolves had run down and killed that morning, and he was calling the other ravens to the feast. Three jet-black birds, among them Tullugak's mate, were walking briskly about over the bay ice hunting a whale carcass. The whale had come ashore months before, providing almost a winter's supply of food for Tullugak and his kin, who lived the year round in the vicinity of the bay. Now the storm had opened a channel into which the shifting ice masses had pushed the dead whale and closed over it. At the welcome food cry of Tullugak, the three ravens sprang into the air and followed him across the tundra to pick off the few shreds of meat that remained on the bones of the caribou.

"Race to the Sea"

LEAPING AND RACING, foaming and swirling, the incoming
flood brought release to the myriads of small fishes that had been
imprisoned in the pond. Now in thousands they poured out of
the pond and out of the marshes. They raced in mad confusion
to meet the clean, cold water. In their excitement they let the
flood take them, toss them, turn them over and over. Reaching
midchannel of the slough they leaped high in the air again and
again, sparkling bits of animate silver, like a swarm of glittering
insects that rose and fell, rose again and fell. There the water
seized them and held them back in their wild dash to the sea, so
that many of them were caught on the slopes of the waves and
held, tails uppermost, struggling helplessly against the might of
the water. When finally the waves released them they raced
down the slough to the ocean, where they knew once more the
rolling breakers, the clean sandy bottoms, the cool green waters.

How did the pond and the marshes hold them all? On they
came, in school after school, flashing bright among the marsh
grasses, leaping and bounding out of the pond. For more than an
hour the exodus continued, with scarcely a break in the hurrying
schools. Perhaps they had come in, many of them, on the last
spring tide when the moon was a pencil stroke of silver in the
sky. And now the moon had grown fat and round and another
spring tide, a rollicking, roistering, rough-and-ready tide, called
them back to the sea again.

On they went, passing through the surf line where the white-
capped waves were tumbling. On they went, most of them, past
the smoother green swells to the second line of surf, where shoals
tripped the waves coming in from the open sea and sent them

sprawling in white confusion. But there were terns fishing above the surf, and thousands of the small migrants went no farther than the portals of the sea.*

"Birth of a Mackerel"

The life of the open sea — miles beyond sight of land — is various, strangely beautiful, and wholly unknown to all but a fortunate few. Book Two is the story of a true sea rover — a mackerel — from birth in the great ocean nursery of the surface waters, through all the vicissitudes of early life among the drifting plankton herds and youth in a sheltered New England harbor, to membership in a wandering school of mackerel subject to the depredations of fish-eating birds, large fishes, and man.

BETWEEN the Chesapeake Capes and the elbow of Cape Cod the place where the continent ends and the true sea begins lies from fifty to one hundred miles from the tide lines. It is not the distance from shore, but the depth, that marks the transition to the true sea; for wherever the gently sloping sea bottom feels the weight of a hundred fathoms of water above it, suddenly it begins to fall away in escarpments and steep palisades, descending abruptly from twilight into darkness.

In the blue haze of the continent's edge the mackerel tribes lie in torpor during the four coldest months of winter, resting from

---

* This is the passage referred to on page 7 where Rachel wrote to a friend, "Don't ever dream I wondered at your tears."

the eight months of strenuous life in the upper waters. On the threshold of the deep sea they live on the fat stored up from a summer's rich feeding, and toward the end of their winter's sleep their bodies begin to grow heavy with spawn.

In the month of April the mackerel are roused from their sleep as they lie at the edge of the continental shelf, off the Capes of Virginia. Perhaps the currents that drift down to bathe the resting places of the mackerel stir in the fish some dim perception of the progress of the ocean's seasons — the old, unchanging cycle of the sea. For weeks now the cold, heavy surface water — the winter water — has been sinking, slipping under and displacing the warmer bottom water. The warm water is rising, carrying into the surface rich loads of phosphates and nitrates from the bottom. Spring sun and fertile water are wakening the dormant plants to a burst of activity, of growth and multiplication. Spring comes to the land with pale, green shoots and swelling buds; it brings to the sea a great increase in the number of simple, one-celled plants of microscopic size, the diatoms. Perhaps the currents bring down to the mackerel some awareness of the flourishing vegetation of the upper waters, of the rich pasturage for hordes of crustaceans that browse in the diatom meadows and in their turn fill the water with clouds of their goblin-headed young. Soon fishes of many kinds will be moving through the spring sea, to feed on the teeming life of the surface and to bring forth their own young.

Perhaps, also, the currents moving over the place where the mackerel lie carry a message of the inpouring of fresh water as ice and snow dissolve in floods to rush down the coastal rivers to the sea, diminishing ever so slightly its bitter saltiness and attracting the spawn-laden fishes by the lesser density. But however the feeling of awakening spring comes to the dormant fishes, the mackerel stir in swift response. Their caravans begin to form and to move through the dim-lit water, and by thousands and hundreds of thousands they set out for the upper sea.

About a hundred miles beyond the place where the mackerel winter, the sea rises out of the deep, dark bed of the open Atlantic and begins its own climb up over the muddy sides of the continental slope. In utter blackness and stillness the sea climbs those hundred miles, rising from depths of a mile or more until black begins to fade to purple, and purple to deep blue, and blue to azure.

At one hundred fathoms the sea rolls over a sharp edge — the rim of the bowl formed by the foundations of the continent — and starts up the gentler acclivity of the continental shelf. Over the shelving edge of the continent, the sea contains for the first time roving herds of fishes that browse over the fertile undersea plains, for in the deep abyss there are only small, lean fishes hunting singly or in small bands for the sparse food. But here the fishes have rich pasturage — meadows of plantlike hydroids and moss animals, clams and cockles that lie passive in the sand; prawns and crabs that start up and dart away before the rooting snout of a fish, like a rabbit before a hound.

Now small, gasoline-engined fishing boats move over the sea and here and there the water pours through the meshes of miles of gill-net webbing suspended from floats or resists the drag of otter trawls over the sandy floor beneath. And now for the first time the gulls' white wings are patterned in numbers on the sky above, for the gulls — except the kittiwakes — hug the fringes of the sea, feeling uneasy on the open ocean.

As the sea comes in over the continental shelf it meets a series of shoals that run parallel to the coast. In the fifty to one hundred miles to tidewater the sea must hurdle each of these shoals or chains of shoals, climbing up the sides of the hills from the surrounding valleys to shelly plateaus a mile or so wide, then on the shoreward side descending again into the deeper shadows of another valley. The plateaus are more fertile than the valleys in the thousand-odd kinds of backboneless animals that fishes live on, and so more and larger fish herds browse on them. Often the water above the shoals is especially rich in the moving clouds of small plants and animals of many different kinds that drift with the currents or swim feebly about in search of food — the wanderers or plankton of the sea.

The mackerel do not follow the road over the hills and valleys of the sea's floor as they leave their wintering grounds and turn shoreward. Instead, as though in eagerness to reach at once the sun-lit upper water, they climb steeply the hundred-fathom ascent to the surface. After four months in the gloom of deep water the mackerel move in excitement through the bright waters of the surface layers. They thrust their snouts out of the water as they swim and behold once more the gray expanse of sea cupped in the paleness of arching sky.

Where the mackerel come to the surface there is no sign by which to distinguish the great sea out of which the sun rises from the lesser sea into which it sets; but without hesitation the schools turn from the deep-blue saline water of the open sea and move toward the coastal waters, paled to greenness by the fresh inpouring of the rivers and bays. The place they seek is a great, irregular patch of water that runs from south by west to north by east, from the Chesapeake Capes to southward of Nantucket. In some places it is only twenty miles from shore, in others fifty or more — the spawning grounds in which, from ancient times, the Atlantic mackerel have shed their eggs.

Throughout all the latter part of April mackerel are rising from off the Virginia Capes and hurrying shoreward. There is a stir of excitement in the sea as the spring migration begins. Some of the schools are small; some are as much as a mile wide and several miles long. By day the sea birds watch them rolling landward like dark clouds across the green of the sea; but at night they pour through the water like molten metal, as by their movements they disturb the myriad luminescent animals of the plankton.

The mackerel are voiceless and they make no sound; yet their passage creates a heavy disturbance in the water, so that schools of launce and anchovies must feel the vibrations of an approaching school a long way off and hurry in apprehension through the green distances of the sea; and it may be that the stir of their passage is felt on the shoals below — by the prawns and crabs that pick their way among the corals, by the starfish creeping over the rocks, by the sly hermit crabs, and by the pale flowers of the sea anemone.

As the mackerel hurry shoreward they swim in tier above tier. Throughout those weeks when the fish are rolling in from the open sea the scattered shoals between the edge of the continent and the shore are often darkened as the earth was once dimmed by the passing of another living cloud — the flights of the passenger pigeons.

In time the shoreward-running mackerel reach the inshore waters, where they ease their bodies of their burden of eggs and milt. They leave in their wake a cloud of transparent spheres of infinitesimal size, a vast, sprawling river of life, the sea's counterpart of the river of stars that flows through the sky as the Milky Way. There are known to be hundreds of millions of eggs to the square mile, billions in an area a fishing vessel could cruise over in an hour, hundreds of trillions in the whole spawning area.

After spawning, the mackerel turn toward the rich feeding grounds that lie to seaward of New England. Now the fish are bent only on reaching the waters they knew of old, where the small crustaceans called Calanus move in red clouds through the water. The sea will care for their young, as it cares for the young of all other fishes, and of oysters and crabs and starfish, of worms and jellyfish and barnacles.

∽∽∽

So it came about that Scomber, the mackerel, was born in the surface waters of the open sea, seventy miles south by east from the western tip of Long Island. He came into being as a tiny globule no larger than a poppy seed, drifting in the surface layers of pale-green water. The globule carried an amber droplet of oil that served to keep it afloat and it carried also a gray particle of living matter so small that it could have been picked up on the point of a needle. In time this particle was to become Scomber, the mackerel, a powerful fish, streamlined after the manner of his kind, and a rover of the seas.

The parents of Scomber were fish of the last big wave of mackerel migration that came in from the edge of the continental shelf in May, heavy with spawn and driving rapidly shoreward. On the fourth evening of their journey, in a flooding current straining to landward, the eggs and milt had begun to flow from their bodies into the sea. Somewhere among the forty or fifty thousand eggs that were shed by one of the female fish was the egg that was to become Scomber.

There could be scarcely a stranger place in the world in which to begin life than this universe of sky and water, peopled by strange creatures and governed by wind and sun and ocean currents. It was a place of silence, except when the wind went whispering or blustering over the vast sheet of water, or when sea gulls came down the wind with their high, wild mewing, or when whales broke the surface, expelled the long-held breath, and rolled again into the sea.

The mackerel schools hurried on into the north and east, their journey scarcely interrupted by the act of spawning. As the sea birds were finding their resting places for the night on the dark water plains, swarms of small and curiously formed animals stole into the surface waters from hills and valleys lying in darkness far below. The night sea belonged to the plankton, to the diminutive worms and the baby crabs, the glassy, big-eyed shrimp, the young barnacles and mussels, the throbbing bells of the jellyfish, and all the other small fry of the sea that shun the light.

It was indeed a strange world in which to set adrift anything so fragile as a mackerel egg. It was filled with small hunters, each of which must live at the expense of its neighbors, plant and animal. The eggs of the mackerel were jostled by the newly hatched young of earlier spawning fishes and of shellfish, crustaceans, and worms. The larvae, some of them only a few hours old, were swimming along in the sea, busily seeking their food. Some snatched out of the water with pincered claws anything small enough to be overpowered and swallowed; others seized any prey less swift and agile than themselves in biting jaws or sucked into cilium-studded mouths the drifting green or golden cells of the diatoms.

The sea was filled, too, with larger hunters than the microscopic larvae. Within an hour after the parent mackerel had gone away, a horde of comb jellies rose to the surface of the sea. The comb jellies, or ctenophores, looked like large gooseberries, and they swam by the beating of plates of fused hairs or cilia, set in eight bands down the sides of the transparent bodies. Their substance was scarcely more than that of sea water, yet each of them ate many times its own bulk of solid food in a day. Now they were rising slowly toward the surface, where the millions of new-spawned mackerel eggs drifted free in the upper layers of the sea. They twirled slowly back and forth on the long axes of their bodies as they came, flashing a cold, phosphorescent fire. Throughout the night the ctenophores flicked the waters with their deadly tentacles, each a slim, elastic thread twenty times the length of the body when extended. And as they turned and twirled and flashed frosty green lights in the black water, jostling one another in their greed, the drifting mackerel eggs were swept up in the silken meshes of the tentacles and carried by swift contraction to the waiting mouths.

Often during this first night of Scomber's existence the cold, smooth body of a ctenophore collided with him or a searching tentacle missed by a fraction of an inch the floating sphere in which the speck of protoplasm had already divided into eight parts, thus beginning the development by which a single fertile cell would swiftly be transformed into an embryo fish.

Of the millions of mackerel eggs drifting alongside the one

that was to produce Scomber, thousands went no farther than the first stages of the journey into life until they were seized and eaten by the comb jellies, to be speedily converted into the watery tissue of their foe and in this reincarnation to roam the sea, preying on their own kind.

Throughout the night, while the sea lay under a windless sky, the decimation of the mackerel eggs continued. Shortly before dawn the water began to stir to a breeze from the east and in an hour was rolling heavily under a wind that blew steadily to the south and west. At the first ruffling of the surface calm the comb jellies began to sink into deep water. Even in these simple creatures, which consist of little more than two layers of cells, one inside the other, there exists the counterpart of an instinct of self-preservation, causing them in some way to sense the threat of destruction which rough water holds for so fragile a body.

In the first night of their existence more than ten out of every hundred mackerel eggs either had been eaten by the comb jellies or, from some inherent weakness, had died after the first few divisions of the cell.

Now, the rising up of a strong wind blowing to southward brought fresh dangers to the mackerel eggs, left for the time being with few enemies in the surface waters about them. The upper layers of the sea streamed in the direction urged upon them by the wind. The drifting spheres moved south and west with the current, for the eggs of all sea creatures are carried help-lessly wherever the sea takes them. It happened that the south-west drift of the water was carrying the mackerel eggs away from the normal nursery grounds of their kind into waters where food for young fish was scarce and hungry predators abundant. As a result of this mischance fewer than one egg in every thousand was to complete its development.

On the second day, as the cells within the golden globules of the eggs multiplied by countless divisions, and the shieldlike forms of embryo fish began to take shape above the yolk spheres, hordes of a new enemy came roving through the drifting plankton. The glassworms were transparent and slender creatures that cleaved the water like arrows, darting in all directions to seize fish eggs, copepods, and even others of their own kind. With their fierce heads and toothed jaws they were terrible as dragons to the smaller beings of the plankton, although as men measure they were less than a quarter of an inch long.

The floating mackerel eggs were scattered and buffeted by the dartings and rushes of the glassworms, and when the driftings of current and tide carried them away to other waters a heavy toll of the mackerel had been taken as food.

Again the egg that contained the embryonic Scomber had drifted unscathed while all about him other eggs had been seized and eaten. Under the warm May sun the new young cells of the egg were stirred to furious activity — growing, dividing, differentiating into cell layers and tissues and organs. After two nights and two days of life, the threadlike body of a fish was taking form within the egg, curled halfway around the globe of yolk that gave it food. Already a thin ridge down the midline showed where a stiffening rod of cartilage — forerunner of a backbone — was forming; a large bulge at the forward end showed the place of the head, and on it two smaller outpushings marked the future eyes of Scomber. On the third day a dozen V-shaped plates of muscle were marked out on either side of the backbone; the lobes of the brain showed through the still-transparent tissues of the head; the ear sacs appeared; the eyes neared completion and showed dark through the egg wall, peering sightlessly into the surrounding world of the sea. As the sky lightened preparatory to the fifth rising of the sun a thin-walled sac beneath the head — crimson tinted from the fluid it contained — quivered, throbbed, and began the steady pulsation that would continue as long as there was life within the body of Scomber.

Throughout that day development proceeded at a furious pace, as though in haste to make ready for the hatching that was soon to come. On the lengthening tail a thin flange of tissue appeared — the fin ridge from which a series of tail finlets, like a row of flags stiff in the wind, was later to be formed. The sides of an open groove that traversed the belly of the little fish, beneath and protected by the plate of more than seventy muscle segments, grew steadily downward and in midafternoon closed to form the alimentary canal. Above the pulsating heart the mouth cavity deepened, but it was still far short of reaching the canal.

Throughout all this time the surface currents of the sea were pouring steadily to the southwest, driven by the wind and carrying with them the clouds of plankton. During the six days since the spawning of the mackerel the toll of the ocean's predators had continued without abatement, so that already more than half of the eggs had been eaten or had died in development.

It was the nights that had seen the greatest destruction. They had been dark nights with the sea lying calm under a wide sky. On those nights the little stars of the plankton had rivaled in number and brilliance the constellations of the sky. From underlying depths the hordes of comb jellies and glassworms, copepods and shrimps, medusae of jellyfish, and translucent winged snails had risen into the upper layers to glitter in the dark water.

When the first dilution of blackness came in the east, warning of the dawn into which the revolving earth was carrying them, strange processions began to hurry down through the water as the animals of the plankton fled from the sun that had not yet risen. Only a few of these small creatures could endure the surface waters by day except when clouds deflected the fierce lances of the sun.

In time Scomber and the other baby mackerel would join the hurrying caravans that moved down into deep green water by day and pressed upward again as the earth swung once more into darkness. Now, while still confined within the egg, the embryonic mackerel had no power of independent motion, for the eggs remained in water of a density equal to their own and were carried horizontally in their own stratum of the sea.

On the sixth day the currents took the mackerel eggs over a

large shoal thickly populated with crabs. It was the spawning season of the crabs — the time when the eggs, that had been carried throughout the winter by the females, burst their shells and released the small, goblin-like larvae. Without delay the crab larvae set out for the upper waters, where through successive moltings of their infant shells and transformations of appearance they would take on the form of their race. Only after a period of life in the plankton would they be admitted to the colony of crabs that lived on that pleasant undersea plateau.

Now they hastened upward, each newborn crab swimming steadily with its wandlike appendages, each ready to discern with large black eyes and to seize with sharp-beaked mouth such food as the sea might offer. For the rest of that day the crab larvae were carried along with the mackerel eggs, on which they fed heavily. In the evening the struggle of two currents — the tidal current and the wind-driven current — carried many of the crab larvae to landward while the mackerel eggs continued to the south.

There were many signs in the sea of the approach to more southern latitudes. The night before the appearance of the crab larvae the sea had been set aglitter over an area of many miles with the intense green lights of the southern comb jelly Mnemiopsis, whose ciliated combs gleam with the colors of the rainbow by day and sparkle like emeralds in the night sea. And now for the first time there throbbed in the warm surface waters the pale southern form of the jellyfish Cyanea, trailing its several hundred tentacles through the water for fish or whatever else it might entangle. For hours at a time the ocean seethed with great shoals of salpae — thimble-sized, transparent barrels hooped in strands of muscle.

On the sixth night after the spawning of the mackerel the tough little skins of the eggs began to burst. One by one the tiny fishlets, so small that the combined length of twenty of them, head to tail, would have been scarcely an inch, slipped out of the confining spheres and knew for the first time the touch of the sea. Among these hatching fish was Scomber.

He was obviously an unfinished little fish. It seemed almost that he had burst prematurely from the egg, so unready was he to care for himself. The gill slits were marked out but were not cut through to the throat, so were useless for breathing. His mouth was only a blind sac. Fortunately for the newly hatched fishlet, a supply of food remained in the yolk sac still attached to him, and on this he would live until his mouth was open and functioning. Because of the bulky sac, however, the baby mackerel drifted upside down in the water, helpless to control his movements.

The next three days of life brought startling transformations. As the processes of development forged onward, the mouth and gill structures were completed and the finlets sprouting from back and sides and underparts grew and found strength and certainty of movement. The eyes became deep blue with pigment, and now it may be that they sent to the tiny brain the first messages of things seen. Steadily the yolk mass shrank, and with its loss Scomber found it possible to right himself and by undulation of the still-rotund body and movement of the fins to swim through the water.

Of the steady drift, the southward pouring of the water day after day, he was unconscious, but the feeble strength of his fins was no match for the currents. He floated where the sea carried him, now a rightful member of the drifting community of the plankton.

"The Abyss"

For Book Three ("River and Sea") there remained the gently sloping sea bottom that forms the rim or shelf of the continent, the steep descent of the continental slopes, and finally the abyss or the deep sea. Fortunately there is one creature whose life embraces all these in a history without parallel in the annals of sea or land. This creature is the eel . . . Other fish run out of the bays and sounds in the fall, but only far enough to find warm water in which to winter. But the eels go on, to a deep abyss near the Sargasso Sea, where they spawn and die. From this strange world of the deep sea the young eels return alone each spring to the coastal rivers.

BILLIONS OF YOUNG EELS — billions of pairs of black, pin-prick eyes peering into the strange sea world that overlay the abyss. Before the eyes of the eels, clouds of copepods vibrated in their ceaseless dance of life, their crystal bodies catching the light like dust motes when the blue gleam came down from above. Clear bells pulsated in the water, fragile jellyfish adjusted to life where five hundred pounds of water pressed on every square inch of surface. Fleeing before the descending light, shoals of ptero-pods, or winged snails, swept down from above before the eyes of the watching eels, their forms glistening with reflected light like a rain of strangely shaped hailstones — daggers and spirals and cones of glassy clearness. Shrimps loomed up — pale ghosts in the dim light. Sometimes the shrimps were pursued by pale fishes, round of mouth and flabby of flesh, with rows of light organs set like jewels on their gray flanks. Then the shrimps often expelled jets of luminous fluid that turned to a fiery cloud to blind and confuse their enemies. Most of the fishes seen by the eels wore silver armor, for silver is the prevailing color or badge of those waters that lie at the end of the sun's rays. Such were the small dragonfish, long and slender of form, with fangs glistening in their opened mouths as they roamed through the water in an endless pursuit of prey. Strangest of all were the fishes, half as long as a man's finger and clothed in a leathery skin, that shone with turquoise and amethyst lights and gleamed like quicksilver over their flanks. Their bodies were thin from side to side and tapered to sharp edges. When enemies looked down from above, they saw nothing, for the backs of the hatchet-fish were bluish black that was invisible in the black sea. When sea hunters looked up from below, they were confused and could not distinguish their prey with certainty, for the mirrorlike flanks of the hatchetfish reflected the blueness of the water and their outlines were lost in a shimmer of light.

The young eels lived in one layer or tier of a whole series of horizontal communities that lay one below the other, from the nereid worms that spun their strands of silk from frond to frond of the brown sargassum weed floating on the surface to the sea spiders and prawns that crawled precariously over the deep and yielding oozes of the floor of the abyss.

Above the eels was the sunlight world where plants grew, and small fishes shone green and azure in the sun, and blue and crystal jellyfish moved at the surface.

Then came the twilight zone where fishes were opalescent or silver, and red prawns shed eggs of a bright orange color, and round-mouthed fishes were pale, and the first light organs twinkled in the gloom.

Then came the first black layer, where none wore silvery sheen or opalescent luster, but all were as drab as the water in which they lived, wearing monotones of reds and browns and blacks whereby they might fade into the surrounding obscurity and defer the moment of death in the jaws of an enemy. Here the red prawns shed deep-red eggs, and the round-mouthed fishes were black, and many creatures wore luminous torches or a multitude of small lights arranged in rows or patterns that they might recognize friend or enemy.

Below them lay the abyss, the primeval bed of the sea, the deepest of all the Atlantic. The abyss is a place where change comes slow, where the passing of the years has no meaning, nor the swift succession of the seasons. The sun has no power in those depths, and so their blackness is a blackness without end, or beginning, or degree. No beating of tropical sun on the surface miles above can lessen the bleak iciness of those abyssal waters that varies little through summer or winter, through the years that melt into centuries, and the centuries into ages of geologic time. Along the floor of the ocean basins, the currents are a slow creep of frigid water, deliberate and inexorable as the flow of time itself.

Down beneath mile after mile of water — more than four miles in all — lay the sea bottom, covered with a soft, deep ooze that had been accumulating there through eons upon eons of time. These greatest depths of the Atlantic are carpeted with red clay, a pumicelike deposit hurled out of the earth from time to time by submarine volcanoes. Mingled with the pumice are spherules of iron and nickel that had their origin on some far-off sun and once rushed millions of miles through interstellar space, to perish in the earth's atmosphere and find their grave in the deep sea. Far up on the sides of the great bowl of the Atlantic the bottom oozes are thick with the skeletal remains of minute sea creatures of the surface waters — the shells of starry Foraminifera and the limy remains of algae and corals, the flintlike skeletons of Radiolaria and the frustules of diatoms. But long before such delicate structures reach this deepest bed of the abyss, they are dissolved and made one with the sea. Almost the only organic remains that have not passed into solution before they reach these cold and silent deeps are the ear bones of whales and the teeth of sharks. Here in the red clay, in the darkness and stillness, lies all that remains of ancient races of sharks that lived, perhaps, before there were whales in the sea; before the giant ferns flourished on the earth or ever the coal measures were laid down. All of the living flesh of these sharks was returned to the sea millions of years before, to be used over and over again in the fashioning of other creatures, but here and there a tooth still lies in the red-clay ooze of the deep sea, coated with a deposit of iron from a distant sun.

CHAPTER 6

WASHINGTON:
WAR AND POSTWAR

UNDER THE SEA-WIND was published on November 1, 1941, the eve of Pearl Harbor. Referring to its publication, Rachel Carson later remarked: "The world received the event with superb indifference." The first year's sales amounted to 1348 copies; the total, six years later, was still less than 1600. Her earnings, including fees for use of extracts in other publications and a small payment for an edition in German, came to under a thousand dollars. No wonder she advised a friend and author to try writing magazine articles rather than books, since she knew from sad experience that books did not pay: "Instead of another book now, have you thought of doing some magazine articles? I am going to sound very materialistic, but after all if one is to live even in part by writing, he may as well look at the facts. Except for the rare miracles where a book becomes a 'best seller,' I am convinced that writing a book is a very poor gamble financially. This is based not only on my own experience (which, heaven knows, confirms it fully) but on what friends in the publishing business tell me. The average book will earn its author very little more than one magazine article placed with the 'right' magazine."

Although Rachel Carson was deeply disappointed in the sales

of *Under the Sea-Wind*, she found comfort in the enthusiastic response of the scientific community. "I have been so pleased," she wrote her publisher, "with the reception the purely scientific people, who so often have little patience with popularizations of science, have given the book." She quoted an example. "Dr. Hubbs is one of the leading fishery biologists, who is apt to be caustic in his comments, so his commendations meant a good deal to me." Other reviews were equally good, as were the personal reactions of leading naturalists. "Last week," she wrote, "I heard Dr. [Arthur A.] Allen (the Cornell ornithologist whose very nice comment on the book you may remember) lecture in Constitution Hall. I met him afterward and had a very pleasant chat. One of the things he said was that the book 'will be as good ten years from now as it is today.' " She was also glad to hear that there was to be an edition in Braille and Talking Books: "It is nice to think of having a chance to tell blind people something about the ocean, and perhaps opening up for them wholly new vistas of thought."

The following October, *Under the Sea-Wind* was made a selection of the Scientific Book Club. Best of all was the choice of two chapters by Dr. William Beebe for his anthology, *The Book of Naturalists*. This was the beginning of a long and fruitful friendship.

∾∾∾

Meanwhile, Rachel Carson's job in Washington became increasingly demanding as all government departments were mobilized for the war effort. In 1940, the Bureau of Fisheries (in the Department of Commerce) had been merged with the Biological Survey (in the Department of Agriculture), to form the Fish and Wildlife Service, under the Department of the Interior. Ira N. Gabrielson, former chief of the Biological Survey, was appointed director. (A position which he held until 1946, when he was succeeded by Albert M. Day.) Dr. Gabrielson remembers Rachel Carson as a well-trained biologist with a gift for expression not always found in scientists or in government employees. She was, he recalls, extremely shy: almost unable to get the words out when she came to him to ask for a writing job. This is hardly to be wondered at, considering that she was young, inexperienced and, above all, entering a man's world; she was one of the first two women ever to be hired by the Fish and Wildlife Service in other than a clerical capacity. Her shyness, however, was apparently no hindrance to her career, as she worked her way up the bureaucratic ladder: Assistant Aquatic Biologist (1942–43); Associate Aquatic Biologist (1943–45); Aquatic Biologist (1945–46); Information Specialist (1946–49); Biologist and Chief Editor from 1949 till her resignation from the Service in 1952. From the beginning, her work was concerned with publications. For example, she did most of the editorial work for the *Progressive Fish-Culturist*, which had a circulation among professionals of some 3500 copies. She was a firm editor, and had little patience with second-rate work. No time-wasting was allowed. But if she was demanding of her associates, she nevertheless managed to make them like it — no doubt because she was even more demanding of herself. Always calm and polite in her official dealings with writers, she would later blow off steam in private if they were incompetent.

Her own major contribution to government publications began shortly after the beginning of the war. At first she was not too happy with her department's role in the war effort. On March 15, 1942, she wrote to a friend: "Yesterday, after being victim of a sort of cat-and-mouse game for three months, we received final orders to go to Chicago . . . I am quite distressed about it, mostly for personal reasons like leaving behind certain people, but there seems to be nothing to do but go along. In many ways, I'd rather get into some sort of work that had more immediate value in relation to the war, but in boondoggling, official Washington, I don't know how to find it. Really, seeing the things that I do here in the Government makes one very disheartened for the future."

The move to Chicago was a wartime measure, presumably to relieve the shortage of office space in Washington. It did not actually take place until the end of the summer, and as far as Rachel Carson's office was concerned was of short duration; she was back in Maryland by mid-spring of 1943. Meanwhile she had been "exceedingly busy with two manuscripts for early government publication." These were Conservation Bulletins Nos. 33 and 34: *Food from the Sea: Fish and Shellfish of New England* and *Food from Home Waters: Fishes of the Middle West,* both of which appeared in 1943. They were followed by similar bulletins on the South and Middle Atlantic coasts. These booklets, averaging around fifty or sixty pages each, are crammed with facts, yet written in a manner that the American housewife could understand. The objective was to augment our wartime food supply — particularly of proteins — by popularizing little-known seafoods, and thereby take some of the pressure off familiar fishes such as cod and haddock, that were suffering from overexploitation. Her introductory note shows her approach: "Before we can try new foods, we must know what they are — something of their nutritive value, where they come from, how market supplies vary with the season. Our enjoyment of these foods is heightened if we also know something of the creatures from which they are derived, how and where they live, how they are caught, their habits and migrations."

While these bulletins were essentially handbooks of information, written for a practical purpose, they contain occasional pages of vivid exposition rarely found among the products of the Government Printing Office. Take for example this brief life history of the clam, in *Food from the Sea:*

The Clam

During the summer months the water over the flats is often teeming with the minute, swimming forms that are embryo clams. These tiny creatures are swept in and out by the changing tides, and are carried up and down the coast by prevailing currents and eddies. Each of the embryos is about ⅟₃₀₀ of an inch long and swims through the water by a spinning motion. At this stage they are very sensitive to temperature changes, and a long, cold rain may kill them by the thousand. Probably many are eaten by small jellyfish, comb jellies, and larval fishes. Those that survive develop a muscular "foot" (the digging tool of the adult clam), a siphon or breathing tube, and gills. Meanwhile the swimming organ, a small pad covered with rapidly beating hairs, gradually shrivels away, and some time between the third and sixth days of life the young clam is no longer able to swim, but sinks to the bottom.

Since some spawning of clams continues throughout the entire period from about the first of June to the end of August, there is also during this time a light but more or less constant rain of young clams descending from the overlying water onto the bottom, for some of the young are reaching the end of the swimming stage almost every day. Sometimes large numbers settle on eel grass and seaweeds, and thick colonies of them may populate certain shore areas, leaving other areas practically barren. Probably these thickly settled areas are places where eddying currents have concentrated large numbers of swimming young.

When it descends to the underlying bottom the young clam is only about as large as a sand grain. Instead of burrowing at once into the bottom it spins a tough thread (known as a byssus) and anchors itself to a bit of seaweed, a stone, or a shell, and so keeps its position during the tidal ebb and flow. At slack water it may cast off the anchor line and creep about on its muscular foot; but soon it secretes another thread, although it may continue to crawl about in various directions at the end of its tether. At this stage the young clams have no protection against enemies that creep about over the bottom or swim above it, for the shell is thin and brittle. Crabs and small fishes may eat them, but probably the greatest damage is done by young starfish, which are spawned about the same time as the clams and settle to the bottom with them. The infant starfish are able to attack young clams and force open their shells in the same way that the adults attack grown shellfish.

Some time before the shell has become ¼-inch long, the young clam begins to dig among the sand grains with its sharp foot, gradually working the shell down into the bottom. Usually this first descent is only a trial venture, and the young clam may come out of its shallow burrow and wander about for a time, only to reimbed itself once more. Within the burrow it anchors itself by byssus threads, which may be secreted until the shell is at least ½-inch long. About this stage the clam makes its final descent, when it loses its power to secrete threads through the disappearance of the byssus gland. It never again leaves its subterranean chamber of its own accord.

ᔇᔇᔇ

In these years during and immediately after the war, Rachel Carson was in the classic position of the would-be writer who cannot afford the time for creative work. Her job at the Fish and Wildlife Service allowed her little literary outlet. Her salary was modest, and she had a household to support. She decided to take her own advice and see if she could supplement her government pay by writing magazine articles during evenings and weekends.

Fortunately there were at Simon and Schuster two members of the staff who were interested in her problem: her editor Maria Lieper, and Sonia Bleeker (Mrs. Herbert Zim), whose job selling subsidiary rights to the firm's books had given her broad experience in the periodical market. "Sunnie" Bleeker was soon acting virtually as her literary agent, explaining the complications of the magazine business, suggesting the most likely outlets, offering occasional editorial advice, estimating probable fees. With her encouragement, Rachel wrote an article on oysters which the *Reader's Digest* considered but eventually turned down. It was not, she realized, her kind of writing. "I hardly know how to be more informative," she wrote to Sunnie, "without changing the tone of the thing. As you know, it was written to the *Digest's* specification of 'lively reading.'" More to her taste was a plan — alas never realized — for a series of monthly articles on outdoor nature, tied in with the seasons. "While it is relatively easy to write about the oddities in nature, which we stressed in the oyster piece, my real interest is not in the believe-it-or-not type of thing, but in developing a deeper appreciation of nature."

Meanwhile she had to write for the market. In late 1944, almost precisely three years after publication of *Under the Sea-Wind*, she broke into the *Reader's Digest* with a story about bats and their use of "radar" to avoid obstacles in the dark. She referred to this later as "representative of a different kind of writing I have occasionally indulged in for practical reasons." It is a piece of clear and competent exposition, with no claim to literary distinction. She submitted it to *This Month*, which did not respond, and then to the *Digest*, which eventually did. "Dear Sunnie," wrote the grateful author. "This is to tell you at the earliest possible moment that your excellent advice, given more than a month ago, worked out perfectly. Today's mail brought word from the *Reader's Digest* that they are using the bat article, and a check for $200. [The final price was $500.] I want to remind you that this good fortune is entirely due to you, for I should never have had the courage to withdraw the article from *This Month* and approach the *Digest* on it without your advice and moral support. I hope you know how much I appreciate it." Nor was the article unrelated to the war effort. The navy decided to reprint it for recruiting purposes, as "one of the clearest expositions of radar yet made available for public consumption."

As the war drew toward an end, Rachel Carson felt increasingly restless in her job, and eager to break away. "I'm definitely in the mood to make a change of some sort," she wrote to Sunnie Bleeker, "preferably to something that will give me more time for my own writing. At this stage, that seems the prime necessity."

Money continued to be a problem. Not long after the sale of the bat article to *Reader's Digest*, another magazine offered $55 for a short piece on the chimney swift. Rachel had just had a minor operation, and was feeling strapped: "I don't call $55 a good fee . . . but I am really in a quandary. When I think about my hospital and doctors' bills I'm inclined to grab the $55 rather than gamble on placing it somewhere else." Grab it she did.

Through the good offices of Quincy Howe and Lincoln Schuster, she applied for an editorial job at the *Digest*, but there was no opening for her. Next, she turned to Dr. William Beebe, who had already shown such interest in her writing. She hoped that he might be able to find something for her with the New York Zoological Society, which had recently announced expanded activities in the field of public education in natural history and conservation: "As you may remember, I have been with the Fish and Wildlife Service as a biologist and writer for nearly ten years. Currently, I have been in charge of informational matters related to the wartime fishery program. This specific assignment will soon come to an end. While I am offered a reasonably attractive future with the Service, for some time I have felt disinclined to continue longer in a government agency. Frankly, I don't want my own thinking in regard to 'living natural history' to become set in the molds which hard necessity sometimes imposes upon government conservationists! I cannot write about these things unless I can be sincere. So if a broader field is open I should certainly want to consider its possibilities." Dr. Beebe did his best: "You should have no trouble fulfilling every requirement if there is any opening anywhere." But there was not. One more try: the National Audubon Society. Her letter of application, written in November of 1945, gives a good summary of her writing experience up to that time: "I have done one book in which birds figure rather prominently — *Under the Sea-Wind* (S & S, 1941) from which Beebe recently reprinted a couple of chapters in his *Book of Naturalists*. In the magazine field, I have written for the *Atlantic, Collier's, Coronet, Transatlantic, Nature Magazine,* and a few others. For the government, I have done a series of Conservation Bulletins on the fishes and fisheries of the various regions, as well as turning out quantities of press releases and other short things." Again no luck. Over a year later, she was complaining to a friend: "No, my life isn't at all well ordered and I don't know where I am going! I know that if I could choose what seems to me the ideal existence, it would be just to live by writing. But I have done far too little to dare risk it. And all the while my job with the Service grows and demands more and more of me, leaving less time that I could put on my own writing. And as my salary increases little by little, it becomes even more impossible to give it up! That is my problem right now, and not knowing what to do about it, I do nothing. For the past year or so I have told myself that the job (for the first time in my years with the Service) was giving me the travel I wanted and could not afford on my own and that, temporarily, was compensation for its other demands. But now the man higher up is leaving, and I may have to take his place, which will mean very close confinement to the office, I'm afraid."

Rachel Carson's job was indeed demanding, and destined to become more so, but she never let it become a bore. Shirley Briggs, who joined the Service in 1945, recalls that "her qualities of zest and humor made even the dull stretches of bureaucratic procedure a matter for quiet fun, and she could instill a sense of adventure into the editorial routine of a government department. My office adjoined hers, and this gave me an inaccurate and heady view of government life. With her and Dr. Lionel A. Walford, with whom she shared the office and the task of producing Fish and Wildlife Service publications, a small group used to gather over sandwiches at noon and tea at appropriate intervals. Intransigent official ways, small stupidities, and inept pronouncements were changed from annoyances into sources of merriment. Nothing could pass the wry scrutiny of that gathering and still seem unsurmountable or too frustrating . . . Ruthless with her own writing, she tried equally to raise the standards of the Federal prose she dealt with in her Fish and Wildlife post. The tact and skill with which she tackled uninspired writers was a joy to watch. Her private views were often more pungent."

A practical joke now and then helped to let off steam. Rachel's fellow workers still remember the "Cookbook Hoax": an elaborate plan designed to embarrass a lady in the Chicago office of the Information Section, who had produced a shoddy publication on the cooking of wild game, most of it plagiarized and some of it absurd. They concocted a telegram to the lady, purportedly from a feature writer for a big New York magazine. It informed her that the writer and a photographer were coming out to do an illustrated interview, including photos of a distinctive dish, and named the very day on which Rachel's colleague Bert Walford was indeed scheduled to arrive at the Chicago office. The telegram went on to suggest that the dish should be "field mice for twelve" served with mushrooms and white wine. Unfortunately a legal friend who had agreed to send the telegram from New York remembered that telegraphing under a false name was a penitentiary offense, and so the hoax never came off. But as they later recalled, "we had almost as much fun thinking it up, and imagining the scene."

These early years in Washington, Rachel later remarked, were the only carefree ones she ever had. At home her mother took care of the housework (Rachel hated cooking) and could see to the young nieces when Rachel wanted to go off for the weekend or to attend an evening party. "Looking back at the records," recalls Shirley Briggs, "I was astonished at the number of parties we had. And Rachel was always there if possible. They were mostly the sort of gatherings typical of wartime Washington, and just thereafter, groups of assorted people who had been uprooted from their normal academic or other lives, and gathered at each others' homes to talk and keep up their interests in art or music or writing or whatever they really wanted to get back to . . . Rachel appreciated so many kinds of people, and was always glad to meet new ones and enter into whatever conversation or merriment was going on at these affairs."

With their common interest in hiking and outdoor exploration, Rachel and Shirley seized every opportunity to get into the field — sometimes in line of duty, more often with the local Audubon Society (of whose magazine, *Atlantic Naturalist*, Shirley was to become editor). One of their first trips together was to the Hawk Mountain Sanctuary in Pennsylvania in October 1945, to watch the famous fall migration. Rachel found it an exciting — if somewhat chilly — experience, as shown by these passages from an unpublished sketch:

Road of the Hawks

They came by like brown leaves drifting on the wind. Sometimes a lone bird rode the air currents; sometimes several at a time, sweeping upward until they were only specks against the clouds or dropping down again toward the valley floor below us; sometimes a great burst of them milling and tossing, like the flurry of leaves when a sudden gust of wind shakes loose a new batch from the forest trees . . . On the horizon to the north, formed by a series of seven peaks running almost at right angles to the ridge on which we sit, an indistinct blur takes form against the sky. Second by second the outlines sharpen. Soon the unmistakable silhouette of a hawk is etched on the gray. It is too soon to make out the identifying lines of wing and tail that mark him for one species or another. On he comes, following the left side of the ridge, high up. Sometimes he banks steeply and his outlines melt into the sky. Then a swift wing beat or two and we have him in our glasses again . . .

Now follows a long wait with no more hawks. I settle back against the rock behind me, seeking shelter from the wind, trying vainly to draw some physical comfort from the hard angularity of stone. The cold is bitter. The morning had seemed reasonably mild down in the valley, as we had our quick cups of coffee in the predawn blackness. But here on the mountain top we are in the sweep of all the winds out of a great emptiness of sky, and the cold seeps through to the very marrow of my bones. But cold, windy weather is hawk weather, and so I am glad, although I shiver and my nose reddens, and I look speculatively at my thermos of hot coffee. But that must last the day, and now it is only ten o'clock.

Mists are drifting over the valley. A grayness overhangs all the sky and the clouds seem heavy with unshed rain. It is an elemental landscape — a great rockpile atop a mountain, nearby a few trees that have been stripped and twisted by the mountain winds, a vast, pale, arching sky.

Perhaps it is not strange that I, who greatly love the sea, should find much in the mountains to remind me of it. I cannot watch the headlong descent of the hill streams without remembering that, though their journey be long, its end is in the sea. And always in these Appalachian highlands there are reminders of those ancient seas that more than once lay over all this land. Halfway up the steep path to the lookout is a cliff formed of sandstone; long ago it was laid down under shallow marine waters where strange and unfamiliar fishes swam; then the seas receded, the mountains were uplifted, and now wind and rain are crumbling the cliff away to the sandy particles that first composed it. And these whitened limestone rocks on which I am sitting — these, too, were formed under that Paleozoic ocean, of the myriad tiny skeletons of creatures that drifted in its water. Now I lie back with half closed eyes and try to realize that I am at the bottom of another ocean — an ocean of air on which the hawks are sailing.

∾∾∾

In addition to Audubon Society expeditions, an occasional official assignment broke up the often monotonous office routine. Rachel later recalled one such trip to an area as different from the Appalachians as it could possibly be, where the terrain itself, rather than the ocean of air above it, gave her a "sense of the sea on land." This was the vast, watery grassland of the Florida Everglades, now a national park but at that time under the jurisdiction of the Fish and Wildlife Service.

The Heart of the Everglades

Two of us were staying at a hotel in Miami Beach, visiting various wildlife areas in the vicinity. When we heard about Mr. Don Poppenhager and his wonderful "glades buggy," we decided to try to arrange a trip. Mr. Poppenhager had never taken a woman into the swamp and at first he was hesitant. He warned us that it was a very uncomfortable experience; we assured him we could take it and really wanted to go. So he agreed to meet us at a little store on the Tamiami Trail kept by a character known as Ma Szady.

I think our elegant Miami Beach hotel had been a little suspicious of our comings and goings on strange errands and in strange costumes, but the morning we left for the Everglades trip was almost too much for them. One of the Fish and Wildlife men was to pick us up at 5 a.m. and take us over the trail. This was in the summer, and a tropical darkness still hung over Miami at that hour. Not wanting to arouse the hotel, Shirley and I crept down the stairs laden with all our strange gear. As we tiptoed through the lobby, the head of a very sleepy but thoroughly suspicious clerk rose above the desk. "Yer not checking out, are yuh?" he asked. I don't think his estimate of us rose when a very noisy, 2-ton government truck roared down the street and stopped at the hotel for its passengers.

The glades buggy that was waiting for us was a wonderful conveyance. It was built something like a tractor, with six pairs of very large wheels. Its engine was completely naked and exposed, and during the trip blasted its heat on the three of us perched on the buggy's single seat. There were various tools — pliers, screw drivers, etc., in a little rack against the motor block, and from time to time Mr. Poppenhager leaned out as we jogged along and turned something or jabbed at the motor. It seemed to be in a perpetual state of boiling over; and now and then Mr. P. would stop and get out with a tin can and dip up some water — there was water everywhere — and pour into the radiator. Usually he would drink a little — "the best water in the world" he would say.

There was a curious sense of the sea there in the heart of the Everglades. At first I couldn't analyze it but I felt it strongly. There is first of all a sense of immense space, from the utter flatness of the land and the great expanse of sky. The feeling of space is almost the same as at sea. The cloud effects were beautiful and always changing; then rain came over the grass, making a beautiful soft play of changing color — all gray and soft green. And again I found myself remembering rain at sea, dimpling the soft gray sheet of water. And in the Everglades the coral rock is always cropping out — underlying the water and raised in jagged boulders among the grass. Once that rock was formed by coral animals, living in a shallow sea that covered this very place. There is today the feeling that the land has formed only the thinnest veneer over this underlying platform of the ancient sea — that at any time the relations of sea and land might again be reversed.

And as we traveled from one to another of the "hammocks" of palmetto and other trees that rise here and there in the great sea of grass, we thought irresistibly of islands in the ocean. Except for scattered cypresses, all the trees of this part of the Everglades are concentrated in the hammocks, which form where depressions in the rock accumulate a little soil. Everywhere else, there is only rock, water, and grass . . .

To us the whole area seemed as trackless and as lacking in landmarks as the sea, but our guide knew exactly where he was going. Our only bad moments came later in the afternoon, when there began to be some question whether we had enough gas to get us back to the Trail. Mosquitoes had been with us all day, settling in clouds every time we stopped moving. So the thought of a night in the swamp wasn't pleasant. However, we made it about dusk, just as the Game Warden and the Fish and Wildlife patrolmen were beginning to line up cars along the Trail to guide us back by their headlights.

∽∾∽

Shirley Briggs recorded in her diary a more modest trip in mid-April of 1946, when she and Rachel were gathering material for the first of the Conservation in Action booklets* on Chincoteague Island, along the Maryland coast. "Off at 6, reaching Chincoteague about 1:30 . . . the refuge manager took us out by motorboat — involving wading ashore, our tennis shoes got mighty cold e'er the day was over. Photographed clammers and oysterers, climbed the lighthouse, dug clams, went on a wild hell-for-leather ride in his army CR car thru the woods to reach 2 horses mired in the tidal flats." Four more days were spent exploring, birding, photographing on the island. And no sooner were they back home than they were off again, this time on a shad boat. Life was not all paperwork.

As Shirley Briggs later recalled, most of Rachel's exploring of the natural world was necessarily near home: first in western Pennsylvania, then in Maryland and Maine. "This did not re-

* See pages 100–108.

flect lack of enthusiasm for travel to farther places, but rather the circumstances of her work and family responsibilities through the years. For her, though, there was surely more to be found in a weekend jaunt to Ocean City, Maryland, or Hawk Mountain, Pennsylvania, than many find in remote and glamorous tours. In her book, *The Sense of Wonder*, she told her ways to introduce a child to nature — storms and night as well as summer sunshine. We who were included in her own expeditions learned a great deal about many aspects of our world, but most of all a way of seeing, alert for every impression, with keen delight in all manner of small creatures as well as the vast horizons and far reaches."

Among Rachel Carson's unpublished papers are a few fragments, written during these years, that express this delight in the sights and sounds of nature to be found just beyond one's doorstep. They were later to be used in *The Sense of Wonder*:

If I had been asked a month ago, I would have said my back yard was a peaceful enough place at night. That was before I had gone exploring in it with a flashlight, and had seen how the bushes, the jungles of moss and grass, and even the woodpile were filled with hunters. After an hour of exploring by flashlight, you realize as never before how alive the night is. It is alive with a thousand watchful eyes. It is filled with the tenseness of the weak who must be swift to evade their stronger enemies. It is vibrant with the stealth and cunning of those who must stalk their prey to live.

Here on my woodpile I have become acquainted with half a dozen spiders, permanent, respectable residents who have spun their funnel webs in the dark interstices between the split oak logs. In the daytime I can see the spiders lying back in the deep throats of their funneled webs, watchful, perhaps, but quiescent. Yet as my flashlight sweeps their webs at night, I have many a time seen a spider dash out across the floor of his web in hot pursuit of some insect who had been unfortunate enough to blunder against the web in the darkness. One of these spiders I came to know rather well. Every night I visited the woodpile

I made a point of peeping down her funnel to see whether she was still there. One night I was startled to see a strange spider — a larger, hairier, more sinister looking creature occupying the funnel. Holding the light so that it would illuminate the whole depth of the web, I saw, deep in the funnel, a little body that looked like the remains of a spider. I could only surmise that some dark internecine tragedy had overtaken my friend.

About this same time, her pleasure in the voices of the night took a new turn:

"What do you know about insect voices?" I suddenly demanded one August night of a friend far better versed in insect lore than I.

It was a question that had lain unasked in some recess of my mind almost as long as I can remember. No one with the slightest awareness of the natural world about him can have failed to be conscious in some degree of that insect chorus that fills the night with its throbbing rhythm from midsummer until frost. But of the individual voices, or better, the individual instruments that make up that elemental earth orchestra, my ignorance had been complete and abysmal until that sudden, unpremeditated question made me determined to find the answer.

And so began what has been one of the most fascinating and satisfying of all my interests in the world of nature.

Characteristically, her determination to learn as much as she could about the natural world around her never obscured her appreciation of its mystery and beauty. Naturalist and poet went hand in hand as she listened to the crickets on a summer's night:

Most haunting of all is the one I call the fairy bellringer. I have never found him — I'm not sure I want to. For his voice, and surely he himself, are so ethereal, so delicate, so otherworldly, that he should remain invisible, as he has through all the nights I have searched for him.

It is impossible to listen to his whispered chiming in the marigold bed and keep your mind on the sober facts of natural history. Your brain may tell you that you are listening to the stridulations of the snowy tree cricket, but though you try to be ever so matter of fact, you will be able to think of nothing but fairies when you hear it. It is exactly the sound that should come from a bell held in the hand of the tiniest elf — inexpressibly clear and silvery, so faint, so barely-to-be-heard, so ghostly, that you hold your breath as you bend closer to the green glades from which the fair chiming comes.

Yet "summer's lease hath all too short a date." The sadness of autumn is expressed in these two short paragraphs entitled "October Night":

Tonight I stepped out into the garden at dusk, and walked down the path where the blackened flowers of the wood asters told of the hard frost of last night. I stood under the old oak and listened. There was only silence in the garden. Silence in the tall hedge that separates my place from my neighbors, silence in the forsythias by the porch, silence in the woodpile by the fence and in the maples overhead. My mind had warned me that the frost last night had surely stilled all the little voices that used to greet me there — the insect music of wing rubbed over wing or of legs, like chiton fiddle bows, drawn across the wings — but my heart did not want to believe it.

But tonight there is only silence, a chill that is not wholly of temperature, a queer emptiness. And so I have come back into the house and closed the door on summer. And I have put a fresh log on the fire and sat down to remember the little world into which I stepped last August, my passport a flashlight and my visa a suddenly awakened curiosity about those insect voices which I had heard — and yet not heard — all my life.

For summer holidays, Rachel managed to escape to a wholly different environment. The place she chose was to have a lasting influence on both her life and her writing. In July 1946 she rented a cabin on the Sheepscot River near Boothbay, Maine. "Of course it is not what we would call a river at home," she wrote to Shirley Briggs, "for it is presumably briny as the ocean, and has a ten or twelve foot tidal range. Our little place is on the very edge of the water — if you jumped out of the windows on one side you would fall in. And in front there are only a few feet of grass to the water's edge. The cabin is built against a rocky hillside with spruces and birches around it. With few exceptions, the only sounds are the lapping of water, the cries of gulls, herons, and ospreys, sometimes the tolling of a bell buoy, and — when the wind is right, the very distant sound of surf. And about sunset, we always hear something that I take to be a hermit thrush over on the Island [Indiantown Island]. I have never before heard the hermits, so am not sure, but it sounds the way one ought to sound.

"The most common little birds are warblers. There is a wonderful pine woods up over the hill, all carpeted with reindeer moss and full of the most wonderful smells when the sun is hot on the evergreens. It is a happy hunting ground for warblers, and you can almost always hear their lispy little voices in the trees overhead, and with luck you can get the glasses on them. Unfortunately for the length of my bird list, almost every warbler I see is a black-throated green, but I have also added the myrtle, magnolia, chestnut-sided, and parula, as well as yellowthroats and redstarts. For very close bird neighbors, we have a phoebe nesting under the eaves of the cabin, and a song sparrow who evidently regards this place as his, but generously lets us use it, and throws in plenty of songs for good measure. To reach a rocky ocean shore, we have to drive probably five miles to the nearest one and nearer ten to the prettiest — Ocean Point.*

The latter has some good tide pools which I have as yet investigated only in a general way, but this week I plan to get there at extreme low tide, which is best for finding creatures . . . It is nice to lie on your back and watch the birds overhead. On warm sunny days the gulls go so high they look about the size of stars. Sometimes a dark star comes into sight, and that is an osprey.

---

* Scene of the "fairy cave" later described in the opening pages of *The Edge of the Sea* — see page 166.

"From all this you will know that the only reason I will ever come back is that I don't have brains enough to figure out a way to stay here the rest of my life. At least I know now that my greatest ambition is to be able to buy a place here and then manage to spend a great deal of time in it — summers at least!" *

Among Rachel Carson's unpublished papers is a sketch of Indiantown Island: the rhythm of life as she observed it during the still summer days and in the early evening hours when the whole landscape came alive. She entitled it "An Island I Remember."

* This ambition was finally fulfilled seven years later when the proceeds from *The Sea Around Us* enabled her to buy land and build a summer cottage on the edge of the Sheepscot River, in West Southport.

CHAPTER 7

"An Island I Remember"

IT WAS only a small island, perhaps a mile long and half as wide. The face it presented to the mainland shore was a dark wall of coniferous forest rising in solid, impenetrable blackness to where the tops of the spruces feathered out into a serrate line against the sky. There was no break in that wall anywhere that I could see, no suggestion of paths worn through island forests, no invitation to enter. At high tide the sea came up almost to the trees, with only little patches of light colored rock showing at the water line, like white daubs made by a painter's brush. As the tide ebbed and the water dropped lower on the rocks, the white patches grew and merged with each other, exposing the solid granite foundations of the island, so that now there was a high rocky rampart, on which grew the living green wall of the forest.

There was perhaps a quarter of a mile of water between the island and the mainland shore where our cabin stood, its screened porch at the sea wall and its back against a steep hillside where ferns were dark among the rocks and the branches of great hemlocks reached down to touch the ground. Day after day the island lay under the summer sun, with no sound coming from it, and nothing moving at the visible edges of the forest. On every low tide I could see a solemn line of cormorants standing on a rocky ledge that ran out from the south end of the island, their long necks extended skyward. The gulls were less broodingly protective of the approaches to the island forest, their presence about the shores of the island more casual as they perched on the weed-covered rocks while waiting for the turn of the tide.

About sundown the island, that had lain so silent all day long, began to come to life. Then the forms of large, dark birds could be seen moving among its trees, and hoarse cries that brought to mind thoughts of ancient, reptilian monsters came across the water. Sometimes one of the birds would emerge from the shadows and fly across to our shore, then revealing itself as a great blue heron out for an evening's fishing.

It was during those early evening hours that the sense of mystery that invested the island drew somehow closer about it, so that I wished even more to know what lay beyond the wall of dark spruces. Was there somewhere within it an open glade that held the sunlight? Or was there only solid forest from shore to shore? Perhaps it was all forest, for the island voice that came to us most clearly and beautifully each evening was the voice of a forest spirit, the hermit thrush. At the hour of the evening's beginning its broken, silvery cadences drifted with infinite deliberation across the water. Its phrases were filled with a beauty and a meaning that were not wholly of the present, as though the thrush were singing of other sunsets, extending far back beyond his personal memory, through eons of time when his forebears had known this place, and from spruce trees long since returned to earth had sung the beauty of the evening.

It was in the evenings, too, that I came to know the herring gulls as I had never known them before. The harbor gull — the gull of the fish wharves — is an opportunist. He sits with his fellows on the roofs above the harbor, or each on his wharf piling, and waits, knowing at what hour the refuse will be discharged from the fish house, or when the first of the returning fishing boats will appear on the horizon, to be met with excited

cries. But the gulls of the island were different. They were fishermen, and like the men who handle the nets, they lived by their
own toil.

I suppose a certain amount of regular fishing went on during
the day, but I was especially aware of the excitement that attended the runs of young herring that came into our cove each
evening.

It is strange to reflect on that twilight migration of the young
herring that by day have moved widely through the coastal waters, but now are drawn, as the water darkens to black and silver,
to follow the channels between the rocky foundations of the
islands.

We would know the herring were coming by watching the behavior of the gulls. Most of the late afternoon they would have
dozed on their rocky perches along the shore of the island. But
as sunset neared and the shadows of the spruces began to build
dark spires in the water, a stir of excitement would pass among
the gulls. There would be a good deal of flying up and down the
channel, as though scouts were coming and going. It seemed
that some intelligence of the movements of the fish was being
spread among the birds. More and more of the gulls would join
in the scouting parties, until the whole flock was in movement,
their sharp, staccato cries coming across the water.

When the water was glassy calm, holding the colors of the
evening sky on its surface, we could time as exactly as the gulls
the arrival of the herring in our cove. Suddenly the silken sheet
would be dimpled by a thousand little noses pushing against the
water film. It would be streaked by a thousand little ripples
moving eagerly toward the shore. It would be shot through by a
thousand silver needles as the fish, swimming just beneath the
surface, disturbed the placid sheet. Then the herring would
begin flipping into the air. It seemed it was always out of the
corner of your eye that you saw them, and you never quite knew
where to look for the next little herring skipping recklessly into

the air in a sort of back somersault. They did it as though it were great fun — this rash defying of a strange and hostile element, the air. I believe it was a sort of play indulged in by these young children of the herring. They looked like silvery coins skipped along the surface. I never actually saw any of the youngsters caught in the air by a gull, but the quick eyes of the birds must certainly have been attracted by the bright flashes.

The gulls would greet the arrival of the herring schools with a frenzy of excitement, swooping, plunging, crying loudly. A gull does not dive as a tern does; he swoops and, not quite alighting, plucks his fish from the water. It takes a good eye and good timing. It is less graceful than the beautiful, clean dive of a tern, but perhaps it requires equal skill.

A night I especially remember there had been a large run of herring into the cove and it had come somewhat later than usual. The gulls, apparently determined to make their catch despite the gathering darkness, fished on until it was hard to understand how they could possibly see the fish. We could see their moving forms against the island — white, mothlike figures against the dark backdrop of the island forest, fluttering to and fro and all the while uttering their cries, in a scene out of some weird shadow world.

On sunny days the gulls would go aloft to ride the warm, ascending air currents. Up and up, sailing around in slow, wide circles, until they were almost lost to sight. I used to lie on my back on the dock, relaxing in the warm sunshine, and watch the gulls above me in the blue sky. Some were so high they were only white stars wheeling slowly in orbits of their own making.

It was possible to do a good deal of birding by ear alone, lying there on the dock half asleep. Once the sound had been identified by squinting through half-opened eyes, I knew without looking that the mouselike rustling and patter of very small feet on the dock, skirting my head and passing just beyond my outstretched arm, was the song sparrow on whose territory we were living. I knew that the soft "whuff, whuff" overhead was the wing beat of a gull, the bird passing so close that I could easily hear the sound of air sliding over the feathered wing surfaces. The gulls' wings made a dry sound, very different from the wet, spattering wing beat of a cormorant that had just risen from the water, and whose precipitate flight down the cove sounded like a wet dog shaking himself.

Often, as I lay there, I could hear the high, peeping whistle of an osprey, and opening my eyes, would see him coming down along the inner shore of the island. I think a pair of them had a nest somewhere up north of the island; when they carried fish, they were always going north.

And then there were the sounds of other, smaller birds — the rattling call of a kingfisher that perched, between forays after fish, on the posts of the dock; the call of the phoebe that nested under the eaves of the cabin; the redstarts that foraged in the birches on the hill behind the cabin and forever, it seemed to me, asked each other the way to Wiscasset, for I could easily twist their syllables into the query, "Which is Wiscasset? Which is Wiscasset?"

Sometimes the still water of the passage would be rippled, then broken, by the sleek, round head of a seal. Swimming up-current, his nostrils and forehead protruding, his passage sent diverging ripples running in silken V's toward the opposite shores. After looking gravely about him with soft, dark eyes, surveying for a moment the world of sun and air, the seal would disappear as silently as he had come, returning to the soft green lights, the seaweeds streaming from sunken rocks, the little silver gleams of fleeting fishes. There is always something of mystery about these mammals of the sea. Akin to ourselves in most of the biological processes, warm-blooded, possessing a hairy covering, suckling their young, yet they are at home in an element to which we can make only the briefest of visits.

Sometimes I would watch the island from the hill that sloped up from the water line to a wooded crest from which could be seen the cove and all the outlying islands. It was fun to climb the hill, carpeted so thickly with gray-green reindeer moss, studded with pine and spruce and low-growing juniper. On the sunny slopes the moss was so dry that it crunched underfoot like very cold snow, but in the deep shade it was soft and spongy. Beardlike tufts of the strange Usnea moss or old-man's-beard hung from the pines, a suggestion that the beautiful parula warbler might be about, for the parulas nest in pendant clumps of this moss.

And indeed the woods there on the hillside were bright with the moving, flitting forms of many warblers — the exquisite powder-blue parula with his breast band of orange and magenta; the Blackburnian, like flickering flames in the spruces; the myrtle, flashing his yellow rump patch. But most numerous of all was the trim little black-throated green warbler, whose dreamy, nostalgic song drifted all day long through the woods, little wisps of song lingering like bits of fog in the tree tops. Perhaps because I so invariably heard it in those woods, when I now recall the song in memory, it always brings with it a vivid picture of that sunny hill splashed with the dark shadows of the evergreens, and the scent of all the heady, aromatic, bitter-sweet fragrances compounded of pine and spruce and bayberry, warmed by the sun through the hours of a July day.

CHAPTER 8

CONSERVATION IN ACTION

EARLY IN 1947, a book appeared that Rachel Carson greeted
with joy and immediately recommended to her birding companions: *Spring in Washington* by Louis J. Halle, a young writer and
amateur naturalist at the State Department. She apparently regarded the author, whom she had not met, with a certain awe.
Their first encounter, on an early morning bird walk in mid-May
along the Chesapeake and Ohio Canal, was described by Shirley
Briggs in a letter written next day: "It was a cold morning —
thick frost abounded. The weather was splendid, though —
clear and warmer later . . . Presently we met two men, be-
decked with binoculars, and exchanged greetings. We were
watching a great swarm of swallows on the river, over the rapids,
and these men noted a couple of species we had missed . . . As
we proceeded on our separate ways, Ray and I remarked that one
man looked very like the picture of Mr. Halle, and we hoped it
was, indeed, he. We ventured out on the breakwater of the
Feeder Lock, and there found a rifle shell and the sandpiper
which it had killed. We had heard shots earlier, and were properly indignant that anyone had killed a bird on a sanctuary area,
and a sandpiper especially, which is always inviolate. After giving the little creature decent burial, we poked about in the brush

by the rapids, and saw a great many buntings. It was here that I scored my greatest triumph of the day. I had two close and unmistakable views of the prothonotary warbler. As I read the book, *Spring in Washington*, I find that I saw it in quite the right place, though I had not had any idea of finding it there this morning . . .

"As we retraced our steps, we saw the same two men coming back down the towpath, and this time Ray mustered her courage and asked the one if he were Mr. Halle. He was. We introduced ourselves, and had a pleasant little chat. He was sure he had seen some pine siskins among the goldfinches at Seneca, but he couldn't believe his eyes, because this is supposed to be far from their range. Ray was delighted to be able to tell him that she has had pine siskins coming to her feeder all winter, last seen ten days ago. He was elated to learn this, so we parted with great goodwill. We feared the poor man would be ruing his indiscretion in writing the book — all his favorite haunts now becoming overrun with his new public."

Three weeks later Rachel received a more formal introduction to Louis Halle through the good offices of their mutual friend, Edwin Way Teale. Teale had published his *Grassroot Jungles* in 1937 (the same year that *The Atlantic Monthly* printed "Undersea") and had followed it with three other volumes which combined the arts of writing and nature photography with singular success. He was now engaged on the first of the books on the four seasons which were to make him one of America's most popular writers in the field of natural history.

Twenty years after the event, Louis Halle recalled this memorable meeting:

Halle's Recollections

It was in the spring of 1947, in Washington, D.C., that I received a phone call from Edwin Way Teale. He and his wife were passing through on that trip from Florida to New England that he later memorialized in *North with the Spring*. Could I have lunch with them, he asked, to meet a friend who worked in the Department of the Interior, was interested in nature, and had read a recently published book of mine called *Spring in Washington*? So the four of us had lunch together, and that was how I met the Teales' friend, a Miss Carson.

Miss Carson was quiet, diffident, neat, proper, and without any affectation. My recollection is that she had not yet passed the age when one might refer to her as a "girl," although "young lady" might have been more appropriate in her case. There was something about her of the nineteenth century, of the times when there really had been young ladies. She had dignity; she was serious; and, as with Lear's Cordelia, "her voice was ever soft, gentle and low."

My recollection, which was to prove embarrassing later, was that she sought this meeting to ask my advice on how to develop a good literary style. This was a cherished compliment in itself; but I could not then know how great a compliment it really was, because all I knew of her at the time was that she was one of the "government girls" with which Washington swarmed. (It was also a very special compliment to be asked for advice on the art of writing in the presence of Teale, one of the most accomplished living writers in the field of nature.) To me, however it was more than just a compliment. For years I had been over my head in love with the English language, as I still am, and here was this government girl earnestly asking me to speak to her about my love.

It is probably just as well that I don't remember what I said. When, some three years later, a book called *The Sea Around Us* came out I discovered that I was the one who should have been listening while she did the talking. At the very least, we should have been talking together as fellow craftsmen, not as teacher and pupil. Typically, however, it was she who had put herself in the role of pupil. Later I almost felt as if I had been tricked, although she could not have tricked anyone in her whole life, such was her seriousness and integrity.

I never got to know her well. She was one of the persons I occasionally saw to say "hello" to, and I recall that my wife and I, during a visit to Washington after we had moved away, had tea with her and her mother at their house in Silver Spring. She was then paying a common penalty of fame, for she had become a public institution without having the facilities of an institution. She was daily overwhelmed by mail from her readers, mail that such a conscientious person would feel obliged to answer in detail. But she did not have the research assistants and the secretaries that, as a national institution, she needed. I doubt, moreover, that she would have enjoyed running herself as one runs a business. She could not have got away from being a simple human being; she could not have made herself behave like an institution.

One final memory that provides an echo of our first meeting. It had been my fortune to discover the nest of the first veeries known to breed in Washington or anywhere near it, and to follow the increase in nesting veeries over the first few years, while they were becoming the common breeding birds they now are. All this was duly reported in *Atlantic Naturalist*. One spring day Rachel phoned me, told me she had never seen a veery or heard one sing, and asked me to arrange a meeting. On a Sunday morning, then, I took her out into upper Rock Creek Park, where she listened to that phantom song,* as evanescent as breath on a windowpane, with precisely the same air of seeking knowledge with which she had once listened to a youngish man (himself as unaware as the veery) discoursing on the possibilities of the language.

I remember her as always attentive, always listening, always

---

* Years later, when she had become familiar with the song of this thrush at her place in Maine, Rachel Carson wrote: "To my ear, there is no other bird song of such unearthly beauty."

wanting to know. The French existentialists (none of whom, I suspect, has ever gone to a bird for knowledge) talk a great deal about living the "authentic" life. But Rachel Carson exemplified it.

∽∽∽

Unfortunately not all members of the local Audubon Naturalist Society, of which Rachel was a director, were so congenial, and some seemed more concerned with internal power politics than with birds. Rachel once remarked jokingly that she planned to make her fortune by writing another *Forever Amber*, based on characters she had met through the society. But what really distressed her was the successful effort of one aggressive faction to "pack" the annual meeting and thus keep some of the most distinguished members off the board. Characteristically, she chose not to resign, but to stick it out. Already in these early days she was a firm and spirited battler for her beliefs, which she fought for with zest once the issue was clear.

This firmness became ever more essential in her official job, the responsibilities of which increased with the expansion of the Fish and Wildlife's information service. In reply to an inquiry from a women's study group on "Women in Government," she summarized her official duties: "My job consists of general direction of the publishing program of the Service — working with authors in planning and writing their manuscripts, reviewing manuscripts submitted, and overseeing the actual editing and preparation of the manuscript for the printer. I have a staff of six assistants who handle the various details of this sort, including planning or executing illustrations, selecting appropriate type faces, plannings, general page layouts and design. It is really just the work of a small publishing house." *

* Her work in providing information on wildlife and conservation matters apparently extended beyond her official duties. The late Howard Zahniser, lobbyist and executive director of the Wilderness Society, recalled that Rachel had ghost-written many congressional speeches while she was with the Service; and added how happy he was, when her own books were published, to see her receive the personal recognition she deserved.

United States government publications, however useful, have seldom been noteworthy for their literary distinction or charm of format. When Rachel Carson became editor for the Fish and Wildlife Service, she welcomed the chance to show that good writing and printing were possible in the Washington bureaucracy, even though this occasionally involved conflict with the Government Printing Office. Her opportunity came when the Service, under the directorship of Albert M. Day, undertook to publish a series of illustrated booklets on the national wildlife refuges. Following passage of the Migratory Bird Conservation Act, a system of such refuges from the Atlantic Coast to California had been instituted in the early 1930s. The prime mover was Jay N. "Ding" Darling, then Chief of the Biological Survey, a fighting conservationist famous for his cartoons in defense of ducks and other wildlife. By the late 1940s there were some three hundred such refuges in existence, about two hundred of which were devoted to the protection of migratory waterfowl.

Under the supervision of the assistant director, Clarence Cottam (who many years later was so closely associated with *Silent Spring*), Rachel Carson was given responsibility for the new series of twelve booklets, which had the overall title "Conservation in Action." In stating the philosophy behind the enterprise, she expresses — without using the word — the ecological point of view, which was not so commonplace a generation ago as it is today:

The Western Hemisphere has a relatively short history of the exploitation of its natural resources by man. This history, though short, contains many chapters of reckless waste and appalling destruction. Entire species of animals have been exterminated, or reduced to so small a remnant that their survival is doubtful. Forests have been despoiled by uncontrolled and excessive cutting of lumber, grasslands have been destroyed by overgrazing. These and other practices have afflicted us with all the evils of soil erosion, floods, destruction of agricultural lands, and loss of wildlife habitats.

All the people of a country have a direct interest in conservation. For some, as for the commercial fishermen and trappers, the interest is financial. For others, successful conservation means preserving a favorite recreation — hunting, fishing, the study and observation of wildlife, or nature photography. For others, contemplation of the color, motion, and beauty of form in living nature yields aesthetic enjoyment of as high an order as music or painting. But for all the people, the preservation of wildlife and wildlife habitat means also the preservation of the basic resources of the earth, which men, as well as animals, must have in order to live. Wildlife, water, forests, grasslands — all are parts of man's essential environment; the conservation and effective use of one is impossible except as the others also are conserved.

We in the United States have been slow to learn that our wildlife, like other forms of natural wealth, must be vigorously protected if we are to continue to enjoy its benefits. The present generation has seen the awakening of a vital conservation sentiment.

. . . Like the resource it seeks to protect, wildlife conservation must be dynamic, changing as conditions change, seeking always to become more effective. We have much to accomplish before we can feel assured of passing on to future generations a land as richly endowed in natural wealth as the one we live in.

Needless to say, she welcomed the field trips that were involved. Most were on the Atlantic coast, but one took her as far west as Oregon. In September 1946 she spent about two weeks at the Parker River Refuge on the Massachusetts coast at the New Hampshire border, gathering material. "Of course I'd like to spend all my time doing just that sort of thing," she wrote to a friend, "but our budget is not likely to permit very much of it."

The Conservation in Action booklets are long out of date; they were tools for a specific purpose, not contributions to literature. A few passages will be enough to show how superior they were in style — and therefore in effectiveness — to the typical government publication. Here is a view of Plum Island, a spot cherished for its wildlife and natural beauty since the days of the Puritans:*

From PLUM ISLAND

Plum Island, the heart of the Parker River Refuge, is a long, narrow, coastal island. It begins where the Merrimack pours its waters into the Atlantic and ends about 9 miles to the south at Ipswich Bay. To get a panoramic view of Plum Island, climb one of the highest sand dunes . . . As your eyes range from east to west, you see five totally different kinds of country as the birds would classify it, five different zones of life each containing a different community of animal life. These regions are the ocean beach, the dunes, the thickets, the salt meadows, and the tidal flat of the salt marsh creeks.

Eastward from our observation point is the immensity of the Atlantic, nothing but water between you and Spain. Outlined by the white surf lines, a sandy beach runs the length of the island . . . On the landward edge of the beach, where the beachgrass Ammophila and the silvery-leaved dusty miller have begun to anchor the shifting grains, the dunes begin. Their contours are often steep, and as you look southward over the expanse of sand hills you see that the dune zone is pitted with many sandy depressions like bomb craters, their conical sides almost bare of plant growth. Except in these places, the dunes are widely covered with a low, sage-green carpet of the plant Hudsonia, helping to hold the shifting sand and prevent the sea

* One recalls the famous description by Samuel Sewell, who (anticipating the objectives of the Fish and Wildlife Service by two centuries) felt secure in his Christian inheritance "As long as *Plum Island* shall faithfully keep the commanded Post; Notwithstanding all the hectoring Words, and hard Blows of the proud and boisterous Ocean; As long as any Salmon, or Sturgeon shall swim in the stream of *Merrimack*, or any Perch, or Pickeril, in *Crane Pond*; As long as the Sea-Fowl shall know the Time of their coming, and not neglect seasonably to visit the Places of their Acquaintance . . ."

beach from engulfing the land. A scattered growth of bayberry and poison ivy begins midway across the dunes, gradually becomes more dense, and merges with the thickets that run down the center of the island. Cranberries grow abundantly in the low, wet places among the sand hills.

The shrubs, vines, and small trees that form the zone of thickets — the midrib of the island — are the home of the small land birds . . . Deer find good browsing here, as well as places of concealment from the casual eye. Most abundant plants are wild rose, sumac, beach plum, bayberry, black alder, chokecherry, pitch pine, aspen, and the ever present greenbrier.

Lying to the west, almost like another vast green sea, are the salt meadows. The winding Plum Island River, the lower reaches of the Parker, and all their small meandering tributaries traverse the marshes with an intricate series of open-water canals. Scattered ponds or potholes bring down the migrating wildfowl to feed on the water plants that grow in them.

Look out over the marshes when the tide is high and you see nothing but grass and water. But look again when the tide is on the ebb and you will see that every creek has a border of black mud. At dead low tide the small creeks are completely drained; even the large ones have only a central channel in the midst of a great expanse of mud. These are the clam flats, home of the softshell clam.

≈≈≈

Another refuge nearer home was Chincoteague, Virginia, at the southern end of Assateague Island on the Maryland line. Here — as mentioned above — Rachel had spent happy hours with Shirley Briggs, gathering material for the first of the Conservation in Action booklets; during the dark days before her death, she joined the fight for its preservation. Here is her description of bird life at the refuge during the cycle of the year:

From CHINCOTEAGUE

The changing seasons at Chincoteague are reflected in the changing populations of the birds. The summer months are quiet.
Except for a few black ducks and a handful of blue-winged teal,
the thousands of waterfowl that wintered on the refuge have
gone north. They are now dispersed over an immense area, from
Greenland to Alaska. The migratory flights of waterfowl from
the south have paused briefly at the refuge and now they, too, are
gone.

Up in the marshes around Ragged Point the black ducks have
been nesting. In April you might have found their nests here
and there under the bayberries; in June the broods of ducklings,
with their mothers, begin to appear in the slashes. Around the
Levels there are a few broods of the blue-winged teal, making its
first slow comeback as a nesting bird in this region after years of
scarcity. And early almost any morning of the summer you could
see a bittern slinking through the tall salt meadow grass or hear
the sharp clatter of the rails.

August passes into September, with its briskly cooler nights
and shortening days. Since July the shore birds have been returning from the north, and now the beaches and the mud flats are
crowded with them. September brings the first of the returning
waterfowl, and toward the end of the month flocks of small land
bird migrants appear. One morning tree swallows by the thousand are lined up, wing to wing, on the Coast Guard telephone
wires for miles along the beach. Heavy flights of robins and flick-
ers pass through; hawks—mostly the narrow-winged falcons and
the accipiters—sweep down the coast toward the south. Then in
October, when the marshes are silvered with frost in the mornings, the waterfowl begin to pour in from the north. Crossing
the Levels, you see flights of pintails circling the marshes, dropping down into the ponds. After a night of heavy migration, the

refuge suddenly takes on new life as flocks of canvasbacks, red-heads, teal, and baldpates rise into the air in noisy thousands.

Offshore, beyond the white lines of breakers, great numbers of sea ducks appear. Rafts of scoters parallel the beach from one end of the refuge to the other. Old squaws and goldeneyes congregate in the nearly landlocked harbor of Assateague Anchorage, following the oyster dredgers. These sea ducks flock around the boats so closely they are almost run down, diving for the small sea creatures and plants stirred up by the dredges. Canada geese are increasing day by day, flocking in to the Levels and Toms Cove, a few settling in around the marshes of Ragged Point and Sheep Ridge.

Through October, November, and into December the flights of waterfowl increase. Brant gather in the Anchorage, a few whistling swans appear in the Levels. The snow geese drift in, having made the long flight from Greenland and the islands of the Arctic Sea, with only one or two stops anywhere on the continent of North America.

Some of the waterfowl and all of the shore birds continue south after resting and feeding on the refuge. Other waterfowl remain, some of almost every Atlantic coast species. At Chincoteague the winters are not, as a rule, severe. The blizzards and the heavy freezes that sometimes lock the Chesapeake in ice from shore to shore are here tempered by the bordering sea, and it is a rare winter when there is not plenty of open water on the refuge where the ducks can get at the widgeon grass and the sea lettuce, and plenty of snow-free marsh where the geese can pull up the roots of the salt meadow grasses.

The turn of the year finds about 30,000 ducks wintering on the refuge itself, another 10,000 or so on the bordering ocean and Chincoteague Bay. As for the geese, a fairly mild winter may see nearly 10,000 of them on the refuge — perhaps 5000 snow geese, several thousand brant, a thousand Canadas. Black duck, baldpate, and pintail are more numerous than any other kinds of fresh-water ducks; scoters and scaups outnumber all other sea ducks.

March is the time of transformation, the month when the great migrations start. Flock after flock, the ducks, geese, and swans leave for the north. Others come in from the south, linger briefly, move on. By late April, all the waterfowl are gone, except for a few black ducks, teal, and baldpates.

April is the month of the shore birds. Although on an occasional day in March you may hear the high, clear whistle of the yellowlegs, the full tide of the shore bird migration does not reach the refuge until April. The piping, Wilson's, and killdeer plovers, the willet, the spotted sandpiper, and the oystercatcher stay throughout the summer as nesting birds. There are also little colonies of nesting terns, laughing gulls, and black skimmers on the beach at the southern end of the refuge, known as Fishing Point. But for the most part the activities of the refuge have reached their lowest point by midsummer — the ebb between the flood tides of migration.

ऽ∞ऽ

Finally, here is the passage Rachel Carson referred to when she wrote to the blind girl about the importance of sounds in reconstructing one's surroundings. It is from the booklet on the Mattamuskeet Wildlife Refuge off the North Carolina coast. She is describing flocks of whistling swans — next to trumpeter swans, the largest of American waterfowl — and great concentrations of Canada geese.

From MATTAMUSKEET

A large flock of swans is noisy and their voices are a typical winter sound on the refuge. The mingled chorus of swan voices is something like the sound of geese, although somewhat softer. The name "whistling swan" is given because of a single high note sometimes uttered — a sound that suggests a woodwind instrument in its quality. The trumpeter has a deeper, more resonant voice because of an anatomical peculiarity — the windpipe has an extra loop. Trumpeters are never found on the Atlantic coast, however.

After a long history of persecution by man, all wild swans now enjoy complete protection in the United States, Alaska, and Canada. As though sensing this security, the swans at Mattamuskeet show very little fear of people and allow themselves to be approached much more closely than the geese. Five to ten thousand swans usually winter here, feeding in shallow water areas about the southern and eastern shores of the lake. It is possible to see a flock of 500 swans at one time, magnificent in their gleaming white plumage. Sometimes the swans feed or rest in family groups in which the young birds or cygnets may be identified by their gray color.

For the Canada geese of the Atlantic coast, Mattamuskeet is one of the chief wintering places, with a population of about forty to sixty thousand of these handsome birds from November to the middle of March.

Magnificent though the swans are, the person who visits Mattamuskeet in midwinter is likely to come away with impressions of geese uppermost in his mind. Throughout much of the day, their wings pattern the sky above you. Underlying all the other sounds of the refuge is their wild music, rising at times to a great, tumultuous crescendo, and dying away again to a throbbing undercurrent.

Guided by the voices of the birds, you walk out along the banks of one of the canals about sunrise. A steady babble of goose voices tells you of a great concentration of the birds on the lake, probably off the end of the canal. At intervals the sound swells as though a sudden excitement had passed through the flock, and at each such increase in the sound a little party of birds takes off from the main flock and moves away to some favored feeding ground. As you stand quietly in the thickets along the canal, they pass so close overhead that you can hear their wings cutting the air, and see their plumage tinged with golden brown by the early morning sun.

〜〜〜

While she was still at work on the refuge booklets, and carrying a heavy load as overall editor of Fish and Wildlife publications, Rachel Carson was quietly preparing to write another book of her own: a book that would change the course of her life, and make publishing history. Her colleague Bob Hines recalls bringing her stacks of books from the local libraries, piling them on the back seat of her car when she drove home at the end of the afternoon, and exchanging them for a new load a few days later. Many of them were highly technical volumes. She would read far into the night, taking notes, wrestling with a subject so vast as to intimidate all but the most confident of authors. Modest though she was in manner, she did not underestimate her talent, or her perseverance. Both in professional training and in literary skill, she had the tools to create one of the great books about the sea.

CHAPTER 9

AT WORK ON
THE SEA AROUND US

WHILE "UNDERSEA," published in *The Atlantic Monthly*, led directly to the writing of Rachel Carson's first book, *Under the Sea-Wind*, this short essay also contained the germ of *The Sea Around Us*, which appeared a full decade later. As we have seen, she considered *Under the Sea-Wind* only a partial answer to Hendrik van Loon's question about what was going on in the uttermost depths of the ocean. Though it had been a financial failure, she was determined to do something more substantial and lasting than magazine articles, and was soon planning a far more ambitious book. It would bring into focus both the emotional ties with the sea that she had felt since childhood, and the wealth of knowledge she had acquired since she chose marine zoology as her career. It would reflect the vast strides in oceanography made during the war, which her position with the government gave her a rare opportunity to appreciate. (For example, she sat in on top-level conferences weighing the effects of ocean currents on military operations.) And she knew where to go for help; specialists here and abroad were within her reach: "To cope alone and unaided with a subject so vast, so complex, and so infinitely mysterious as the sea would be a task not only cheerless but impossible, and I have not attempted it."

One of those who gave her most encouragement was William Beebe, famous for his research and writings in many branches of natural history, but best known to the public for his undersea explorations in diving suit and bathysphere. Dr. Beebe, who had chosen the life history of the eels in *Under the Sea-Wind* for inclusion in *The Book of Naturalists*, continued to be a source of stimulation in the new enterprise. On September 6, 1948, she wrote to him describing her work in progress: "The book I am writing is something I have had in mind for a good while. I have had to wait to undertake it until at least a part of the wartime oceanographic studies should be published, for I wanted it to reflect some of the new concepts of the ocean which that research has developed. Now there seems to be enough to go ahead on. As for its audience, I think it would strike somewhere between the books by R. E. Coker and Ferdinand Lane — rather nearer the latter, yet I hope to give it a somewhat deeper significance, while still writing for the nontechnical reader. I am much impressed by man's dependence upon the ocean, directly, and in thousands of ways unsuspected by most people. These relationships, and my belief that we will become even more dependent upon the ocean as we destroy the land, are really the theme of the book and have suggested its tentative title, 'Return to the Sea.' "

It was an overwhelming job: "More than once I asked myself why I should have even undertaken such a task."

People often ask me [she wrote years later] how long I worked on *The Sea Around Us*. I usually reply that in a sense I have been working on it all my life, although the actual writing of the book occupied only about three years. As a very small child I was fascinated by the ocean, although I had never seen it. I dreamed of it and longed to see it, and I read all the sea literature I could find. In college I drifted naturally enough into biology and soon came to specialize in marine zoology. I spent several summers at the Marine Biological Laboratory at Woods

Hole, Massachusetts, where I was almost literally surrounded by the ocean. There I could see the racing tidal currents pouring through the "Hole" or watch the waves breaking at Nobska Point after a storm, and there I first became really aware of the unseen ocean currents, for masses of drifting sargassum weed would come in from the distant Gulf Stream after a storm, and tropical creatures like the beautiful Portuguese man-of-war were carried in from the warm rivers offshore.

At Woods Hole, too, I first had an introduction to a large library specializing in the field that so fascinated me. It was immensely exciting to discover the rich but greatly scattered information about the sea that was contained in both old and new books, and in the bewildering variety of scientific journals that the excellent library of the Marine Biological Laboratory contains. I used to spend long hours searching for the answers to questions that filled my mind. At that time I had not the slightest idea that one day my own book about the sea would stand on the shelves of that same library, but I am sure that the genesis of *The Sea Around Us* belongs to that first year at Woods Hole, when I began storing away facts about the sea — facts discovered in scientific literature or by personal observation and experience . . .

The backbone of the work was just plain hard slogging — searching in the often dry and exceedingly technical papers of scientists for the kernels of fact to weld into my profile of the sea. I believe I consulted, at a minimum, somewhat more than a thousand separate printed sources. In addition to this, I corresponded with oceanographers all over the world and personally discussed the book with many specialists. A difficult task was transformed into a richly rewarding experience by the generous help and encouragement of leading oceanographers everywhere. Librarians of special collections, both government and private, searched out for me many obscure documents, and dealers in old and rare books located certain old oceanographic volumes that I needed for my working library. The eagerness of all these people to help was really a very heartwarming experience.

Among the many notable persons who gave her advice and assistance were Robert Cushman Murphy of the American Museum of Natural History (who over a decade later went to bat for *Silent Spring*), Thor Heyerdahl, author of *Kon-Tiki*, and most importantly, Henry B. Bigelow of Harvard. "Bigelow," she wrote, "is probably the best known and most beloved figure on oceanography the world over, and he has been extraordinarily good to me." * Another expert who helped her beyond the call of duty was Arthur McBride, curator of the Marine Studios in Florida. To him she wrote: "To say that I am grateful for your help is a vast understatement, but somehow the English language seems inadequate to thank a man who spent his Fourth of July writing — by hand — a 16-page letter in answer to the questions of a stranger. If I had had any idea you would give me such a wealth of detail I would have lacked the courage to ask so many questions, but the material was exactly what I needed . . ."

In the summer of 1948, when she had compiled a tentative list of chapters, the author decided to put the work in the hands of a professional literary agent. She made her choice with care. After several interviews, she selected Marie Rodell, who had been recommended to her by a mutual friend, Charles Alldredge (Senator Kefauver's press aide during the vice-presidential campaign). A former writer and book editor, Mrs. Rodell had recently gone into the agency business. Thus began a partnership and intimate friendship that endured for the rest of Rachel Carson's life, and — as the monumental and detailed correspondence between them shows — became a leading factor in her subsequent success.

The first order of business was to find a publisher for the new project. (Relations with Simon and Schuster had slowly deteriorated following the commercial failure of *Under the Sea-Wind*, changes in office staff, and various unfortunate incidents to do with remaindering and subsidiary sales.) A legend persists in the publishing trade that the manuscript of *The Sea Around Us* was

* The revised edition of *The Sea Around Us*, published in 1961, is dedicated to Dr. Bigelow.

read and turned down by all sorts of myopic publishers before it finally found a home. The truth is less dramatic. There was one rejection: the publishers to whom the project was first submitted declined on the grounds that they could not reach a decision about so great an undertaking from reading only an outline and sample chapter. Rachel Carson's response to the turndown was not characteristic of most authors. She wrote to Mrs. Rodell: "My rather absurd reaction to your news . . . was that I should try to console *you* about it, feeling that you were more disappointed than I. Of course I admit it would have been nice to have them clamoring for the book, but somehow the news did not depress me." The author tended to sympathize with their view: perhaps the outline looked too formidable; and the sample chapter, on islands, was scarcely representative. She decided to hold back on further submissions for the moment: "Therefore I shall retire to my secret cave, emerging when I have a decent batch of manuscript finished." Four months later she had almost a third of the book in rough draft, and was feeling much better about the whole thing. "At least what I'm writing now is *me*, even if somewhat different from what I once thought it would be." This shift from the conventional approach to something more personal, often with a certain agony, was characteristic of her method. After some further work had been done on them, these chapters were submitted to the Oxford University Press. Their reports were favorable; their editor, Philip Vaudrin, had a successful visit with the author; and finally, in June of 1949, a contract was signed.

Meanwhile research for the book took a more dramatic turn, thanks to a meeting with Dr. Beebe. In April 1949 Rachel Carson had "a grand visit" with him in New York: "As a result of our talk, I don't dare finish this book without getting under water, and he has me practically on the way to Bermuda, where he will make all sorts of advance arrangements so that I'll be sure of meeting the proper sharks, octopuses, etc." Later she decided on Florida rather than Bermuda for this first "Great Undersea Adventure," as she jokingly called it, which took place in July. Not being an experienced swimmer — much less diver — she only went about fifteen feet below the surface in her diving helmet, with lead weights on her feet. She was, she admitted, a little nervous, but all went well: it gave her a firsthand look at a world she already knew so intimately. "There I learned what the surface of the water looks like from underneath and how exquisitely delicate and varied are the colors displayed by the animals of the reef, and I got the feeling of the misty green vistas of a strange, nonhuman world."

A much more rugged adventure followed later that month. As a part of her job, Rachel Carson had occasionally gone out for short cruises on fishing boats or research vessels. Now she arranged to take a real deep-sea voyage. Five years later, she recalled the incident in vivid detail:

Aboard the Albatross

While I was doing information work for Fish and Wildlife, the Service required a research vessel for work at sea, specifically on the famous fishing ground known as Georges Bank, that lies some 200 miles east of Boston, and south of Nova Scotia. Some of the valuable commercial fishes are becoming scarce on the Bank, and the Service is trying to find the reason. The *Albatross III*, as this converted fishing trawler was called, operated out of Woods Hole, making repeated trips to Georges. She was making a census of the fish population; this was done by fishing according to a systematic plan over a selected series of stations. Of course, various scientific data on water temperature and other matters were collected too.

It was decided finally — and I might have had something to do with originating the idea — that perhaps I could do a better job of handling publications about the *Albatross* if I had been out on her. But there was one great obstacle. No woman had ever been on the *Albatross*. Tradition is important in the government, but fortunately I had conspirators who were willing to help me shatter precedent. But among my male colleagues who had to sign the papers, the thought of one woman on a ship with some fifty men was unthinkable. After much soul searching, it was decided that maybe *two* women would be all right, so I arranged with a friend, who was also a writer, to go with me. Marie [Rodell] thought she would write a piece about her experiences and declared that her title would be: "I Was a Chaperone on a Fishing Boat." *

And so one July day we sailed from Woods Hole into ten days of unusual adventure. This is not the place to tell about the scientific work that was done — but there was a lighter side, especially for us who were mere observers, and there were unforgettable impressions of fishing scenes; of fog on Georges, where the cold water and the warm air from the Gulf Stream are perpetually at war at that season of the year; and of the unutterable loneliness of the sea at night as seen from a small vessel.

---

* From *Marie Rodell's Albatross Diary*
Woods Hole, 7/26 — I arrived in Woods Hole at four-thirty; Rachel met me at the station and took me to the Residence, where we were to spend the night — a grim old wooden structure that houses the employees of the U.S. Fisheries labs. After supper, we went round to the wharf and had our first look at the *Albatross III.*

No one could call her pretty. The forward well was heaped with the nets; at the invitation of the third mate, who introduced himself, we clambered over them and were taken up to the wheelhouse. All the modern improvements: Loran radio direction finder, ship-to-shore radio telephone, Sperry gyroscope compass; depth recorder. The third mate filled up our ears with horror stories. "Always hang on to something," he warned us; "the water coming over the decks can bang you about a lot." From the wheelhouse, he pointed down to an open hatch in the center of the forward deck; we could see a spindly ladder leading down. "That's where you eat," he said, and bowed us off the ship with sadistic pleasure. We then went over to see Rachel's friends the Goltsoffs; he is the world's foremost expert on oysters. He spent a happy hour regaling us with the horrors that have befallen the *Albatross* and those aboard her — broken noses, smashed hands — "Never a trip without an accident," he said happily. I was by now in a full-fledged panic, even though I knew everyone was doing this deliberately. We fell asleep that night planning what food to take aboard so we wouldn't have to go down that ladder in a storm. What a pair of landlubbers!

As to the lighter side — a fishing trawler is not exactly a luxury liner, and both of us were on our mettle to prove that a woman could take it without complaining. Hardly had the coast of Massachusetts disappeared astern when some of the ship's officers began to give us a vivid picture of life aboard. The *Albatross*, they told us, was a very long and narrow ship and rolled like a canoe in a sea, so that everyone got violently seasick. They described some of the unpleasant accidents that sometimes occur in handling the heavy gear. They told us about the bad food. They made sure we understood that the fishing process went on night and day, and that it was very noisy. Well — not all the things those Job's comforters predicted came true, but a great many of them did. However, we learned in those ten days that one gets used to almost anything.

We learned about the fishing the very first night. After steaming out through Nantucket Channel late in the afternoon, we were to reach our first fishing station about midnight. Marie and I had gone to bed and were sound asleep when we heard a crash, presumably against the very wall of our cabin, that brought us both upright in our bunks. Surely we had been rammed by another vessel. Then a series of the most appalling bangs, clunks, and rumbles began directly over our heads, a rhythmic thundering of machinery that would put any boiler factory to shame. Finally it dawned on us that this was fishing! It also dawned on us that this was what we had to endure for the next ten nights. If there had been any way to get off the *Albatross* then I'm sure we would have taken it.

At breakfast the next morning there were grins on the faces of the men. "Hear anything last night?" they asked. Both of us wore our most demure expressions. "Well," said Marie, "once we thought we heard a mouse, but we were too sleepy to bother." They never asked us again. And after a night or two we really did sleep through the uproar like old salts.

One of the most vivid impressions I carried away from the *Al-*

batross was the sight of the net coming in with its load of fish. The big fishing trawlers such as this one drag a cone-shaped net on the floor of the ocean, scraping up anything lying on the bottom or swimming just above it. This means not only fish, but also crabs, sponges, starfish and other life of the sea floor. Much of the fishing was done in depths of about 100 fathoms, or 600 feet. After a half hour of trawling the big winches would begin to haul in the cables, winding them on steel drums as they came aboard. There is a marker on every hundred fathoms of cable, so one can tell when to expect the big net to come into view, still far down in the green depths.

I think that first glimpse of the net, a shapeless form, ghostly white, gave me a sense of sea depths that I never had before. As the net rises, coming into sharper focus, there is a stir of excitement even among the experienced fishermen. What has it brought up?

No two hauls are quite alike. The most interesting ones came from the deeper slopes. Georges Bank is like a small mountain resting on the floor of a surrounding deeper sea — most of the fishing is done on its flat plateaus, but sometimes the net is dragged down on the slopes near the mountain's base. Then it brings up larger fish from these depths. There is a strange effect, caused by the sudden change of pressure. Some of the fish become enormously distended and float helplessly on their backs. They drift out of the net as it nears the surface, but they are quite unable to swim down.

Then one sees the slender shapes of sharks moving in to the kill. There was something very beautiful about those sharks to me — and when some of the men got out rifles and killed them for "sport" it really hurt me.

In those deep net hauls, too, there were often the large and grotesque goosefish or angler fish. The angler has a triangular shape, and it enormous mouth occupies most of the base of the triangle. It lives on the floor of the sea, preying on other fish.

The anglers always seemed to have been doing a little fishing of
their own as the net came up, and sometimes the tails of two or
three large cod would be protruding from their mouths.

Sometimes at night we would go up on the deck to watch the
fishing. Then the white splash of electric light on the lower deck
was the only illumination in a world of darkness and water. It
was a colorful sight, with the men in their yellow oilskins and
their bright flannel shirts, all intensified and made somehow dramatic by the blackness that surrounded them.

There is something deeply impressive about the night sea as
one experiences it from a small vessel far from land. When I
stood on the after deck on those dark nights, on a tiny man-made
island of wood and steel, dimly seeing the great shapes of waves
that rolled about us, I think I was conscious as never before that
ours is a water world dominated by the immensity of the sea.

∾∾∾

Rachel's life on shore was less colorful and more frustrating. The
year during which the manuscript was finally completed — i.e.,
the second half of 1949 and the first half of 1950 — turned out
to be a period of increasing stress. The last stages of gestation and
delivery of a book are generally rough enough on the author, whatever the external circumstances; and in Rachel Carson's case the
circumstances were anything but ideal. Following the *Albatross*
trip, work on the manuscript was interrupted by house hunting
and moving (in late September the family moved to another
house in Silver Spring) and the illness of one of her two nieces
who, with Rachel's mother, made up the household at that time.
She did manage to get a leave from the Fish and Wildlife Service for the month of October, but then it took her almost another month to get caught up after her return. She was not one
to complain; most of her correspondence with Marie Rodell,
with whom she kept in close touch, was calm and factual, concerned with the countless details involved in the final revision of

her manuscript. In early November 1949, she wrote: "I have done the chapter on waves, but it is over long and very unevenly written, requiring a lot of work before it will do. Have finished the chapter on currents, which seems reasonably satisfactory. I'm now struggling with the tides, and this proves to be the most cussedly troublesome chapter in the book. This is the one I'd particularly like your advice about. Despite everything, it begins to seem as though the book might some day be finished — that never has seemed possible to me until now. I go back Monday for the rest of November; then presumably will take December." Later that month: "I don't know what's happened to the time since I came back to the office — or rather, I do know! For the first time in a good many weeks, I can wake up mornings without feeling as though I had a ton of bricks on me." In December she took some more time off to complete the first five or six chapters of the book, but this was not enough: "I had so hoped to have all of these chapters absolutely finished before returning to the office Monday, and am a little discouraged that they are not. There has proved to be more to do on them than I thought; then after a week or more of fierce concentration I get so weary and whole days are lost."

By mid-February of 1950 the pressure was building up almost beyond endurance: "None of the present or future is very favorable for the last desperate push, but I am grimly determined to finish somehow. I feel now that I'd die if this went on much longer!" A month later she wrote to Marie Rodell: "Sorry, no chapter today. Last night I went to bed early in an appalling state of exhaustion, but got little good of it because I've reached the point of being unable to sleep. But I dare say I shall live through it." As an aftermath of her leave, she was having to take office work home nights and weekends. "Not a single morning bird walk," she wrote in May, "and spring almost gone! I am really upset about it, but don't seem to have the energy to tuck that in, too." Affairs in the office would be "in a hellish state" until the year's manuscripts were all at the printer's — perhaps not until the end of June. "Then we shall all quietly relapse into a sanitarium, if I am not there already owing to the added strain of my own literary affairs."

In July 1950 the complete manuscript of *The Sea Around Us* was handed over to the Oxford Press. The event was almost an anticlimax. After having lived with it so long, the author — like most authors — had a sense of loss as well as of accomplishment. "Oddly enough," she remarked, "I am less relieved at being delivered of my book than I expected to be."

CHAPTER 10

FAME

THE COMPLETION of the manuscript did not, of course, automatically solve all Rachel Carson's problems. Money continued to be short. Dr. Beebe, among others, was aware of her situation. He had urged her to get her head literally under water. At the same time, he had taken steps to keep her head financially above it by recommending her for a Eugene F. Saxton Memorial Fellowship — an award providing assistance to creative writers, given in memory of the late editor of Harper and Brothers. With the backing of other distinguished naturalists and writers, including Edwin Way Teale,* this finally came through just before the *Albatross* adventure.

Another possible source of income was "first serial" publication — i.e., sales of chapters to the magazines in advance of book publication. As I have said, the legend of the book manuscript's rejection by numerous publishers is quite without foundation. On the other hand, the wholesale rejection of advance chapters by most of the leading magazines is, in retrospect, astonishing.

* On December 7, 1951, Teale ended a letter to Rachel Carson's mother: "I talked to William Beebe the other day. I think we are going to have engraved on our gravestones: 'Recommended Rachel Carson for Two Fellowships!' " The other was a fellowship from the Guggenheim Foundation awarded to her for her next book project, *The Edge of the Sea* — which, however, she returned when income from *The Sea Around Us* indicated that it would not be needed.

Since *The Atlantic Monthly* had started the author on her career by publishing "Undersea" twelve years before, they were
naturally given first offer: initially of a small section that was
finished before the rest, then, a year later, of seven completed
chapters. After holding the latter material for almost two
months, the editors turned it down in favor of "a seafaring adventure" that had come in meanwhile.

Marie Rodell continued to submit chapters to all the likely
popular magazines, including *Harper's, American Mercury, The
Saturday Evening Post, Collier's, The National Geographic;* as
well as more specialized journals like *Scientific American, Natural History, Yachting,* and so on — fifteen or twenty in all. The
response was a steady stream of rejections. But eventually her
persistence was rewarded. Her first success was the sale of a
chapter to the *Yale Review.* Publication of this chapter before
the close of 1950 made it possible for Rachel Carson to apply for
— and win — the George Westinghouse Science Writing Award
of the American Association for the Advancement of Science for
the "finest example of science writing in any American magazine
in 1950": a distinguished honor as well as a substantial addition
to her current income.

Another chapter was sold to *Science Digest.* Then the light-
ning struck from a surprising quarter. Edith Oliver of *The New
Yorker* was delighted with the chapters that she read. She recommended the material warmly to the editor, William Shawn.
He shared her enthusiasm; he felt that this was not just a good
book, but a great one. The material was quite different from anything the magazine had published in its long and distinguished
career. Eventually *The New Yorker* printed approximately half
of the book as a three-part "Profile of the Sea." Mr. Shawn made
the condensation himself. The response to this profile was greater
than to any other piece they had ever printed. Many of her fan
letters asked whether it was going to appear as a book. The value
of this introduction of Rachel Carson to *New Yorker* readers, in

terms of launching the book itself, can never be accurately as-
sessed, but it must have been enormous.

Other chapters not included in the *New Yorker* profile were
sold to *Atlantic Naturalist, Nature Magazine,* and, oddly enough,
Vogue. Up to now, the author had been living on a narrow margin: for example, when she had the chance to buy back the publishing rights of *Under the Sea-Wind* from Simon and Schuster
for $150, she felt that she was "much too broke" to do so (though
she did acquire them later, and the book was reissued by the Oxford Press to join *The Sea Around Us* on the best-seller list).
With the sale of *The Sea Around Us* to *The New Yorker,* her
situation materially improved; their payment amounted to approximately a full year's salary from her government job. The
story of this sale, incidentally, provides a striking example of Rachel Carson's integrity. *The New Yorker's* initial offer was con-
tingent on postponement of book publication, since their own
schedule was full for a year ahead. Despite the large sums involved, Rachel said no; her first obligation was to the Oxford
Press, who had already delayed their publication because of her
being late with the script. Only when *The New Yorker* rear-
ranged their schedules next day did she accept.

The artist in paint has one great advantage over the artist in
words. Once a picture is finished, he is done with it. Not so the
writer. There are more decisions to make, more things that can
go wrong between typescript and bound book than anyone but a
publisher (or a concerned author) can imagine. One crucial decision is of course the title. A title which seems inevitable once a
book has become a best seller is often the end product of months
of worry and indecision — of nights with Bartlett and days with
Burton Stevenson (the Bible and Shakespeare are pretty well
used up) in search of the perfect phrase. *The Sea Around Us* is a
case in point. A score of possible titles were considered, debated,
discarded: "Return to the Sea," "Mother Sea," "Biography of
the Sea," "The Story of the Sea," "The Empire of the Sea" and

on and on — including, in a moment of desperation, "Sea Without End." "The perfect book title seems to be still eluding us," wrote the author, "and I have an unhappy feeling that we will think of it about publication day. Current suggestions from irreverent friends and relatives include 'Out of My Depth' and 'Carson at Sea.' If they would only employ their brains constructively." As the manuscript neared completion, she wrote her editor at Oxford Press: "We have made so many title suggestions that I'm afraid I have lost track — did we ever mention 'The Sea Around Us'?" It had been mentioned once; now, on second look, it seemed by far the best choice. So at last the matter was settled.

As a professional editor, whose job involved all aspects of publishing, Rachel Carson had stronger opinions than most authors about the design and manufacture of her book. To cite just one passage from the voluminous correspondence with her editor at Oxford Press: "You and I have agreed that every care must be taken to avoid the physical appearance of a textbook. Yet I think this is exactly the impression conveyed by the use of the bold and starkly severe sans serif type for the half title pages. In my office we use sans serif a great deal, and with pleasing effect, but for technical material. I can think of any number of textbooks of modern design that have Metro or some other sans serif headings. But not a book like mine! I do hope you will substitute something like Baskerville or Garamond or Granjon, and also in crease the size . . .

"It would be very sad if, after all the good things that have happened before publication, this book should be dismissed as another 'introduction to oceanography.' "

She made a similar point in connection with some last-minute additions. "I think what I am trying to get at in these additions is the introduction of the idea that my real preoccupation is not with 'pure' or abstract science, but that I am the sort who wants above all to get out and enjoy the beauty and wonder of the nat-

ural world, and who resorts only secondarily to the laboratory
and library for explanations. I believe what I have added may
suggest — without baldly stating — such emotional as well as intellectual appreciation."

She need not have worried. The emotional appeal of the book
was instantly apparent, and more "good things" began to happen
the moment advance copies were available for reading. As publication day approached, a ground swell of interest built up. Being
herself an expert on waves, she realized that something pretty
dramatic was about to take place. Enthusiastic comments kept
flowing in, often from surprising quarters: "Alice Longworth
phoned in a state of great excitement. She had spent the night
reading *The Sea* — finishing at 5 a.m. — then read it a second
time. Said it was 'the most marvelous thing she had ever
read! . . .'" Meanwhile the three-part profile in *The New
Yorker* was bringing in stacks of fan mail. The National Press
Club asked her to be their honor guest. "Heavens," she wrote,
"is this all about me — it is really ridiculous!"

The Sea Around Us was to be launched by the publishers with
a big party in Washington. Early in June, two weeks before publication, Rachel Carson escaped for a brief rest to her favorite
beach in Beaufort, North Carolina, where she happily wore out
the seat of her pants on barnacle-covered rocks, "getting acquainted with a whole village of sea anemones, crabs and so on
. . . I spent the morning on a shoal near here, wading around
in water up to my knees, not a human soul in sight. It was really
delightful, but in the process my legs got absolutely cooked . . .
my face and arms have fared better, but are considerably weath-
ered-looking. So I'm thanking my stars I didn't buy a pink dress
for the party, or a lavender or a yellow one, but something nice
and neutral . . ."

She learned that the *Saturday Review of Literature* planned a
feature review, with her picture on the cover. "I shall await the
Saturday Review of July 7 with some apprehension. Are they

doing me against a background of squids, spouting whales, etc.? Really, I grow more astounded by events every day. Maybe it is because a book, once it's between covers, seems to have very little to do with me. I felt that about *Under the Sea-Wind,* and perhaps more about this one. It's just itself — well, sort of as a child is different from its parents. I'm pleased to have people say nice things about the book, but all this stuff about me seems odd, to say the least."

The Sea Around Us was published on July 2, 1951. The rest, as they say, is history. From the day of publication, the only problem (other than some trouble over defective binding) was to keep the book in stock; Oxford Press had printed conservatively, and were immediately caught short. Reviews were prominent and enthusiastic. The Book-of-the-Month Club made it an alternate selection; the *Reader's Digest* ran an abridgement. In England it was published by Staples. (After the Oxford Press in London had declined it on the grounds that they had a competing book about the sea.) Foreign publishers picked it up: eventually it would appear in thirty-two languages around the world.

The publicity was not all pleasure. Having been a notably private person all her life, Rachel Carson was now faced with the painful duty of making public appearances and speaking before large groups. At first she didn't think that she could do it. The moment of decision arrived when Irita Van Doren, editor of the New York *Herald Tribune Books,* invited her to address a "book-and-author luncheon" in New York City. Marie Rodell, who was staying with her on the Maine coast when the invitation arrived, remembers her stepping into a public telephone booth, armed with a fistful of nickels and a determination to decline. But Mrs. Van Doren — who was a hard woman to refuse — somehow charmed her into it. She decided to make her talk as informal as possible; and by including a sound recording of clicking shrimps and other undersea noises, she was able to keep it fairly short. All went well. The ice had been broken.

On September 3, Rachel wrote to her friend Nada Kramar, the Washington bookseller: "I know you will be excited about the big news that came to me today: *The Sea Around Us* moves to top place on the *Times* best-seller list next Sunday, September 9! Of course Oxford, Marie Rodell, and even the author are feeling pretty good about it." On November 8 total sales reached 100,-000 copies; just before Christmas it was selling at the rate of 4000 copies a day. The *Times* Christmas poll voted it "the outstanding book of the year." It was to stay on the best-seller list for eighty-six weeks.

೧೦೧

The following spring Rachel Carson received the John Burroughs Medal,* awarded each year for a book of outstanding literary quality in the field of natural history. And more important commercially, she received the book trade's annual accolade, the National Book Award. Her brief response is an eloquent statement of both her literary aims and her philosophy of life:

National Book Award Acceptance Speech

Writing a book has surprising consequences and the real education of the author perhaps begins on publication day. I, as author, did not know how people would react to a book about the ocean. I am still finding out.

When I planned my book, I knew only that a fascination for

---

* This came as no surprise. I doubt that most authors even know when their books are being considered for the Burroughs Medal. But Rachel Carson, for all her apparent modesty, was quite sophisticated in such matters. The previous summer she had written to her editor at the Oxford Press: "I have heard several bits of gossip to the effect that the Burroughs Medal people would like to consider my book for next year's award — all quite unofficial and off-the-record, of course, but from good sources. Perhaps you can see to it that advance copies are in the proper hands early enough to assure consideration. I can get you the names of the Directors if you do not have them. . . . Just between us, I think my next book will come much closer to the Burroughs tradition, but we need not tell them about that."

the sea and a compelling sense of its mystery had been part of my
own life from earliest childhood. So I wrote what I knew about
it, and also what I thought and felt about it.

Many people have commented with surprise on the fact that a
work of science should have a large popular sale. But this notion,
that "science" is something that belongs in a separate compart-
ment of its own, apart from everyday life, is one that I should
like to challenge. We live in a scientific age; yet we assume that
knowledge of science is the prerogative of only a small number of
human beings, isolated and priestlike in their laboratories. This
is not true. The materials of science are the materials of life itself. Science is part of the reality of living; it is the what, the how,
and the why of everything in our experience. It is impossible to
understand man without understanding his environment and the
forces that have molded him physically and mentally.

The aim of science is to discover and illuminate truth. And
that, I take it, is the aim of literature, whether biography or history or fiction; it seems to me, then, that here can be no separate
literature of science.

My own guiding purpose was to portray the subject of my sea
profile with fidelity and understanding. All else was secondary. I
did not stop to consider whether I was doing it scientifically or
poetically; I was writing as the subject demanded.

The winds, the sea, and the moving tides are what they are. If
there is wonder and beauty and majesty in them, science will
discover these qualities. If they are not there, science cannot create them. If there is poetry in my book about the sea, it is not
because I deliberately put it there, but because no one could
write truthfully about the sea and leave out the poetry.

There has also been a certain amount of surprise that a book in
which human beings play little part should have been widely
read. Like most authors, I have received many letters from readers, and perhaps you would be interested in the clues they offer.
These letters started coming with the publication of *The New*

Yorker profile, and they have never stopped. They come from all sorts of people, from college presidents to fishermen and from scientists to housewives. Most of these people say that it is because the book has taken them away from the stress and strain of human problems . . . that they have welcomed it.

They suggest that they have found refreshment and release from tension in the contemplation of millions and billions of years — in the long vistas of geologic time in which men had no part — in the realization that, despite our own utter dependence on the earth, this same earth and sea have no need of us.

"This sort of thing," wrote one reader, "helps one reduce so many of our man-made problems to their proper proportions."

Another said: "I am overwhelmed with a sense of the vastness of the sea, and properly humble about our own goings-on."

Such letters make me wonder if we have not too long been looking through the wrong end of the telescope. We have looked first at man with his vanities and greed, and at his problems of a day or a year; and then only, and from this biased point of view, we have looked outward at the earth and at the universe of which our earth is so minute a part. Yet these are the great realities, and against them we see our human problems in a new perspective. Perhaps if we reversed the telescope and looked at man down these long vistas, we should find less time and inclination to plan for our own destruction.

By the first of March, 1952, *The Sea Around Us* had sold a total of over 200,000 copies; it would pass the quarter-million mark well before the end of the year. The author took special pride in having bettered the record of Thor Heyerdahl's *Kon-Tiki* for consecutive appearances as the number one national best seller. "It will be nice," she wrote her publisher, "if *The Sea* stays on top for at least a couple of weeks more, so that we can have the satisfaction of being first for an unbroken half year. What was *Kon-Tiki's* record?" *

Now was the moment — when the tide was at the flood — to reissue *Under the Sea-Wind*. The publishing rights had been acquired from Simon and Schuster. On April 13, 1952, Oxford brought out the new edition — in a smaller format than the wide-margined original, and without the illustrations. The Book-of-the-Month Club made it an alternate selection for June, *Life* printed Part 1, and almost 40,000 copies of this once neglected book were sold before publication. So for a while Rachel Carson enjoyed the perhaps unique distinction of having two books simultaneously on the nonfiction best-seller list.

Honors continued to pour in. Rachel's own college, Pennsylvania College for Women (now Chatham College) conferred on her the degree of Doctor of Literature; Oberlin gave her a Doctor of Science. (Thus neatly bracketing her two careers.) She re-

---

* The relation between the two authors was one of mutual admiration, as the following exchange shows:

Dear Mr. Heyerdahl:

I have just asked my publishers, Oxford Press, to send you an advance copy of my new book, *The Sea Around Us*, and am writing now to add my sincere thanks for the help you gave me by answering all my questions a year or more ago. You will see that I made use of this material in my second chapter.

I have been so delighted by the wonderful success of *Kon-Tiki* and I want to add my congratulations to the many thousands you must be receiving. I had read your magazine pieces with great interest, but when the book itself came out I could scarcely put it down, wanting to read right on to the end — and yet not wanting the end to come! It is not only a gripping story; I consider it (and have so said in my own list of readings) one of the truly great books of the sea. You have somehow managed to get into it the elemental quality such a book must have, and the feeling of the timeless, cosmic forces that rule the sea.

Again, thanks for your help on my book, and best wishes for the continued success of *Kon-Tiki*.

Sincerely,
Rachel Carson

Dear Miss Carson:

This is only a note to thank you for your kindness in sending me your wonderful book. I am in the midst of writing an ethnographic work but could not drop your book when I picked it up. It does good to see that a serious and conscientious writer can grasp the fascinating sides of the science and beauty of the sea and its story in such a way as you have mastered it. My heartiest congratulations.

Sincerely,
Thor Heyerdahl

ceived an award from the Garden Club of America and was
made a Fellow of the Royal Society of Literature in England.
Meanwhile she had been obliged to turn down any number of
attractive invitations. "All of these invitations, no matter how
pleasant, would absolutely wreck the writing program I am now
laying out. What has gone on in the last six months is all very
fine, but enough is enough!" And while she could not but enjoy
her fame, her patience wore thin when she thought that she was
being exploited. "In acquiescing on the California publicity,"
she wrote to Marie Rodell, "I feel that I must make one stipula-
tion: I am to be consulted before any schedule is regarded as
final. In Cleveland and in Pittsburgh I was left at the mercy of a
bunch of eager beavers who thought only of how many minutes
the day contained and how many events they could cram into it,
and as a result I came home in a state of utter exhaustion. I will
not submit to anything like that again."

One result of all this publicity she had not foreseen: that the
people who read the book would be curious about the author.
"That was very naïve of me, I suppose," she recalled later, "but
it had never occurred to me, for example, that people would go
to great lengths just to have a look at someone whose book was a
best seller. A few months after *The Sea* was published, I was on
a long southern field trip for my new book. In a strange town, I
went into a beauty shop, and while I was sitting under the drier
— which until then I had considered an inviolate sanctuary —
the proprietor came over, turned off the drier, and said: 'I hope
you don't mind, but there is someone who wants to meet you.' I
admit I felt hardly at my best, with a towel around my neck and
my hair in pin curls. At another place during the same trip, a
knock came at the door of our motor court early one morning.
When my mother opened the door, a determined woman
pushed past her and presented two books for autographing to an
author who was still abed, and, if the truth must be told, very
much annoyed.

"When part of my book appeared as a Profile of the Sea in

The New Yorker, a large proportion of the readers who wrote to the editors of the magazine demanded a profile of Rachel Carson. One wrote: 'Please let me know in a hurry who Rachel Carson is. That girl keeps me awake night after night.'

"In publishing the book, Oxford University Press didn't foresee all this clamor and failed to put my picture on the jacket. So the field was open for all sorts of speculation — what did I look like, how old was I, how did I happen to discover the sea?

"Among male readers there was a certain reluctance to acknowledge that a woman could have dealt with a scientific subject. Some, who apparently had never read the Bible enough to know that Rachel is a woman's name, wrote: 'I assume from the author's knowledge that he must be a man.' Another, addressing me properly as *Miss* Rachel Carson, nevertheless began his letter 'Dear Sir:' He explained his salutation by saying that he had always been convinced that the males possess the supreme intellectual powers of the world, and he could not bring himself to reverse his conviction.

"Then others assumed that, since I knew enough to write *The Sea,* I must be gray-haired and venerable. One of my unknown correspondents wrote that I was probably just what he was looking for as a wife — except that to have learned all I put in the book must have taken a long time and perhaps I was too old for him. I think I could have qualified, but that was one of life's opportunities I passed by.

"Even in my publishing house, those who hadn't met me while I was writing the book seemed to expect something quite different from the reality. One of the editors said to me: "You are such a surprise to me. I thought you would be a very large and forbidding woman." [For Shirley Briggs's cartoon of "Rachel as her readers seem to imagine her," see the illustrations following page 238.]

Another result of this sudden fame was, not surprisingly, interest on the part of Hollywood. The idea of a film based on *The*

Sea Around Us was already in Rachel's mind. Six months before the book appeared, she had written to Marie Rodell: "Speaking of pipe dreams — you may think me utterly mad but after some comment that was made the other day about movie rights I've been thinking, well, why not a documentary on the sea? I don't see why it couldn't be every bit as good as *The River*. After all, lots of movies have rather a casual resemblance to the books on which they are based. My imagination has been running on about this, and if you think it not too utterly fantastic I will let it continue to do so. I should think it would stress the impact of marine matters on human affairs and it seems to me that, with the world situation again making us more ocean-conscious, it could well be very worth doing. Maybe a sort of Pare Lorentz-ish narration, which I wouldn't mind trying to do myself. Well, with that I shall go back to the salt mines!"

Now, a year and a half later, RKO's purchase of the motion picture rights seemed like realization of the dream. But when the author saw the film and read the script, which had been rewritten in the studio, it began to look more like a nightmare. She and Marie Rodell submitted a long list of scientific errors which they insisted be corrected before the picture was released. (One of Mrs. Rodell's terse comments on the script is worth quoting: "page 18 — 'The ever active arts of wooing and eating' strikes me as really an extraordinary phrase.") And though the Hollywood *Reporter* called *The Sea Around Us* an "awesome spectacle," and it won an Oscar for the year's best full-length documentary film, Rachel was never happy — to put it mildly — with her single Hollywood experience.

ကကက

To pick a chapter that is "representative" of *The Sea Around Us* is impossible; the narrative is far too wide ranging and various for that. Every reader will have his favorite. Mine, if I had to choose, is probably "The Birth of An Island." It was one of the first sections of the book to be completed, and it stands up particularly well as an independent essay. Moreover, there are few facts or statistics that require revision as the result of research during the twenty-odd years since it was first published.

As noted above, "The Birth of An Island" was published by the *Yale Review* in December 1950, and won the Westinghouse award. (Parts of it also appeared in *The Wood Thrush*, as *Atlantic Naturalist* was then entitled.) "Authors' judgments are notoriously poor, I know," wrote Rachel Carson some months before it appeared, "but I've always liked that chapter."

CHAPTER 11

FROM *THE SEA AROUND US*

"The Birth of an Island"

Many a green isle needs must be
In the deep, wide sea . . .
SHELLEY

MILLIONS of years ago, a volcano built a mountain on the floor of the Atlantic. In eruption after eruption, it pushed up a great pile of volcanic rock, until it had accumulated a mass a hundred miles across at its base, reaching upward toward the surface of the sea. Finally its cone emerged as an island with an area of about 200 square miles. Thousands of years passed, and thousands of thousands. Eventually the waves of the Atlantic cut down the cone and reduced it to a shoal — all of it, that is, but a small fragment which remained above water. This fragment we know as Bermuda.

With variations, the life story of Bermuda has been repeated by about every one of the islands that interrupt the watery expanses of the oceans far from land. For these isolated islands in the sea are fundamentally different from the continents. The major land masses and the ocean basins are today much as they have been throughout the greater part of geologic time. But islands are ephemeral, created today, destroyed tomorrow. With few exceptions, they are the result of the violent, explosive, earth-shaking eruptions of submarine volcanoes, working perhaps for millions of years to achieve their end. It is one of the paradoxes in the ways of earth and sea that a process seemingly so destructive, so catastrophic in nature, can result in an act of creation.

Islands have always fascinated the human mind. Perhaps it is the instinctive response of man, the land animal, welcoming a brief intrusion of earth in the vast, overwhelming expanse of sea. Here in a great ocean basin, a thousand miles from the nearest continent, with miles of water under our vessel, we come upon an island. Our imaginations can follow its slopes down through darkening waters to where it rests on the sea floor. We wonder why and how it arose here in the midst of the ocean.

The birth of a volcanic island is an event marked by prolonged and violent travail: the forces of the earth striving to create, and all the forces of the sea opposing. The sea floor, where an island begins, is probably nowhere more than about fifty miles thick — a thin covering over the vast bulk of the earth. In it are deep cracks and fissures, the results of unequal cooling and shrinkage in past ages. Along such lines of weakness the molten lava from the earth's interior presses up and finally bursts forth into the sea. But a submarine volcano is different from a terrestrial eruption, where the lava, molten rocks, gases, and other ejecta are hurled into the air through an open crater. Here on the bottom of the ocean the volcano has resisting it all the weight of the ocean water above it. Despite the immense pressure of, it may be, two or three miles of sea water, the new volcanic cone builds upward toward the surface, in flow after flow of lava. Once within reach of the waves, its soft ash and tuff are violently attacked, and for a long period the potential island may remain a shoal, unable to emerge. But, eventually, in new eruptions, the cone is pushed up into the air and a rampart against the attacks of the waves is built of hardened lava.

Navigators' charts are marked with numerous, recently discovered submarine mountains. Many of these are the submerged remnants of the islands of a geologic yesterday. The same charts show islands that emerged from the sea at least fifty million years ago, and others that arose within our own memory. Among the undersea mountains marked on the charts may be the islands of tomorrow, which at this moment are forming, unseen, on the floor of the ocean and are growing upward toward its surface.

For the sea is by no means done with submarine eruptions; they occur fairly commonly, sometimes detected only by instruments, sometimes obvious to the most casual observer. Ships in volcanic zones may suddenly find themselves in violently disturbed water. There are heavy discharges of steam. The sea appears to bubble or boil in a furious turbulence. Fountains spring from its surface. Floating up from the deep, hidden places of the actual eruption come the bodies of fishes and other deep-sea creatures, and quantities of volcanic ash and pumice.

One of the youngest of the large volcanic islands of the world is Ascension in the South Atlantic. During the Second World War the American airmen sang

> If we don't find Ascension
> Our wives will get a pension

this island being the only piece of dry land between the hump of Brazil and the bulge of Africa. It is a forbidding mass of cinders, in which the vents of no less than forty extinct volcanoes can be counted. It has not always been so barren, for its slopes have yielded the fossil remains of trees. What happened to the forests no one knows; the first men to explore the island, about the year 1500, found it treeless, and today it has no natural greenness except on its highest peak, known as Green Mountain.

In modern times we have never seen the birth of an island as large as Ascension. But now and then there is a report of a small island appearing where none was before. Perhaps a month, a year, five years later, the island has disappeared into the sea again. These are the little, stillborn islands, doomed to only a brief emergence above the sea.

About 1830 such an island suddenly appeared in the Mediterranean between Sicily and the coast of Africa, rising from 100-fathom depths after there had been signs of volcanic activity in the area. It was little more than a black cinder pile, perhaps 200 feet high. Waves, wind, and rain attacked it. Its soft and porous materials were easily eroded; its substance was rapidly eaten away and it sank beneath the sea. Now it is a shoal, marked on the charts as Graham's Reef.

Falcon Island, the top of a volcano projecting above the Pacific nearly two thousand miles east of Australia, suddenly disappeared in 1913. Thirteen years later, after violent eruptions in the vicinity, it as suddenly rose again above the surface and remained as a physical bit of the British Empire until 1949. Then it was reported by the Colonial Under Secretary to be missing again.

Almost from the moment of its creation, a volcanic island is foredoomed to destruction. It has in itself the seeds of its own dissolution, for new explosions, or landslides of the soft soil, may violently accelerate its disintegration. Whether the destruction of an island comes quickly or only after long ages of geologic time may also depend on external forces: the rains that wear away the loftiest of land mountains, the sea, and even man himself.

South Trinidad, or in the Portuguese spelling, "Ilha Trinidade," is an example of an island that has been sculptured into bizarre forms through centuries of weathering — an island in which the signs of dissolution are clearly apparent. This group of volcanic peaks lies in the open Atlantic, about a thousand miles northeast of Rio de Janeiro. E. F. Knight wrote in 1907 that Trinidad "is rotten throughout, its substance has been disintegrated by volcanic fires and by the action of water, so that it is everywhere tumbling to pieces." During an interval of nine years between Knight's visits, a whole mountainside had collapsed in a great landslide of broken rocks and volcanic debris.

Sometimes the disintegration takes abrupt and violent form.

The greatest explosion of historic time was the literal eviscera-tion of the island of Krakatoa. In 1680 there had been a premon-itory eruption on this small island in Sunda Strait, between Java and Sumatra in the Netherlands Indies. Two hundred years later there had been a series of earthquakes. In the spring of 1883, smoke and steam began to ascend from fissures in the vol-canic cone. The ground became noticeably warm, and warning rumblings and hissings came from the volcano. Then, on 27 Au-gust, Krakatoa literally exploded. In an appalling series of erup-tions, that lasted two days, the whole northern half of the cone was carried away. The sudden inrush of ocean water added the fury of superheated steam to the cauldron. When the inferno of white-hot lava, molten rock, steam, and smoke had finally sub-sided, the island that had stood 1400 feet above the sea had be-come a cavity a thousand feet below sea level. Only along one edge of the former crater did a remnant of the island remain.

Krakatoa, in its destruction, became known to the entire world. The eruption gave rise to a hundred-foot wave that wiped out villages along the Strait and killed people by tens of thou-sands. The wave was felt on the shores of the Indian Ocean and at Cape Horn; rounding the Cape into the Atlantic, it sped northward and retained its identity even as far as the English Channel. The sound of the explosions was heard in the Philip-pine Islands, in Australia, and on the Island of Madagascar, nearly 3000 miles away. And clouds of volcanic dust, the pulver-ized rock that had been torn from the heart of Krakatoa, as-cended into the stratosphere and were carried around the globe to give rise to a series of spectacular sunsets in every country of the world for nearly a year.

Although Krakatoa's dramatic passing was the most violent eruption that modern man has witnessed, Krakatoa itself seems to have been the product of an even greater one. There is evi-dence that an immense volcano once stood where the waters of Sunda Strait now lie. In some remote period a titanic explosion blew it away, leaving only its base represented by a broken ring of islands. The largest of these was Krakatoa, which, in its own demise, carried away what was left of the original crater ring. But in 1929 a new volcanic island arose in this place — Anak Krakatoa, Child of Krakatoa.

Subterranean fires and deep unrest disturb the whole area occupied by the Aleutians. The islands themselves are the peaks of a thousand-mile chain of undersea mountains, of which volcanic action was the chief architect. The geologic structure of the ridge is little known, but it rises abuptly from oceanic depths of about a mile on one side and two miles on the other. Apparently this long narrow ridge indicates a deep fracture of the earth's crust. On many of the islands volcanoes are now active, or only temporarily quiescent. In the short history of modern navigation in this region, it has often happened that a new island has been reported but perhaps only the following year could not be found.

The small island of Bogoslof, since it was first observed in 1796, has altered its shape and position several times and has even disappeared completely, only to emerge again. The original island was a mass of black rock, sculptured into fantastic, tower-like shapes. Explorers and sealers coming upon it in the fog were reminded of a castle and named it Castle Rock. At the present time there remain only one or two pinnacles of the castle, a long spit of black rocks where sea lions haul out, and a cluster of higher rocks resounding with the cries of thousands of sea birds. Each time the parent volcano erupts, as it has done at least half a dozen times since men have been observing it, new masses of steaming rocks emerge from the heated waters, some to reach heights of several hundred feet before they are destroyed in fresh explosions. Each new cone that appears is, as described by the volcanologist Jaggar, "the live crest, equivalent to a crater, of a great submarine heap of lava six thousand feet high, piled above the floor of Bering Sea where the Aleutian mountains fall off to the deep sea."

One of the few exceptions to the almost universal rule that oceanic islands have a volcanic origin seems to be the remarkable and fascinating groups of islets known as the Rocks of St. Paul. Lying in the open Atlantic between Brazil and Africa, St. Paul's Rocks are an obstruction thrust up from the floor of the ocean into the midst of the racing Equatorial Current, a mass against which the seas, which have rolled a thousand miles unhindered, break in sudden violence. The entire cluster of rocks covers not more than a quarter of a mile, running in a curved line like a horseshoe. The highest rock is no more than sixty feet above the sea; spray wets it to the summit. Abruptly the rocks dip under water and slope steeply down into great depths. Geologists since the time of Darwin have puzzled over the origin of these black, wave-washed islets. Most of them agree that they are composed of material like that of the sea floor itself. In some remote period, inconceivable stresses in the earth's crust must have pushed a solid rock mass upward more than two miles.

So bare and desolate that not even a lichen grows on them, St. Paul's Rocks would seem one of the most unpromising places in the world to look for a spider, spinning its web in arachnidan hope of snaring passing insects. Yet Darwin found spiders when he visited the Rocks in 1833, and forty years later the naturalists of H.M.S. *Challenger* also reported them, busy at their web-spinning. A few insects are there, too, some as parasites on the sea birds, three species of which nest on the Rocks. One of the insects is a small brown moth that lives on feathers. This very nearly completes the inventory of the inhabitants of St. Paul's Rocks, except for the grotesque crabs that swarm over the islets, living chiefly on the flying fish brought by the birds to their young.

St. Paul's Rocks are not alone in having an extraordinary assortment of inhabitants, for the faunas and floras of oceanic islands are amazingly different from those of the continents. The pattern of island life is peculiar and significant. Aside from forms recently introduced by man, islands remote from the continents are never inhabited by any land mammals, except sometimes the one mammal that has learned to fly — the bat. There are never any frogs, salamanders, or other amphibians. Of reptiles, there may be a few snakes, lizards, and turtles, but the more remote the island from a major land mass, the fewer reptiles there are, and the really isolated islands have none. There are usually a few species of land birds, some insects, and some spiders. So remote an island as Tristan da Cunha in the South Atlantic, 1500 miles from the nearest continent, has no land animals but these: three species of land birds, a few insects, and several small snails.

With so selective a list, it is hard to see how, as some biologists believe, the islands could have been colonized by migration across land bridges, even if there were good evidence for the existence of the bridges. The very animals missing from the islands are the ones that would have had to come dry-shod, over the hypothetical bridges. The plants and animals that we find on oceanic islands, on the other hand, are the ones that could have come by wind or water. As an alternative, then, we must suppose that the stocking of the islands has been accomplished by the strangest migration in earth's history — a migration that began long before man appeared on earth and is still continuing, a migration that seems more like a series of cosmic accidents than an orderly process of nature.

We can only guess how long after its emergence from the sea an oceanic island may lie uninhabited. Certainly in its original state it is a land bare, harsh, and repelling beyond human experience. No living thing moves over the slopes of its volcanic hills; no plants cover its naked lava fields. But little by little, riding on the winds, drifting on the currents, or rafting in on logs, floating brush, or trees, the plants and animals that are to colonize it arrive from the distant continents.

So deliberate, so unhurried, so inexorable are the ways of na-

Aged about ten

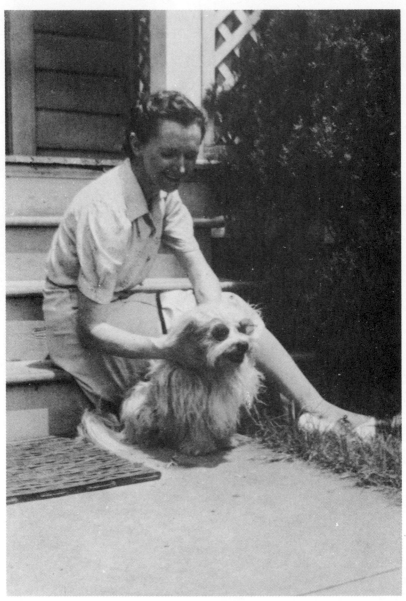

The young biologist

On Hawk Mountain, 1945

One night the mackerel came upon an abandoned gill net swaying in the water. The net was buoyed at the surface by cork floats; and from the cork line it hung down ~~perpendicularly~~ — It like a giant tennis net. Its meshes were 2 inches across so that the yearling mackerel could have slipped through, although larger ~~ones~~ would have been gilled in the twine. Tonight no fish would have tried to pass through the net, for all its meshes were hung with tiny warning lamps. It was as though all the myriad lesser fry of the sea, the animals small as a dust mote, the plants tinier than a drifting ~~and~~ no ocean, seized upon the meshes of the gill net on the one from —— in their flued world and clung to it with protoplasm hair and cilia, with tentacle and —— The gill net glowed like a thing alive; its radiance shown out into the ~~black~~ black sea, shown down into the darkness below, and drew up amphipods and —— , drawn by the light, and these larger creatures also clung to the meshes. the net gave —— to

The original draft of *Under the Sea-Wind*,
with Rachel's sketch of her cat

With Bob Hines in the Florida Keys

At work on *The Edge of the Sea*

The author of *The Sea Around Us*

Woods Hole, Massachusetts, 1951

Jeffie. Taken by Rachel for a valentine, 1954

The woods behind the cottage

The bird-watcher

Among the tide pools

With Roger, 1961

Photograph by Rachel of her shore at West Southport, Maine

Low tide

At the edge of the sea

ture that the stocking of an island may require thousands or millions of years. It may be that no more than half a dozen times in all these eons does a particular form, such as a tortoise, make a successful landing upon its shores. To wonder impatiently why man is not a constant witness of such arrivals is to fail to understand the majestic pace of the process.

Yet we have occasional glimpses of the method. Natural rafts of uprooted trees and matted vegetation have frequently been seen adrift at sea, more than a thousand miles off the mouths of such great tropical rivers as the Congo, the Ganges, the Amazon, and the Orinoco. Such rafts could easily carry an assortment of insect, reptile, or mollusk passengers. Some of the involuntary passengers might be able to withstand long weeks at sea; others would die during the first stages of the journey. Probably the ones best adapted for travel by raft are the wood-boring insects, which, of all the insect tribe, are most commonly found on oceanic islands. The poorest raft travelers must be the mammals. But even a mammal might cover short interisland distances. A few days after the explosion of Krakatoa, a small monkey was rescued from some drifting timber in Sunda Strait. She had been terribly burned, but survived the experience.

No less than the water, the winds and the air currents play their part in bringing inhabitants to the islands. The upper atmosphere, even during the ages before man entered it in his machines, was a place of congested traffic. Thousands of feet above the earth, the air is crowded with living creatures, drifting, flying, gliding, ballooning, or involuntarily swirling along on the high winds. Discovery of this rich aerial plankton had to wait until man himself had found means to make physical invasion of these regions. With special nets and traps, scientists have now collected from the upper atmosphere many of the forms that inhabit oceanic islands. Spiders, whose almost invariable presence on these islands is a fascinating problem, have been captured nearly three miles above the earth's surface. Airmen have passed through great numbers of the white, silken filaments of spiders' "parachutes" at heights of two to three miles. At altitudes of 6000 to 16,000 feet, and with wind velocities reaching 45 miles an hour, many living insects have been taken. At such heights and on such strong winds, they might well have been carried hundreds of miles. Seeds have been collected at altitudes up to 5000 feet. Among those commonly taken are members of the Composite family, especially the so-called "thistle-down" typical of oceanic islands.

An interesting point about transport of living plants and animals by wind is the fact that in the upper layers of the earth's atmosphere the winds do not necessarily blow in the same direction as at the earth's surface. The trade winds are notably shallow, so that a man standing on the cliffs of St. Helena, a thousand feet above the sea, is above the wind, which blows with great force below him. Once drawn into the upper air, insects, seeds, and the like can easily be carried in a direction contrary to that of the winds prevailing at island level.

The wide-ranging birds that visit islands of the ocean in migration may also have a good deal to do with the distribution of plants, and perhaps even of some insects and minute land shells. From a ball of mud taken from a bird's plumage, Charles Darwin raised 82 separate plants, belonging to 5 distinct species! Many plant seeds have hooks or prickles, ideal for attachment to feathers. Such birds as the Pacific golden plover, which annually flies from the mainland of Alaska to the Hawaiian Islands and even beyond, probably figure in many riddles of plant distribution.

The catastrophe of Krakatoa gave naturalists a perfect opportunity to observe the colonization of an island. With most of the island itself destroyed, and the remnant covered with a deep layer of lava and ash that remained hot for weeks, Krakatoa after the explosive eruptions of 1883 was, from a biological standpoint, a new volcanic island. As soon as it was possible to visit it, scientists searched for signs of life, although it was hard to imagine how any living thing could have survived. Not a single plant or animal could be found. It was not until nine months after the eruption that the naturalist Cotteau was able to report: "I only discovered one microscopic spider — only one. This strange pioneer of the renovation was busy spinning its web." Since there were no insects on the island, the web-spinning of the bold little spider was presumably in vain, and, except for a few blades of grass, practically nothing lived on Krakatoa for a quarter of a century. Then the colonists began to arrive — a few mammals in 1908; a number of birds, lizards, and snakes; various mollusks, insects, and earthworms. Ninety per cent of Krakatoa's new inhabitants, Dutch scientists found, were forms that could have arrived by air.

Isolated from the great mass of life on the continents, with no opportunity for the crossbreeding that tends to preserve the average and to eliminate the new and unusual, island life has developed in a remarkable manner. On these remote bits of earth, nature has excelled in the creation of strange and wonderful forms. As though to prove her incredible versatility, almost every island has developed species that are endemic — that is, they are peculiar to it alone and are duplicated nowhere else on earth.

It was from the pages of earth's history written on the lava fields of the Galapagos that young Charles Darwin got his first inkling of the great truths of the origin of species. Observing the strange plants and animals — giant tortoises, black, amazing lizards that hunted their food in the surf, sea lions, birds in extraordinary variety — Darwin was struck by their vague similarity to mainland species of South and Central America, yet was haunted by the differences, differences that distinguish them not only from the mainland species but from those on other islands of the archipelago. Years later he was to write in reminiscence: "Both in space and time, we seem to be brought somewhat near to that great fact — that mystery of mysteries — the first appearance of new beings on earth."

Of the "new beings" evolved on islands, some of the most

striking examples have been birds. In some remote age before there were men, a small, pigeonlike bird found its way to the island of Mauritius, in the Indian Ocean. By processes of change at which we can only guess, this bird lost the power of flight, developed short, stout legs, and grew larger until it reached the size of a modern turkey. Such was the origin of the fabulous dodo, which did not long survive the advent of man on Mauritius. New Zealand was the sole home of the moas. One species of these ostrichlike birds stood twelve feet high. Moas had roamed New Zealand from the early part of the Tertiary; those that remained when the Maoris arrived soon died out.

Other island forms besides the dodo and the moas have tended to become large. Perhaps the Galapagos tortoise became a giant after its arrival on the islands, although fossil remains on the continents cast doubt on this. The loss of wing use and even of the wings themselves (the moas had none) are common results of insular life. Insects on small, wind-swept islands tend to lose the power of flight — those that retain it are in danger of being blown out to sea. The Galapagos Islands have a flightless cormorant. There have been at least fourteen species of flightless rails on the islands of the Pacific alone.

One of the most interesting and engaging characteristics of island species is their extraordinary tameness — a lack of sophistication in dealings with the human race, which even the bitter teachings of experience do not quickly alter. When Robert Cushman Murphy visited the island of South Trinidad in 1913 with a party from the brig *Daisy*, terns alighted on the heads of the men in the whaleboat and peered inquiringly into their faces. Albatrosses on Laysan, whose habits include wonderful ceremonial dances, allowed naturalists to walk among their colonies and responded with a grave bow to similar polite greetings from the visitors. When the British ornithologist David Lack visited the Galapagos Islands, a century after Darwin, he found that the hawks allowed themselves to be touched, and the flycatchers tried to remove hair from the heads of the men for nesting material. "It is a curious pleasure," he wrote, "to have birds of the wilderness settling upon one's shoulders, and the pleasure could be much less rare were man less destructive."

But man, unhappily, has written one of his blackest records as a destroyer on the oceanic islands. He has seldom set foot on an island that he has not brought about disastrous changes. He has destroyed environments by cutting, clearing, and burning; he has brought with him as a chance associate the nefarious rat; and almost invariably he has turned loose upon the islands a whole Noah's Ark of goats, hogs, cattle, dogs, cats, and other nonnative animals as well as plants. Upon species after species of island life, the black night of extinction has fallen.

In all the world of living things, it is doubtful whether there is a more delicately balanced relationship than that of island life to its environment. This environment is a remarkably uniform one. In the midst of a great ocean, ruled by currents and winds that rarely shift their course, climate changes little. There are few natural enemies, perhaps none at all. The harsh struggle for existence that is the normal lot of continental life is softened on the islands. When this gentle pattern of life is abruptly changed, the island creatures have little ability to make the adjustments necessary for survival.

Ernst Mayr tells of a steamer wrecked off Lord Howe Island east of Australia in 1918. Its rats swam ashore. In two years they had so nearly exterminated the native birds that an islander wrote, "This paradise of birds has become a wilderness, and the quietness of death reigns where all was melody."

On Tristan da Cunha almost all of the unique land birds that had evolved there in the course of the ages were exterminated by hogs and rats. The native fauna of the island of Tahiti is losing ground against the horde of alien species that man has introduced. The Hawaiian Islands, which have lost their native plants and animals faster than almost any other area in the world, are a classic example of the results of interfering with natural balances. Certain relations of animal to plant, and of plant to soil, had grown up through the centuries. When man came in and rudely disturbed this balance, he set off a whole series of chain reactions.

Vancouver brought cattle and goats to the Hawaiian Islands, and the resulting damage to forests and other vegetation was enormous. Many plant introductions were as bad. A plant known as the pamakani was brought in many years ago, according to report, by a Captain Makee for his beautiul gardens on the island of Maui. The pamakani, which has light, wind-borne seeds, quickly escaped from the captain's gardens, ruined the pasture lands on Maui, and proceeded to hop from island to island. The CCC boys were at one time put to work to clear it out of the Honouliuli Forest Reserve, but as fast as they destroyed it, the seeds of new plants arrived on the wind. Lantana was another plant brought in as an ornamental species. Now it covers thousands of acres with a thorny, scrambling growth — despite large sums of money spent to import parasitic insects to control it.

There was once a society in Hawaii for the special purpose of introducing exotic birds. Today when you go to the islands, you see, instead of the exquisite native birds that greeted Captain Cook, mynas from India, cardinals from the United States or Brazil, doves from Asia, weavers from Australia, skylarks from Europe, and titmice from Japan. Most of the original bird life has been wiped out, and to find its fugitive remnants you would have to search assiduously in the most remote hills.

Some of the island species have, at best, the most tenuous hold on life. The Laysan teal is found nowhere in the world but on the one small island of Laysan. Even on this island it occurs only on one end, where there is a seepage of fresh water. Probably the total population of this species does not exceed fifty individuals. Destruction of the small swampy bit of land that is its home, or the introduction of a hostile or competing species, could easily snap the slender thread of life.

Most of man's habitual tampering with nature's balance by introducing exotic species has been done in ignorance of the fatal chain of events that would follow. But in modern times, at least, we might profit by history. About the year 1513, the Portuguese introduced goats onto the recently discovered island of St. Helena, which had developed a magnificent forest of gumwood, ebony, and brazilwood. By 1560 or thereabouts, the goats had so multiplied that they wandered over the island by the thousand, in flocks a mile long. They trampled the young trees and ate the seedlings. By this time the colonists had begun to cut and burn the forests, so that it is hard to say whether men or goats were the more responsible for the destruction. But of the result there was no doubt. By the early 1800s the forests were gone, and the naturalist Alfred Wallace later described this once beautiful, forest-clad volcanic island as a "rocky desert," in which the remnants of the original flora persisted only in the most inaccessible peaks and crater ridges.

When the astronomer Halley visited the islands of the Atlantic about 1700, he put a few goats ashore on South Trinidad. This time, without the further aid of man, the work of deforestation proceeded so rapidly that it was nearly completed within the century. Today Trinidad's slopes are the place of a ghost forest, strewn with the fallen and decaying trunks of long-dead trees; its soft volcanic soils, no longer held by the interlacing roots, are sliding away into the sea.

One of the most interesting of the Pacific islands was Laysan, a tiny scrap of soil which is a far outrider of the Hawaiian chain. It once supported a forest of sandalwood and fanleaf palms and had five land birds, all peculiar to Laysan alone. One of them was the Laysan rail, a charming, gnomelike creature no more than six inches high, with wings that seemed too small (and were never used as wings), and feet that seemed too large, and a voice like distant, tinkling bells. About 1887, the captain of a visiting ship moved some of the rails to Midway, about 300 miles to the west, establishing a second colony. It seemed a fortunate move, for soon thereafter rabbits were introduced on Laysan. Within a quarter of a century, the rabbits had killed off the vegetation of the tiny island, reduced it to a sandy desert, and all but exterminated themselves. As for the rails, the devastation of their island was fatal, and the last rail died about 1924.

Perhaps the Laysan colony could later have been restored from the Midway group had not tragedy struck there also. During the war in the Pacific, rats went ashore to island after island from ships and landing craft. They invaded Midway in 1943. The adult rails were slaughtered. The eggs were eaten, and the young birds killed. The world's last Laysan rail was seen in 1944.

The tragedy of the oceanic islands lies in the uniqueness, the irreplaceability of the species they have developed by the slow processes of the ages. In a reasonable world men would have treated these islands as precious possessions, as natural museums filled with beautiful and curious works of creation, valuable beyond price because nowhere in the world are they duplicated. W. H. Hudson's lament for the birds of the Argentine pampas might even more truly have been spoken of the islands: "The beautiful has vanished and returns not."

CHAPTER 12

THE EVOLUTION OF AN IDEA

LIKE MOST creative writers, Rachel Carson had her eye constantly on the future. "I am always more interested in what I am about to do than in what I have already done." The manuscript of *The Sea Around Us* was in fact still some months from completion, and the author still a relatively unknown employee of the Fish and Wildlife Service, when she started planning her next book, to be published five years later as *The Edge of the Sea.* When it was finally done, she saw it as a book that balanced and complemented *The Sea Around Us*; in a sense, as a biological counterpart to its predecessor. In *The Sea Around Us*, she said later: "I dealt chiefly with the physical world of the ocean: its geologic origin, with the dynamics of waves and currents and tides, and with the nature of the unseen world beneath the surface of the ocean. In *The Edge of the Sea* I am telling something of the story of how that marvelous, tough, vital, and adaptable something we know as LIFE has come to occupy one part of the sea world and how it has adjusted itself and survived despite the immense, blind forces acting upon it from every side."

The idea for the book has an amusing origin, involving "blind forces" of which Miss Carson was not aware. It can be traced back to a minor event in which she had no part: a Sunday morn-

ing walk on the outer beaches of Cape Cod near the home of
Rosalind Wilson, then an editor for Houghton Mifflin Company.
The guests on that occasion were distinguished literary figures, but
somewhat lacking in biological sophistication. Seeing the beach
covered with horseshoe crabs, apparently stranded from the previous night's storm, they conscientiously returned them to the
sea, unaware that this intended act of mercy was interrupting the
normal mating procedure. Returning to her office on Monday
morning, Miss Wilson dictated a memorandum to the editor,
suggesting that an author be found to write a layman's handbook
to seashore life that would dispel such ignorance once and for all.
Shortly thereafter, when Rachel Carson met the Houghton Mifflin editors in connection with another project, the proposal was
put to her and she accepted.

The new book was a long time in the making, and, as Rachel
recalled with characteristic understatement, underwent "a certain evolution." "It began," she said, "as a subconscious thought
somewhere deep in my mind that I would one day do a different
sort of book about the shore. [On October 6, 1948, she had
written to Marie Rodell: "Among my remote literary projects is
a book on the lives of shore animals, which Mr. Teale once asked
me to write for his benefit."] I would probably have written some
other books first, but Houghton Mifflin came along about 5 years
ago with an idea they had about a seashore book. (This was before I had completed the ms. of *Sea*.) A contract was signed *
and I was granted a Guggenheim Fellowship to begin field work
on the book. At first we thought of it somewhat in terms of a
guide or field book. Of course it has gone a long way from that.

---

* But not before the author had suffered from the procrastination for which editors are notorious. She wrote to Marie Rodell: "I see that my letter to Mr.
Brooks is dated July 28. I can only assume the gentleman is having a nice long
vacation, but I still think a well-run office would have sent me a note saying so.
However, don't you think we'd better give him through next week, on the assumption he might come back along with everyone else right after Labor Day?
Then if I still hear nothing, I'll send you the file and you can go to work on
him."

"Perhaps I might have chosen some other part of the sea. But the choice of the shore has obvious advantages. First of all, it is a region that may be visited by almost everyone. Therefore the things I describe need not be taken on faith: they can actually be seen by everyone whose curiosity is aroused. Then, too, the shore is a place of special interest. It is a transition zone, that has some of the characteristics of the land and some of the sea. With the rhythm of the tides, rising and falling over the shore, it belongs now to the land, now to the sea. So it is a place that demands every bit of adaptability living things can muster. And by adapting themselves to the shore, sea animals have taken a long step toward adapting themselves to the land. So this is a place where the dramatic process of evolution can actually be observed."

The growth of *The Edge of the Sea* from the original concept to the finished product illustrates the long and often painful "process of evolution" that many good books go through before they see the light. It is a subtle, often barely detectable, process which — like biological evolution — generally takes place not in a steady and orderly fashion, but in irregular leaps. New concepts, new approaches arise continually in the author's mind; many will be discarded as useless, but a few will survive to change the shape and character of the original enterprise. In the hands of a creative writer such changes will be in the direction of originality, leading in some cases to a whole new species of book. As *The Sea Around Us* was *sui generis*, so in the event was its successor.

The original working title was "Guide to Seashore Life on the Atlantic Coast." For each important form of life that was mentioned there would be a "biological sketch . . . which, while brief, suggests a *living creature* and illuminates the basic conditions of its life: why it lives where it does, how it has adapted its structures and habitat to its environment, how it gets food, its life cycle, its enemies, competitors, associates." Her aim was "to take the seashore out of the category of scenery and make it

come alive . . . An ecological concept will dominate the book."
She wrote to Marie Rodell: "I'm getting awfully full of ideas, and
enthusiasm, about the seashore book . . . It would be such fun
to do." But to do it she needed time. In early September she
talked with her immediate superior at the Fish and Wildlife
Service, Alastair McBain, about the possibility of making an ar-
rangement to take three or four months' unpaid leave a year "if
my writing schedule (and finances) warranted it." He was sympathetic to her ambition. The following June (by which time
she had received her Guggenheim Fellowship and a contract for
the new book) she began a year's leave of absence, but she still
hesitated to make a permanent break. On a visit to New York,
shortly after *The Sea Around Us* had become a spectacular success, she asked advice of William Shawn and Edith Oliver: dare
she depend for a living on her pen? She was also concerned not
to appear as if she thought she had outgrown government work.
Finally, before the year had expired, she offered her official resignation, to take effect on June 3, 1952. "Of course the stated and
obvious reason for resigning," she wrote, "is to devote all my
time to writing." So it was, and by then royalties from *The Sea
Around Us* had given her financial independence. But it seems
clear that in any case she would not have been happy for long in
her old job. When Benton McKay, a former automobile sales-
man, became Secretary of the Interior, Albert M. Day, the courageous and highly respected director of the Service was fired.
Rachel Carson was furious. She wrote a letter to the Washington *Post*, which was condensed in the *Reader's Digest* as follows:

> The dismissal of Mr. Albert M. Day as director of the Fish
> and Wildlife Service is the most recent of a series of events that
> should be deeply disturbing to every thoughtful citizen. The
> ominous pattern that is clearly being revealed is the elimination
> from the government of career men of long experience and high
> professional competence and their replacement by political ap-
> pointees. The firing of Mr. Marion Clawson, director of the

Bureau of Land Management, is another example. These actions strongly suggest that the way is being cleared for a raid upon our natural resources that is without parallel within the present century.

The real wealth of the Nation lies in the resources of the earth — soil, water, forests, minerals, and wildlife. To utilize them for present needs while insuring their preservation for future generations requires a delicately balanced and continuing program, based on the most extensive research. Their administration is not properly, and cannot be, a matter of politics.

By long tradition, the agencies responsible for these resources have been directed by men of professional stature and experience, who have understood, respected, and been guided by the findings of their scientists. Mr. Day's career in wildlife conservation began 35 years ago, when, as a young biologist, he was appointed to the staff of the former Biological Survey, which later became part of the Fish and Wildlife Service. During the intervening years, he rose through the ranks occupying successively higher positions until he was appointed director in 1946. He achieved a reputation as an able and fair-minded administrator, with courage to stand firm against the minority groups who demanded that he relax wildlife conservation measures so that they might raid these public resources. Secretary McKay, whose own grasp of conservation problems is yet to be demonstrated, has now decreed that the Nation is to be deprived of these services.

For many years public-spirited citizens throughout the country have been working for the conservation of the natural resources, realizing their vital importance to the Nation. Apparently their hard-won progress is to be wiped out, as a politically minded Administration returns us to the dark ages of unrestrained exploitation and destruction.

It is one of the ironies of our time that, while concentrating on the defense of our country against enemies from without, we should be so heedless of those who would destroy it from within.

Rachel L. Carson

August 1953

〰〰〰

As always, Rachel Carson was concerned from the beginning
with the book as a whole — particularly in this case with the selection of an artist. The planning of design and illustrations, she
knew, should go right along with the writing. Fortunately, the
perfect choice for the assignment was right on hand: her close
friend and longtime colleague, Bob Hines, staff artist for the Fish
and Wildlife Service. Bob would work, not from preserved specimens but from living animals, observed and collected in their
native habitat. Often Rachel and he would spend hours together
on the beaches and rocks and coral reefs. The resultant black
and white pencil drawings combined the factual information
necessary for recognition with a lifelike and artistic quality which
were all the more essential when the book became less of a mere
guide and more of a work of literature.

The spring of 1951 had been occupied with the final publication details of *The Sea Around Us* and preparation of the selections for *The New Yorker*. By June, however, Rachel Carson
was planning her summer field work for the new book: a trip to
Beaufort, North Carolina, to have at least a preliminary look at
its creatures, then to Maine and Cape Cod.

Having become an instant celebrity with the publication of
The Sea Around Us on July 2, she was by midsummer enjoying
(in Bob Hines's words) "a hectic, but wonderful existence."
Years later she recalled "the perfectly appalling volume of mail
that comes to the author of a book on the best-seller list . . .
Remembering the letters that drifted down upon me — like the
never-ending rain of sediments to the flow of the sea — I sometimes wonder how *The Edge of the Sea* ever got written." Honors and obligations had reached overwhelming proportions for
someone whose primary concern was with her current writing. "It
is hard to answer your questions about availability for publicity
matters," she wrote to the publicity director at the Oxford Press,
"except to say that it will continue to be limited. Naturally the
new book is uppermost in my mind and I begrudge time taken

from it." In April of 1952 she was observing and collecting on southern beaches from Charleston to the Florida Keys. Among other things she saw on this trip a clear example of how local environmental conditions, rather than latitude or climate, may be the determining factor in the life of an area. "Coming down the coast yesterday," she wrote, "I visited one of the few (or perhaps the only) outcroppings of rock on this sandy coast, and for a moment felt as if I were in Maine again, for there were the limpets, chitons, periwinkles, etc., of the Maine coast, yet with the blue Gulf Stream water almost washing the rocks." Most of the summer was to be spent at Woods Hole. "I'd rather spend the whole time in Maine, but I need the M.B.L. Library at this point even more than I need the tide pools."

Rachel Carson later described the excitement of working on *The Edge of the Sea* by recalling a remark that had once been made to her and Shirley Briggs when they were studying the marine life of the upper Keys. "On that particular morning we hoped to do a little helmet diving with equipment provided by the University of Miami. We were waiting for a bus to take us to the Yacht Basin where the boat was anchored. We were laden with paraphernalia of all sorts. But especially, I suppose, a certain happy anticipation must have been written on our faces. A stranger who was also waiting for the bus took it all in, then he said to us: 'You girls look as though you were going out to discover a new world.' I think perhaps that remark expressed the keynote of these studies of the shore — the sense of discovery."

But a writing job can also involve real sacrifices. She received a tempting invitation from the Scripps Oceanographic Institute for a trip to the South Pacific, which would have meant interrupting work on the book for two months. "After a dreadful week of thinking one day that the Pacific trip made sense, and the next finding that it didn't — only to have hope revive on the following — I have finally and irrevocably given it up . . . It might not have mattered last winter, but with the book rolling now and in a

very sensitive stage, it would matter a great deal . . . So —
don't get the presses ready for any Samoa saga from me!"

By March 1953 she felt that she was far behind schedule, "but
at least I am in that state of desperate determination that — judging by the past — is likely to bring me through about on time
. . . I am suffering tortures over the manuscript, but I guess that
is a normal sign with me." A week later she described in outline
the material on the Florida Keys, which was turning out to have
a unity of theme that she had found lacking in the early stages.
"As I write of it, it sounds so very easy; why is it such agony to
put on paper?"

About this time the slowly evolving manuscript took a decisive
turn in a direction which was to lead to a quite different book
from the one originally envisioned.

Somewhere along in the Florida Keys chapter [she wrote to me]
I decided that I have been trying for a very long time to write
the wrong kind of book, and in dealing with the corals and mangroves and all the rest I seemed at last to fall into the sort of
treatment that is "right" for me in dealing with this sort of subject. I seem to be doing the same sort of thing for the sand and
feel I can for the marshes, not yet begun. It means that I shall
have to rewrite quite a lot of the rocks chapter — but that is part
of writing, I guess. At any rate this chapter is quite typical of
the book that is shaping up, and I'd like you to read it now.

I think we could say that the book has become an interpretation of four types of shore, the other chapters merely providing
the frame for this, the real heart of the book. As I am now writing, the routine and miscellaneous facts, that were so difficult for
me to incorporate in the text, are now being saved for the cap-
tions of Bob's pictures, or for a tabular summary I'd like to tuck
in at the end of the book. This solution frees my style to be itself; the attempt to write a structureless chapter that was just one
little thumbnail biography after another was driving me mad. I
don't know why I once thought I should do it that way, but I did.

In the beginning I thought of this as a book very different in
kind from *The Sea Around Us*; now it seems to me a sort of

sequel or companion volume, the former dealing with the physical aspects of the sea, this with the biological aspects of at least part of it.

These four types were eventually reduced to three, which — thanks to the configuration and geologic history of the area she was writing about — lent themselves particularly well to the ecological approach, that is, the study of living communities as opposed to merely individual life histories. These three types were the rocky shores north of Cape Cod, where seashore life is adapted to the tides; the sand beaches from there southward, where the dominant force is the waves; and finally the coral and mangrove coasts of the far south, which are governed largely by ocean currents. These environments are found the world over, but the Atlantic coast demonstrates their life patterns "almost with the clarity of a well-conceived scientific experiment."

∽∾∽

One happy result of the success of *The Sea Around Us* was to enable its author to realize her dream of owning a summer home at the edge of the sea. In 1953 she bought a tract of land in West Southport, Maine, overlooking Sheepscot Bay, and built a one-story cottage on the rocks, with only a few steps between the window that faced the sunset and the dark line of high tide. "Writing a book about the shore," she said, "as I am doing now, has given me an excuse to spend a great deal of time in places I love very much . . . I can't think of any more exciting place to be than down in the low-tide world, when the ebb tide falls very early in the morning, and the world is full of salt smell, and the sound of water, and the softness of fog."

The first summer in the new cottage began rather sadly. Owing to the illness of Rachel's mother, they did not move in until July; immediately after their arrival, their beloved cat died of pneumonia, which was a deep grief to them both and caused a temporary relapse on the part of Mrs. Carson. As the summer advanced, however, it became apparent that this was a good place to write a book about the seashore. Her laboratory was at her doorstep, and her research was anything but dull: "Yesterday morning Marjie [her niece] and I went out about seven for the most extraordinary low we've had, and brought back a 10-inch starfish to photograph Roger [Marjie's son] holding it. By the time the fog lifted enough for photography, the tide was too high to return the starfish to his happy home. When we got back from putting M. and R. on the train, the tide was low, but also it was about dark. I took the flashlight and went slithering down to the low tide line and it was quite spooky. The big crabs that usually stay down in crevices and under ledges in the daytime were out scampering around, and a drained anemone cave, by flashlight, with all the anemones hanging down, was quite Charles Addamsish." A month later: "These September spring tides have been wonderful and I have learned a great deal I didn't know before — so that I'm now redoing the rock chapter with more conviction and authority, at least . . . It is nothing to find 30 anemones under one ledge at these low levels; one was 5 inches *across!* My most exciting discovery — and as far as I know it is original, for I have never seen it reported — is that there is a large and thriving fauna living in and under the crusts of Litho-phyllum, etc. Well, you can read about it in *The Edge of the Sea* — in the year 1963."

The shift in the direction of the book involved, of course, a good deal of rethinking and reworking from the start, but at last she was on the right track. Rewriting the rock chapter from her new vantage point was getting results. "For the first time, I'm writing about something while it is right under my nose, and it gives me a very different feeling about it . . . But it is still so terribly slow!"

The Maine cottage had indeed proved to be the fulfillment of a dream. Besides the sea creatures of the tide pools there were loons and seals in the bay within sight of the window, a whale had been playing around at the mouth of the harbor, and a large bull moose and cow had been causing excitement all over South-port Island. Though this was designed as a summer home, Rachel was determined to stay to the last possible moment, until the water supply was turned off for the winter. "The autumn color is becoming vivid everywhere," she wrote in early October, "the blueberry bushes above my shore are all afire. Why do they have to turn off the water, ever?" Two weeks later, "All the color sud-denly became far more intense than it had been so that it is really breathtaking. I'm so glad we stayed to see it. And almost every morning our trees are full of small bird migrants that have come in during the night, so that breakfast has to be eaten with the binoculars in one hand. Yesterday was quite a morning. Besides all the usual warblers, kinglets, and other small fry, we had a small flock of pine grosbeaks in the top of the spruce at the foot of the steps. Then a large flock of geese came down over the bay, and a red-necked grebe fished just off our rocks."

༄༄༄

She was back as early as possible in the spring for a brief visit that led to her first meeting with the American writer whom she most admired, Henry Beston. She wrote to him on May 14, 1954:

Although this letter is a result of a telephone conversation with Carl Buchheister [President of the National Audubon So-ciety], it is, in a way, at least twenty years overdue. It was about that long ago that I discovered *The Outermost House* in a corner of the Pratt Library in Baltimore. I hesitate to guess how many times I have read the book since then, but I don't hesitate to say that I can think of few others that have given me such deep and lasting pleasure, or to which I can return with such assurance of a renewal of my original enjoyment.

While I was writing *Under the Sea-Wind* I spent part of a summer at Woods Hole, and one day drove to Eastham and walked down the beach to find the little house and the surround-ings with which I felt so familiar through your pages. The daughter of one of your Harvard contemporaries, Mr. George Hamilton, was with me.* After that happy experience I wanted to write you, but procrastinated. Then, a year or more ago, some one sent me a clipping of your review of *Under the Sea-Wind* (I had missed the review on its appearance). Let me tell you now, though belatedly, that I found it the most beautiful, perceptive, and deeply satisfying one I had read, and because of my feeling about *The Outermost House*, I was so grateful it was you who had written it.

Recently I acquired a bit of Maine coast at Southport and built a cottage overlooking Sheepscot Bay; last summer we occupied it for the first time — my mother and I. Next week I am going up to open the cottage and spend a few days there. When I was in New York earlier this week, I called Mr. Buchheister to ask whether veeries would be singing this early, and where. He immediately suggested that I ask you about localities. To me the song of the veery is one of the most deeply moving of bird voices, and I should love to hear them again in Maine.

∾∾∾

The embryo book was now clearly recognizable in its new form, and she hoped to wind up the whole job during the following summer: "To do this I have canceled all invitations — both to friends who had thoughts of visiting me and *by* friends who wanted me to do things with them! But it will be wonderful to have the book done!" Some eight months later, she delivered the complete — well, *almost* complete — manuscript. "In thinking how to celebrate this momentous event — the end of simply years of misery — I'm handicapped by the fact that the end seems *never* quite to come!" Her phrase "years of misery" should not, I suggest, be taken too literally. For most talented and painstak-

---

* Now Mrs. Glenn H. Algire. She recalled this trip thirty years later: "I was working in the Fisheries Laboratory at Woods Hole as I did every summer. Rachel had only a few weeks in August but we managed to explore parts of the outer Cape. She was particularly interested in Nauset Beach, especially in seeing Henry Beston's 'outermost house.' She seemed much impressed by the house when we finally found it. I remember her standing looking at it a long time, in complete silence."

ing authors writing is — like love — a bitter-sweet experience. Misery, yes; the only greater misery would be not to write at all.

Characteristically, she wanted to make sure that her partner Bob Hines received due credit. "I hope you are going to give some information on the jacket about the artist as well as the author . . . This, it seems to me, is demanded by the fact that the art is such a substantial part of the book and is so beautifully and satisfyingly done."

Few books of natural history have succeeded so well as *The Edge of the Sea* in bringing to life the total environment with which they deal; in combining scientific fact with personal enthusiasm. Rachel Carson's own comment suggests why.

"I have lived as much of it as possible, working at key spots from Eastport to Key West, spending one summer at Woods Hole where I had many of my subjects under close observation in my own lab and in the waters nearby, and other summers at my own summer home and lab on the Maine coast. It is a subject that is as fresh for me now as it was in the beginning. There is always something new to discover and I never go down to the low tide world without a sense of anticipation. I hope some of the fascination I feel has seeped through into the book. Now at the end of the more than four years, I feel some sense of the relief that is an author's right; but it is relief to be done with the task of writing. I am not weary of the subject. In fact I have my eye on the calendar and am counting the days till I can get back to my own Maine shore and go exploring on the great spring tides that will follow the new moon next month."

No one was better able to appreciate her achievement than Edwin Way Teale. When the first installment of *The Edge of the Sea* appeared in *The New Yorker*, he wrote to her: "You have done it again! The wonderful part of it is that in spite of the strain and struggle and frustration that I know went into shaping the book in its final form there is no hint of 'tired writing' in any of the portion I have read. It is serene and fresh and strong with no residue of fatigue or stress in it — and that, in truth, is a very great accomplishment."

The Edge of the Sea was to bring her two more honors: the Achievement Award of the American Association of University Women and, from the National Council of Women of the United States, the citation for "the outstanding book of the year."

CHAPTER 13

FROM *THE EDGE OF THE SEA*

"The Marginal World"

THE EDGE of the sea is a strange and beautiful place. All through the long history of Earth it has been an area of unrest where waves have broken heavily against the land, where the tides have pressed forward over the continents, receded, and then returned. For no two successive days is the shore line precisely the same. Not only do the tides advance and retreat in their eternal rhythms, but the level of the sea itself is never at rest. It rises or falls as the glaciers melt or grow, as the floor of the deep ocean basins shifts under its increasing load of sediments, or as the earth's crust along the continental margins warps up or down in adjustment to strain and tension. Today a little more land may belong to the sea, tomorrow a little less. Always the edge of the sea remains an elusive and indefinable boundary.

The shore has a dual nature, changing with the swing of the tides, belonging now to the land, now to the sea. On the ebb tide it knows the harsh extremes of the land world, being exposed to heat and cold, to wind, to rain and drying sun. On the flood tide it is a water world, returning briefly to the relative stability of the open sea.

Only the most hardy and adaptable can survive in a region so mutable, yet the area between the tide lines is crowded with plants and animals. In this difficult world of the shore, life displays its enormous toughness and vitality by occupying almost every conceivable niche. Visibly, it carpets the intertidal rocks, or half hidden, it descends into fissures and crevices, or hides under boulders, or lurks in the wet gloom of sea caves. Invisibly, where the casual observer would say there is no life, it lies deep in the sand, in burrows and tubes and passageways. It tunnels into solid rock and bores into peat and clay. It encrusts weeds or drifting spars or the hard, chitinous shell of a lobster. It exists minutely, as the film of bacteria that spreads over a rock surface or a wharf piling; as spheres of protozoa, small as pinpricks, sparkling at the surface of the sea; and as Lilliputian beings swimming through dark pools that lie between the grains of sand.

The shore is an ancient world, for as long as there has been an earth and sea there has been this place of the meeting of land and water. Yet it is a world that keeps alive the sense of continuing creation and of the relentless drive of life. Each time that I enter it, I gain some new awareness of its beauty and its deeper meanings, sensing that intricate fabric of life by which one creature is linked with another, and each with its surroundings.

In my thoughts of the shore, one place stands apart for its revelation of exquisite beauty. It is a pool hidden within a cave that one can visit only rarely and briefly when the lowest of the year's low tides fall below it, and perhaps from that very fact it acquires some of its special beauty. Choosing such a tide, I hoped for a glimpse of the pool. The ebb was to fall early in the morning. I knew that if the wind held from the northwest and no interfering swell ran in from a distant storm the level of the sea should drop below the entrance to the pool. There had been sudden ominous showers in the night, with rain like handfuls of gravel flung on the roof. When I looked out into the early morning the sky was full of a gray dawn light but the sun had not yet risen. Water and air were pallid. Across the bay the moon was a luminous disc in the western sky, suspended above the dim line of distant shore — the full August moon, drawing the tide to the low, low levels of the threshold of the alien sea world. As I watched, a gull flew by, above the spruces. Its breast was rosy with the light of the unrisen sun. The day was, after all, to be fair.

Later, as I stood above the tide near the entrance to the pool, the promise of that rosy light was sustained. From the base of the steep wall of rock on which I stood, a moss-covered ledge jutted seaward into deep water. In the surge at the rim of the ledge the dark fronds of oarweeds swayed, smooth and gleaming as leather. The projecting ledge was the path to the small hidden cave and its pool. Occasionally a swell, stronger than the rest, rolled smoothly over the rim and broke in foam against the cliff. But the intervals between such swells were long enough to admit me to the ledge and long enough for a glimpse of that fairy pool, so seldom and so briefly exposed.

And so I knelt on the wet carpet of sea moss and looked back into the dark cavern that held the pool in a shallow basin. The floor of the cave was only a few inches below the roof, and a mirror had been created in which all that grew on the ceiling was reflected in the still water below.

Under water that was clear as glass the pool was carpeted with green sponge. Gray patches of sea squirts glistened on the ceiling and colonies of soft coral were a pale apricot color. In the moment when I looked into the cave a little elfin starfish hung down, suspended by the merest thread, perhaps by only a single tube foot. It reached down to touch its own reflection, so perfectly delineated that there might have been, not one starfish, but two. The beauty of the reflected images and of the limpid pool itself was the poignant beauty of things that are ephemeral, existing only until the sea should return to fill the little cave.

Whenever I go down into this magical zone of the low water of the spring tides, I look for the most delicately beautiful of all the shore's inhabitants — flowers that are not plant but animal, blooming on the threshold of the deeper sea. In that fairy cave I was not disappointed. Hanging from its roof were the pendent flowers of the hydroid Tubularia, pale pink, fringed and delicate as the wind flower. Here were creatures so exquisitely fashioned that they seemed unreal, their beauty too fragile to exist in a world of crushing force. Yet every detail was functionally useful, every stalk and hydranth and petal-like tentacle fashioned for dealing with the realities of existence. I knew that they were merely waiting, in that moment of the tide's ebbing, for the return of the sea. Then in the rush of water, in the surge of surf and the pressure of the incoming tide, the delicate flower heads would stir with life. They would sway on their slender stalks, and their long tentacles would sweep the returning water, finding in it all that they needed for life.

And so in that enchanted place on the threshold of the sea the realities that possessed my mind were far from those of the land world I had left an hour before. In a different way the same sense of remoteness and of a world apart came to me in a twilight hour on a great beach on the coast of Georgia. I had come down after sunset and walked far out over sands that lay wet and gleaming, to the very edge of the retreating sea. Looking back across that immense flat, crossed by winding, water-filled gullies and here and there holding shallow pools left by the tide, I was filled with awareness that this intertidal area, although abandoned briefly and rhythmically by the sea, is always reclaimed by the rising tide. There at the edge of low water the beach with its reminders of the land seemed far away. The only sounds were those of the wind and the sea and the birds. There was one sound of wind moving over water, and another of water sliding over the sand and tumbling down the faces of its own wave forms. The flats were astir with birds, and the voice of the willet rang insistently. One of them stood at the edge of the water and gave its loud, urgent cry; an answer came from far up the beach and the two birds flew to join each other.

The flats took on a mysterious quality as dusk approached and the last evening light was reflected from the scattered pools and creeks. Then birds became only dark shadows, with no color discernible. Sanderlings scurried across the beach like little ghosts, and here and there the darker forms of the willets stood out. Often I could come very close to them before they would start up in alarm — the sanderlings running, the willets flying up, crying. Black skimmers flew along the ocean's edge silhouetted against the dull, metallic gleam, or they went flitting above the sand like large, dimly seen moths. Sometimes they "skimmed" the winding creeks of tidal water, where little spreading surface ripples marked the presence of small fish.

The shore at night is a different world, in which the very darkness that hides the distractions of daylight brings into sharper focus the elemental realities. Once, exploring the night beach, I surprised a small ghost crab in the searching beam of my torch. He was lying in a pit he had dug just above the surf, as though watching the sea and waiting. The blackness of the night possessed water, air, and beach. It was the darkness of an older world, before Man. There was no sound but the all-enveloping, primeval sounds of wind blowing over water and sand, and of waves crashing on the beach. There was no other visible life — just one small crab near the sea. I have seen hundreds of ghost crabs in other settings, but suddenly I was filled with the odd sensation that for the first time I knew the creature in its own world — that I understood, as never before, the essence of its being. In that moment time was suspended; the world to which I belonged did not exist and I might have been an onlooker from outer space. The little crab alone with the sea became a symbol that stood for life itself — for the delicate, destructible, yet incredibly vital force that somehow holds its place amid the harsh realities of the inorganic world.

The sense of creation comes with memories of a southern coast, where the sea and the mangroves, working together, are building a wilderness of thousands of small islands off the south-western coast of Florida, separated from each other by a tortuous pattern of bays, lagoons, and narrow waterways. I remember a winter day when the sky was blue and drenched with sunlight; though there was no wind one was conscious of flowing air like cold clear crystal. I had landed on the surf-washed tip of one of those islands, and then worked my way around to the sheltered bay side. There I found the tide far out, exposing the broad mud flat of a cove bordered by the mangroves with their twisted branches, their glossy leaves, and their long prop roots reaching down, grasping and holding the mud, building the land out a little more, then again a little more.

The mud flats were strewn with the shells of that small, exquisitely colored mollusk, the rose tellin, looking like scattered petals of pink roses. There must have been a colony nearby, living buried just under the surface of the mud. At first the only creature visible was a small heron in gray and rusty plumage — a reddish egret that waded across the flat with the stealthy, hesitant movements of its kind. But other land creatures had been there, for a line of fresh tracks wound in and out among the mangrove roots, marking the path of a raccoon feeding on the oysters that gripped the supporting roots with projections from their shells. Soon I found the tracks of a shore bird, probably a sanderling, and followed them a little; then they turned toward the water and were lost, for the tide had erased them and made them as though they had never been.

Looking out over the cove I felt a strong sense of the interchangeability of land and sea in this marginal world of the shore, and of the links between the life of the two. There was also an awareness of the past and of the continuing flow of time, obliterating much that had gone before, as the sea had that morning washed away the tracks of the bird.

The sequence and meaning of the drift of time were quietly summarized in the existence of hundreds of small snails — the mangrove periwinkles — browsing on the branches and roots of the trees. Once their ancestors had been sea dwellers, bound to the salt waters by every tie of their life processes. Little by little over the thousands and millions of years the ties had been broken, the snails had adjusted themselves to life out of water, and now today they were living many feet above the tide to which they only occasionally returned. And perhaps, who could say how many ages hence, there would be in their descendants not even this gesture of remembrance for the sea.

The spiral shells of other snails — these quite minute — left winding tracks on the mud as they moved about in search of food. They were horn shells, and when I saw them I had a nostalgic moment when I wished I might see what Audubon saw, a century and more ago. For such little horn shells were the food of the flamingo, once so numerous on this coast, and when I half closed my eyes I could almost imagine a flock of these magnificent flame birds feeding in that cove, filling it with their color. It was a mere yesterday in the life of the earth that they were there; in nature, time and space are relative matters, perhaps most truly perceived subjectively in occasional flashes of insight, sparked by such a magical hour and place.

There is a common thread that links these scenes and memories — the spectacle of life in all its varied manifestations as it has appeared, evolved, and sometimes died out. Underlying the beauty of the spectacle there is meaning and significance. It is the elusiveness of that meaning that haunts us, that sends us again and again into the natural world where the key to the riddle is hidden. It sends us back to the edge of the sea, where the drama of life played its first scene on earth and perhaps even its prelude; where the forces of evolution are at work today, as they have been since the appearance of what we know as life; and where the spectacle of living creatures faced by the cosmic realities of their world is crystal clear.

"Patterns of Shore Life"

THE EARLY HISTORY of life as it is written in the rocks is exceedingly dim and fragmentary, and so it is not possible to say when living things first colonized the shore, nor even to indicate the exact time when life arose. The rocks that were laid down as sediments during the first half of the earth's history, in the Archeozoic era, have since been altered chemically and physically by the pressure of many thousands of feet of super-imposed layers and by the intense heat of the deep regions to which they have been confined during much of their existence. Only in a few places, as in eastern Canada, are they exposed and accessible for study, but if these pages of the rock history ever contained any clear record of life, it has long since been obliterated.

The following pages — the rocks of the next several hundred million years, known as the Proterozoic era — are almost as disappointing. There are immense deposits of iron, which may possibly have been laid down with the help of certain algae and bacteria. Other deposits — strange globular masses of calcium carbonate — seem to have been formed by lime-secreting algae. Supposed fossils or faint impressions in these ancient rocks have been tentatively identified as sponges, jellyfish, or hard-shelled creatures with jointed legs called arthropods, but the more skeptical or conservative scientists regard these traces as having an inorganic origin.

Suddenly, following the early pages with their sketchy records, a whole section of the history seems to have been destroyed. Sedimentary rocks representing untold millions of years of pre-Cambrian history have disappeared, having been lost by erosion or possibly, through violent changes in the surface of the earth, brought into a location that now is at the bottom of the deep sea.

Because of this loss a seemingly unbridgeable gap in the story of life exists.

The scarcity of fossil records in the early rocks and the loss of whole blocks of sediments may be linked with the chemical nature of the early sea and the atmosphere. Some specialists believe that the pre-Cambrian ocean was deficient in calcium or at least in the conditions that make easily possible the secretion of calcium shells and skeletons. If so, its inhabitants must have been for the most part soft-bodied and so not readily fossilized. A large amount of carbon dioxide in the atmosphere and its relative deficiency in the sea would also have affected the weathering of rock, according to geological theory, so that the sedimentary rocks of pre-Cambrian time must have been repeatedly eroded, washed away, and newly sedimented, with consequent destruction of fossils.

When the record is resumed in the rocks of the Cambrian period, which are about half a billion years old, all the major groups of invertebrate animals (including the principal inhabitants of the shore) suddenly appear, fully formed and flourishing. There are sponges and jellyfish, worms of all sorts, a few simple snail-like mollusks, and arthropods. Algae also are abundant, although no higher plants appear. But the basic plan of each of the large groups of animals and plants that now inhabit the shore had been at least projected in those Cambrian seas, and we may suppose, on good evidence, that the strip between the tide lines 500 million years ago bore at least a general resemblance to the intertidal area of the present stage of earth history.

We may suppose also that for at least the preceding half-billion years those invertebrate groups, so well developed in the Cambrian, had been evolving from simpler forms, although what they looked like we may never know. Possibly the larval stages of some of the species now living may resemble those ancestors whose remains the earth seems to have destroyed or failed to preserve.

During the hundreds of millions of years since the dawn of the

Cambrian, sea life has continued to evolve. Subdivisions of the original basic groups have arisen, new species have been created, and many of the early forms have disappeared as evolution has developed others better fitted to meet the demands of their world. A few of the primitive creatures of Cambrian time have representatives today that are little changed from their early ancestors, but these are the exception. The shore, with its difficult and changing conditions, has been a testing ground in which the precise and perfect adaptation to environment is an indispensable condition of survival.

All the life of the shore — the past and the present — by the very fact of its existence there, gives evidence that it has dealt successfully with the sea itself, and the subtle life relationships that bind each living thing to its own community. The patterns of life as created and shaped by these realities intermingle and overlap so that the major design is exceedingly complex.

Whether the bottom of the shallow waters and the intertidal area consists of rocky cliffs and boulders, of broad plains of sand, or of coral reefs and shallows determines the visible pattern of life. A rocky coast, even though it is swept by surf, allows life to exist openly through adaptations for clinging to the firm surfaces provided by the rocks and by other structural provisions for dissipating the force of the waves. The visible evidence of living things is everywhere about — a colorful tapestry of seaweeds, barnacles, mussels, and snails covering the rocks — while more delicate forms find refuge in cracks and crevices or by creeping under boulders. Sand, on the other hand, forms a yielding, shifting substratum of unstable nature, its particles incessantly stirred by the waves, so that few living things can establish or hold a place on its surface or even in its upper layers. All have gone below, and in burrows, tubes, and underground chambers the hidden life of the sands is lived. A coast dominated by coral reefs is necessarily a warm coast, its existence made possible by warm ocean currents establishing the climate in which the coral animals can thrive. The reefs, living or dead, provide a hard surface to which living things may cling. Such a coast is somewhat like one bordered by rocky cliffs, but with differences introduced by smothering layers of chalky sediments. The richly varied tropical fauna of coral coasts has therefore developed special adaptations that set it apart from the life of mineral rock or sand. Because the American Atlantic coast includes examples of all three types of shore, the various patterns of life related to the nature of the coast itself are displayed there with beautiful clarity.

Still other patterns are superimposed on the basic geologic ones. The surf dwellers are different from those who live in quiet waters, even if members of the same species. In a region of strong tides, life exists in successive bands or zones, from the high-water mark to the line of the lowest ebb tides; these zones are obscured where there is a tidal action or on sand beaches where life is driven underground. The currents, modifying temperature and distributing the larval stages of sea creatures, create still another world.

Again the physical facts of the American Atlantic coast are such that the observer of its life has spread before him, almost with the clarity of a well-conceived scientific experiment, a demonstration of the modifying effect of tides, surf, and currents. It happens that the northern rocks, where life is lived openly, lie in the region of some of the strongest tides of the world, those within the area of the Bay of Fundy. Here the zones of life created by the tides have the simple graphic force of a diagram. The tidal zones being obscured on sandy shores, one is free there to observe the effect of the surf. Neither strong tides nor heavy surf visits the southern tip of Florida. Here is a typical coral coast, built by the coral animals and the mangroves that multiply and spread in the calm, warm waters — a world whose inhabitants have drifted there on ocean currents from the West Indies, duplicating the strange tropical fauna of that region.

And over all these patterns there are others created by the sea water itself — bringing or withholding food, carrying substances of powerful chemical nature that, for good or ill, affect the lives of all they touch. Nowhere on the shore is the relation of a creature to its surroundings a matter of a single cause and effect; each living thing is bound to its world by many threads, weaving the intricate design of the fabric of life.

The problem of breaking waves need not be faced by inhabitants of the open ocean, for they can sink into deep water to avoid rough seas. An animal or plant of the shore has no such means of escape. The surf releases all its tremendous energy as it breaks against the shore, sometimes delivering blows of almost incredible violence. Exposed coasts of Great Britain and other eastern Atlantic islands receive some of the most violent surf in the world, created by winds that sweep across the whole expanse of ocean. It sometimes strikes with a force of two tons to the square foot. The American Atlantic coast, being a sheltered shore, receives no such surf, yet even here the waves of winter storms or of summer hurricanes have enormous size and destructive power. The island of Monhegan on the coast of Maine lies unprotected in the path of such storms and receives their waves on its steep seaward-facing cliffs. In a violent storm the spray from breaking waves is thrown over the crest of White Head, about 100 feet above the sea. In some storms the green water of actual waves sweeps over a lower cliff known as Gull Rock. It is about 60 feet high.

The effect of waves is felt on the bottom a considerable distance offshore. Lobster traps set in water nearly 200 feet deep often are shifted about or have stones carried into them. But the critical problem, of course, is the one that exists on or very close to the shore, where waves are breaking. Very few coasts have completely defeated the attempts of living things to gain a foothold. Beaches are apt to be barren if they are composed of loose coarse sand that shifts in the surf and then dries quickly when the tide falls. Others, of firm sand, though they may look barren, actually sustain a rich fauna in their deeper layers. A beach composed of many cobblestones that grind against each other in the surf is an impossible home for most creatures. But the shore formed of rocky cliffs and ledges, unless the surf be of extraordinary force, is host to a large and abundant fauna and flora.

Barnacles are perhaps the best example of successful inhabitants of the surf zone. Limpets do almost as well, and so do the small rock periwinkles. The coarse brown seaweeds called wracks or rockweeds possess species that thrive in moderately heavy surf, while others require a degree of protection. After a little experience one can learn to judge the exposure of any shore merely by identifying its fauna and flora. If, for example, there is a broad area covered by the knotted wrack—a long and slender weed that lies like a tangled mass of cordage when the tide is out—if this predominates, we know the shore is a moderately protected one, seldom visited by heavy surf. If, however, there is little or none of the knotted wrack but instead a zone covered by a rockweed of much shorter stature, branching repeatedly, its fronds flattened and tapering at the ends, then we sense more keenly the presence of the open sea and the crushing power of its surf. For the forked wrack and other members of a community of low-growing seaweeds with strong and elastic tissues are sure indicators of an exposed coast and can thrive in seas the knotted wrack cannot endure. And if, on still another shore, there is little vegetation of any sort, but instead only a rock zone whitened by a living snow of barnacles — thousands upon thousands of them raising their sharp-pointed cones to the smother of the surf — we may be sure this coast is quite unprotected from the force of the sea.

The barnacle has two advantages that allow it to succeed where almost all other life fails to survive. Its low conical shape deflects the force of the waves and sends the water rolling off harmlessly. The whole base of the cone, moreover, is fixed to the rock with natural cement of extraordinary strength; to remove it one has to use a sharp-bladed knife. And so those twin dangers of the surf zone — the threat of being washed away and of being crushed — have little reality for the barnacle. Yet its existence in such a place takes on a touch of the miraculous when we remember this fact: it was not the adult creature, whose shape and firmly cemented base are precise adaptations to the surf, that gained a foothold here; it was the larva. In the turbulence of heavy seas, the delicate larva had to choose its spot on the wavewashed rocks, to settle there, and somehow not be washed away during those critical hours while its tissues were being reorganized in their transformation to the adult form, while the cement was extruded and hardened, and the shell plates grew up about the soft body. To accomplish all this in heavy surf seems to me a far more difficult thing than is required of the spore of a rockweed; yet the fact remains that the barnacles can colonize exposed rocks where the weeds are unable to gain a footing.

The streamlined form has been adopted and even improved upon by other creatures, some of whom have omitted the permanent attachment to the rocks. The limpet is one of these — a simple and primitive snail that wears above its tissues a shell like the hat of a Chinese coolie. From this smoothly sloping cone the surf rolls away harmlessly; indeed, the blows of falling water only press down more firmly the suction cup of fleshy tissue beneath the shell, strengthening its grip on the rock.

Still other creatures, while retaining a smoothly rounded contour, put out anchor lines to hold their places on the rocks. Such a device is used by the mussels, whose numbers in even a limited area may be almost astronomical. The shells of each animal are bound to the rock by a series of tough threads, each of shining silken appearance. The threads are a kind of natural silk, spun by a gland in the foot. These anchor lines extend out in all directions; if some are broken, the others hold while the damaged lines are being replaced. But most of the threads are directed forward and in the pounding of storm surf the mussel tends to swing around and head into the seas, taking them on the narrow "prow" and so minimizing their force.

Even the sea urchins can anchor themselves firmly in moderately strong surf. Their slender tube feet, each equipped with a suction disc at its tip, are thrust out in all directions. I have marveled at the green urchins on a Maine shore, clinging to the exposed rock at low water of spring tides, where the beautiful coralline algae spread a rose-colored crust beneath the shining green of their bodies. At that place the bottom slopes away steeply and when the waves at low tide break on the crest of the slope, they drain back to the sea with a strong rush of water. Yet as each wave recedes, the urchins remain on their accustomed stations, undisturbed.

For the long-stalked kelps that sway in dusky forests just below the level of the spring tides, survival in the surf zone is largely a matter of chemistry. Their tissues contain large amounts of alginic acid and its salts, which create a tensile strength and elasticity able to withstand the pulling and pounding of the waves.

Still others — animal and plant — have been able to invade the surf zone by reducing life to a thin creeping mat of cells. In such form many sponges, ascidians, bryozoans, and algae can endure the force of waves. Once removed from the shaping and conditioning effect of surf, however, the same species may take on entirely different forms. The pale green crumb-of-bread sponge lies flat and almost paper-thin on rocks facing toward the sea; back in one of the deep rock pools its tissues build up into thickened masses, sprinkled with the cone-and-crater structure that is one of the marks of the species. Or the golden-star tunicate may expose a simple sheet of jelly to the waves, though in quiet water it hangs down in pendulous lobes flecked with the starry forms of the creatures that comprise it.

As on the sands almost everything has learned to endure the surf by burrowing down to escape it, so on the rocks some have found safety by boring. Where ancient marl is exposed on the Carolina coast, it is riddled by date mussels. Masses of peat contain the delicately sculptured shells of mollusks called angel wings, seemingly fragile as china, but nevertheless able to bore into clay or rock; concrete piers are drilled by small boring clams; wooden timbers by other clams and isopods. All of these creatures have exchanged their freedom for a sanctuary from the waves, being imprisoned forever within the chambers they have carved.

∽∾∽

The vast current systems, which flow through the oceans like rivers, lie for the most part offshore and one might suppose their influence in intertidal matters to be slight. Yet the currents have far-reaching effects, for they transport immense volumes of water over long distances — water that holds its original temperature through thousands of miles of its journey. In this way tropical warmth is carried northward and arctic cold brought far down toward the equator. The currents, probably more than any other single element, are the creators of the marine climate.

The importance of climate lies in the fact that life, even as broadly defined to include all living things of every sort, exists within a relatively narrow range of temperature, roughly between 32° F. and 210° F. The planet Earth is particularly favorable for life because it has a fairly stable temperature. Especially in the sea, temperature changes are moderate and gradual and many animals are so delicately adjusted to the accustomed water climate that an abrupt or drastic change is fatal. Animals living on the shore and exposed to air temperatures at low tide are necessarily a little more hardy, but even these have their preferred range of heat and cold beyond which they seldom stray.

Most tropical animals are more sensitive to change — especially toward higher temperatures — than northern ones, and this is probably because the water in which they live normally varies by only a few degrees throughout the year. Some tropical sea urchins, keyhole limpets, and brittle stars die when the shallow waters heat to about 99° F. The arctic jellyfish Cyanea, on the other hand, is so hardy that it continues to pulsate when half its bell is imprisoned in ice, and may revive even after being solidly frozen for hours. The horseshoe crab is an example of an animal that is very tolerant of temperature change. It has a wide range as a species, and its northern forms can survive being frozen into ice in New England, while its southern representatives thrive in tropical waters of Florida and southward to Yucatán.

Shore animals for the most part endure the seasonal changes of temperate coasts, but some find it necessary to escape the extreme cold of winter. Ghost crabs and beach fleas are believed to dig very deep holes in the sand and go into hibernation. Mole crabs that feed in the surf much of the year retire to the bottom offshore in winter. Many of the hydroids, so like flowering plants in appearance, shrink down to the very core of their animal beings in winter, withdrawing all living tissues into the basal stalk. Other shore animals, like annuals in the plant kingdom, die at the end of summer. All of the white jellyfish, so common in coastal waters during the summer, are dead when the last autumn gale has blown itself out, but the next generation exists as little plantlike beings attached to the rocks below the tide.

For the great majority of shore inhabitants that continue to live in the accustomed places throughout the year, the most dangerous aspect of winter is not cold but ice. In years when much shore ice is formed, the rocks may be scraped clean of barnacles, mussels, and seaweeds simply by the mechanical action of ice grinding in the surf. After this happens, several growing seasons separated by moderate winters may be needed to restore the full community of living creatures.

Because most sea animals have definite preferences as to aquatic climate, it is possible to divide the coastal waters of eastern North America into zones of life. While variation in the temperature of the water within these zones is in part a matter of the advance from southern to northern latitudes, it is also strongly influenced by the pattern of the ocean currents — the sweep of warm tropical water carried northward in the Gulf Stream, and the chill Labrador Current creeping down from the north on the landward border of the Stream, with complex intermixing of warm and cold water between the boundaries of the currents.

From the point where it pours through the Florida straits up as far as Cape Hatteras, the Stream follows the outer edge of the continental shelf, which varies greatly in width. At Jupiter Inlet on the east coast of Florida this shelf is so narrow that one can stand on shore and look out across emerald-green shallows to the place where the water suddenly takes on the intense blue of the Stream. At about this point there seems to exist a temperature barrier, separating the tropical fauna of southern Florida and the Keys from the warm-temperate fauna of the area lying between Cape Canaveral and Cape Hatteras. Again at Hatteras the shelf becomes narrow, the Stream swings closer inshore, and the northward-moving water filters through a confused pattern of shoals and submerged sandy hills and valleys. Here again is a boundary between life zones, though it is a shifting and far from absolute one. During the winter, temperatures at Hatteras probably forbid the northward passage of migratory warm-water forms, but in summer the temperature barriers break down, the invisible gates open, and these same species may range far toward Cape Cod.

From Hatteras north the shelf broadens, the Stream moves far offshore, and there is a strong infiltration and mixing of colder water from the north, so that the progressive chilling is speeded. The difference in temperature between Hatteras and Cape Cod is as great as one would find on the opposite side of the Atlantic between the Canary Islands and southern Norway — a distance five times as long. For migratory sea fauna this is an intermediate zone, which cold-water forms enter in winter, and warm-water species in summer. Even the resident fauna has a mixed, indeterminate character, for this area seems to receive some of the more temperature-tolerant forms from both north and south, but to have few species that belong to it exclusively.

Cape Cod has long been recognized in zoology as marking the boundary of the range for thousands of creatures. Thrust far into the sea, it interferes with the passage of the warmer waters from the south and holds the cold waters of the north within the long curve of its shore. It is also a point of transition to a different kind of coast. The long sand strands of the south are replaced by rocks, which come more and more to dominate the coastal scene. They form the sea bottom as well as its shores; the same rugged contours that appear in the land forms of this region lie drowned and hidden from view offshore. Here zones of deep water, with accompanying low temperatures, lie generally closer to the shore than they do farther south, with interesting local effects on the populations of shore animals. Despite the deep inshore waters, the numerous islands and the jaggedly indented coast create a large intertidal area and so provide for a rich shore fauna. This is the cold-temperate region, inhabited by many species unable to tolerate the warm water south of the Cape. Partly because of the low temperatures and partly because of the rocky nature of the shore, heavy growths of seaweeds cover the ebb-tide rocks with a blanket of various hues, herds of periwinkles graze, and the shore is here whitened by millions of barnacles or there darkened by millions of mussels.

Beyond, in the waters bathing Labrador, southern Greenland, and parts of Newfoundland, the temperature of the sea and the nature of its flora and fauna are subarctic. Still farther to the north is the arctic province, with limits not yet precisely defined.

Although these basic zones are still convenient and well-founded divisions of the American coast, it became clear by about the third decade of the twentieth century that Cape Cod was not the absolute barrier it had once been for warm-water species attempting to round it from the south. Curious changes have been taking place, with many animals invading this cold-temperate zone from the south and pushing up through Maine and even into Canada. This new distribution is, of course, related to the widespread change of climate that seems to have set in about the beginning of the century and is now well recognized — a general warming-up noticed first in arctic regions, then in subarctic, and now in the temperate areas of northern states. With warmer ocean waters north of Cape Cod, not only the adults but the critically important young stages of various southern animals have been able to survive.

One of the most impressive examples of northward movement is provided by the green crab, once unknown north of the Cape, now familiar to every clam fisherman in Maine because of its habit of preying on the young stages of the clam. Around the turn of the century, zoological manuals gave its range as New Jersey to Cape Cod. In 1905 it was reported near Portland, and by 1930 specimens had been collected in Hancock County, about midway along the Maine coast. During the following decade it moved along to Winter Harbor, and in 1951 was found at Lubec. Then it spread up along the shores of Passamaquoddy Bay and crossed to Nova Scotia.

With higher water temperatures the sea herring is becoming scarce in Maine. The warmer waters may not be the only cause, but they are undoubtedly responsible in part. As the sea herring decline, other kinds of fish are coming in from the south. The menhaden is a larger member of the herring family, used in enormous quantities for manufacturing fertilizer, oils, and other industrial products. In the 1880s there was a fishery for menhaden in Maine, then they disappeared and for many years were confined almost entirely to areas south of New Jersey. About 1950, however, they began to return to Maine waters, followed by Virginia boats and fishermen. Another fish of the same tribe, called the round herring, is also ranging farther north. In the 1920s Professor Henry Bigelow of Harvard University reported it as occurring from the Gulf of Mexico to Cape Cod, and pointed out that it was rare anywhere on the Cape. (Two caught at Provincetown were preserved in the Museum of Comparative

Zoölogy at Harvard.) In the 1950s, however, immense schools of this fish appeared in Maine waters, and the fishing industry began experiments with canning it.

Many other scattered reports follow the same trend. The mantis shrimp, formerly barred by the Cape, has now rounded it and spread into the southern part of the Gulf of Maine. Here and there the soft-shell clam shows signs of being adversely affected by warm summer temperatures and the hard-shell species is replacing it in New York waters. Whiting, once only summer fish north of the Cape, now are caught there throughout the year, and other fish once thought distinctively southern are able to spawn along the coast of New York, where their delicate juvenile stages formerly were killed by the cold winters.

Despite the present exceptions, the Cape Cod–Newfoundland coast is typically a zone of cool waters inhabited by a boreal flora and fauna. It displays strong and fascinating affinities with distant places of the northern world, linked by the unifying force of the sea with arctic waters and with the coasts of the British Isles and Scandinavia. So many of its species are duplicated in the eastern Atlantic that a handbook for the British Isles serves reasonably well for New England, covering probably 80 per cent of the seaweeds and 60 per cent of the marine animals. On the other hand, the American boreal zone has stronger ties with the arctic than does the British coast. One of the large Laminarian seaweeds, the arctic kelp, comes down to the Maine coast but is absent in the eastern Atlantic. An arctic sea anemone occurs in the western North Atlantic abundantly down to Nova Scotia and less numerously in Maine, but on the other side misses Great Britain and is confined to colder waters farther north. The occurrence of many species such as the green sea urchin, the blood-red starfish, the cod, and the herring are examples of a distribution that is circumboreal, extending right around the top of the earth and brought about through the agency of cold currents from melting glaciers and drifting pack ice that carry representatives of the northern faunas down into the North Pacific and North Atlantic.

The existence of so strong a common element between the faunas and floras of the two coasts of the North Atlantic suggests that the means of crossing must be relatively easy. The Gulf Stream carries many migrants away from American shores. The distance to the opposite side is great, however, and the situation is complicated by the short larval life of most species and the fact that shallow waters must be within reach when the time comes for assuming the life of the adult. In this northern part of the Atlantic intermediate way stations are provided by submerged ridges, shallows, and islands, and the crossing may be broken into easy stages. In some earlier geologic times these shallows were even more extensive, so over long periods both active and involuntary migration across the Atlantic have been feasible.

In lower latitudes the deep basin of the Atlantic must be crossed, where few islands or shallows exist. Even here some transfer of larvae and adults takes place. The Bermuda Islands, after being raised above the sea by volcanic action, received their whole fauna as immigrants from the West Indies via the Gulf Stream. And on a smaller scale the long transatlantic crossings have been accomplished. Considering the difficulties, an impressive number of West Indian species are identical with, or closely related to African species, apparently having crossed in the Equatorial Current. They include species of starfish, shrimp, crayfish, and mollusks. Where such a long crossing has been made it is logical to assume that the migrants were adults, traveling on floating timber or drifting seaweed. In modern times, several African mollusks and starfish have been reported as arriving at the Island of St. Helena by these means.

The records of paleontology provide evidence of the changing shapes of continents and the changing flow of the ocean currents, for these earlier earth patterns account for the otherwise mysterious present distribution of many plants and animals. Once, for example, the West Indian region of the Atlantic was in direct communication, via sea currents, with the distant waters of the Pacific and Indian Oceans. Then a land bridge built up between the Americas, the Equatorial Current turned back on itself to the east, and a barrier to the dispersal of sea creatures was erected. But in species living today we find indications of how it was in the past. Once I discovered a curious little mollusk living in a meadow of turtle grass on the floor of a quiet bay among Florida's Ten Thousand Islands. It was the same bright green as the grass, and its little body was much too large for its thin shell, out of which it bulged. It was one of the scaphanders, and its nearest living relatives are inhabitants of the Indian Ocean. And on the beaches of the Carolinas I have found rocklike masses of calcareous tubes, secreted by colonies of a dark-bodied little worm. It is almost unknown in the Atlantic; again its relatives are Pacific and Indian Ocean forms.

And so transport and wide dispersal are a continuing, universal process — an expression of the need of life to reach out and occupy all habitable parts of the earth. In any age the pattern is set by the shape of the continents and the flow of the currents; but it is never final, never completed. On a shore where tidal action is strong and the range of the tide is great, one is aware of the ebb and flow of water with a daily, hourly awareness. Each recurrent high tide is a dramatic enactment of the advance of the sea against the continents, pressing up to the very threshold of the land, while the ebbs expose to view a strange and unfamiliar world. Perhaps it is a broad mud flat where curious holes, mounds, or tracks give evidence of a hidden life alien to the land; or perhaps it is a meadow of rockweeds lying prostrate and sodden now that the sea has left them, spreading a protective cloak over all the animal life beneath them. Even more directly the tides address the sense of hearing, speaking a language of their own distinct from the voice of the surf. The sound of a rising tide is heard most clearly on shores removed from the swell of the open ocean. In the stillness of night the strong waveless surge of a rising tide creates a confused tumult of water sounds — swashings and swirlings and a continuous slapping against the rocky rim of the land. Sometimes there are undertones of murmurings and whisperings; then suddenly all lesser sounds are obliterated by a torrential inpouring of water.

On such a shore the tides shape the nature and behavior of life. Their rise and fall give every creature that lives between the high- and low-water lines a twice-daily experience of land life. For those that live near the low-tide line the exposure to sun and air is brief; for those higher on the shore the interval in an alien environment is more prolonged and demands greater powers of endurance. But in all the intertidal area the pulse of life is adjusted to the rhythm of the tides. In a world that belongs alternately to sea and land, marine animals, breathing oxygen dissolved in sea water, must find ways of keeping moist; the few air breathers who have crossed the high-tide line from the land must protect themselves from drowning in the flood tide by bringing with them their own supply of oxygen. When the tide is low there is little or no food for most intertidal animals, and indeed the essential processes of life usually have to be carried on while water covers the shore. The tidal rhythm is therefore reflected in a biological rhythm of alternating activity and quiescence.

On a rising tide, animals that live deep in sand come to the surface, or thrust up the long breathing tubes or siphons, or begin to pump water through their burrows. Animals fixed to rocks open their shells or reach out tentacles to feed. Predators and grazers move about actively. When the water ebbs away the sand dwellers withdraw into the deep wet layers; the rock fauna brings into use all its varied means for avoiding desiccation. Worms that build calcareous tubes draw back into them, sealing the entrance with a modified gill filament that fits like a cork in a bottle. Barnacles close their shells, holding the moisture around their gills. Snails draw back into their shells, closing the doorlike operculum to shut out the air and keep some of the sea's wetness within. Scuds and beach fleas hide under rocks or weeds, waiting for the incoming tide to release them.

All through the lunar month, as the moon waxes and wanes, so the moon-drawn tides increase or decline in strength and the lines of high and low water shift from day to day. After the full moon, and again after the new moon, the forces acting on the sea to produce the tide are stronger than at any other time during the month. This is because the sun and moon then are directly in line with the earth and their attractive forces are added together. For complex astronomical reasons, the greatest tidal effect is exerted over a period of several days immediately after the full and the new moon, rather than at a time precisely coinciding with these lunar phases. During these periods the flood tides rise higher and the ebb tides fall lower than at any other time. These are called the "spring tides" from the Saxon "sprungen." The word refers not to a season, but to the brimming fullness of the water causing it to "spring" in the sense of a strong, active movement. No one who has watched a new-moon tide pressing against a rocky cliff will doubt the appropriateness of the term. In its quarter phases, the moon exerts its attraction at right angles to the pull of the sun so the two forces interfere with each other and the tidal movements are slack. Then the water neither rises as high nor falls as low as on the spring tides. These sluggish tides are called the "neaps" — a word that goes back to old Scandinavian roots meaning "barely touching" or "hardly enough."

On the Atlantic coast of North America the tides move in the so-called semidiurnal rhythm, with two high and two low waters in each tidal day of about 24 hours and 50 minutes. Each low tide follows the previous low by about 12 hours and 25 minutes, although slight local variations are possible. A like interval, of course, separates the high tides.

The range of tide shows enormous differences over the earth as a whole and even on the Atlantic coast of the United States there are important variations. There is a rise and fall of only a foot or two around the Florida Keys. On the long Atlantic coast of Florida the spring tides have a range of 3 to 4 feet, but a little to the north, among the Sea Islands of Georgia, these tides have an 8-foot rise. Then in the Carolinas and northward to New England they move less strongly, with spring tides of 6 feet at Charleston, South Carolina, 3 feet at Beaufort, North Carolina, and 5 feet at Cape May, New Jersey. Nantucket Island has little tide, but on the shores of Cape Cod Bay, less than 30 miles away, the spring tide range is 10 to 11 feet. Most of the rocky coast of New England falls within the zone of the great tides of the Bay of Fundy. From Cape Cod to Passamaquoddy Bay the amplitude of their range varies but is always considerable: 10 feet at Provincetown, 12 at Bar Harbor, 20 at Eastport, 22 at Calais. The conjunction of strong tides and a rocky shore, where much of the life is exposed, creates in this area a beautiful demonstration of the power of the tides over living things.

As day after day these great tides ebb and flow over the rocky rim of New England, their progress across the shore is visibly marked in stripes of color running parallel to the sea's edge. These bands, or zones, are composed of living things and reflect the stages of the tide, for the length of time that a particular level of shore is uncovered determines, in large measure, what can live there. The hardiest species live in the upper zones. Some of the earth's most ancient plants — the blue-green algae — though originating eons ago in the sea, have emerged from it to form dark tracings on the rocks above the high-tide line, a black zone visible on rocky shores in all parts of the world. Below the black zone, snails that are evolving toward a land existence browse on the film of vegetation or hide in seams and crevices in the rocks. But the most conspicuous zone begins at the upper line of the tides. On an open shore with moderately heavy surf, the rocks are whitened by the crowded millions of the barnacles just below the high-tide line. Here and there the white is interrupted by mussels growing in patches of darkest blue. Below them the seaweeds come in — the brown fields of the rockweeds. Toward the low-tide line the Irish moss spreads its low cushioning growth — a wide band of rich color that is not fully exposed by the sluggish movements of some of the neap tides, but appears on all of the greater tides. Sometimes the reddish brown of the moss is splashed with the bright green tangles of another seaweed, a hairlike growth of wiry texture. The lowest of the spring tides reveal still another zone during the last hour of their fall — that sub-tide world where all the rock is painted a deep rose hue by the lime-secreting seaweeds that encrust it, and where the gleaming brown ribbons of the large kelps lie exposed on the rocks.

With only minor variations, this pattern of life exists in all parts of the world. The differences from place to place are related usually to the force of the surf, and one zone may be largely suppressed and another enormously developed. The barnacle zone, for example, spreads its white sheets over all the upper shore where waves are heavy, and the rockweed zone is greatly reduced. With protection from surf, the rockweeds not only occupy the middle shore in profusion but invade the upper rocks and make conditions difficult for the barnacles.

Perhaps in a sense the true intertidal zone is that band between high and low water of the neap tides, an area that is completely covered and uncovered during each tidal cycle, or twice during every day. Its inhabitants are the typical shore animals and plants, requiring some daily contact with the sea but able to endure limited exposure to land conditions.

Above high water of neaps is a band that seems more of earth than of sea. It is inhabited chiefly by pioneering species; already they have gone far along the road toward land life and can endure separation from the sea for many hours or days. One of the barnacles has colonized these higher high-tide rocks, where the sea comes only a few days and nights out of the month, on the spring tides. When the sea returns it brings food and oxygen, and in season carries away the young into the nursery of the surface waters; during these brief periods the barnacle is able to carry on all the processes necessary for life. But it is left again in an alien land world when the last of these highest tides of the fortnight ebbs away; then its only defense is the firm closing of the plates of its shell to hold some of the moisture of the sea about its body. In its life brief and intense activity alternates with long periods of a quiescent state resembling hibernation. Like the plants of the Arctic, which must crowd the making and storing of food, the putting forth of flowers, and the forming of seeds into a few brief weeks of summer, this barnacle has drastically adjusted its way of life so that it may survive in a region of harsh conditions.

Some few sea animals have pushed on even above high water of the spring tides into the splash zone, where the only salty moisture comes from the spray of breaking waves. Among such pioneers are snails of the periwinkle tribe. One of the West Indian species can endure months of separation from the sea. Another, the European rock periwinkle, waits for the waves of the spring tides to cast its eggs into the sea, in almost all activities except the vital one of reproduction being independent of the water.

Below the low water of neaps are the areas exposed only as the rhythmic swing of the tides falls lower and lower, approaching the level of the springs. Of all the intertidal zone this region is linked most closely with the sea. Many of its inhabitants are offshore forms, able to live here only because of the briefness and infrequency of exposure to the air.

The relation between the tides and the zones of life is clear, but in many less obvious ways animals have adjusted their activities to the tidal rhythm. Some seem to be a mechanical matter of utilizing the movement of water. The larval oyster, for example, uses the flow of the tides to carry it into areas favorable for its attachment. Adult oysters live in bays or sounds or river estuaries rather than in water of full oceanic salinity, and so it is to the advantage of the race for the dispersal of the young stages to take place in a direction away from the open sea. When first hatched the larvae drift passively, the tidal currents carrying them now toward the sea, now toward the headwaters of estuaries or bays. In many estuaries the ebb tide runs longer than the flood, having the added push and volume of stream discharge behind it, and the resulting seaward drift over the whole two-week period of larval life would carry the young oysters many miles to sea. A sharp change of behavior sets in, however, as the larvae grow older. They now drop to the bottom while the tide ebbs, avoiding the seaward drift of water, but with the return of the flood they rise into the currents that are pressing upstream, and so are carried into regions of lower salinity that are favorable for their adult life.

Others adjust the rhythm of spawning to protect their young from the danger of being carried into unsuitable waters. One of the tube-building worms living in or near the tidal zone follows a pattern that avoids the strong movements of the spring tides. It releases its larvae into the sea every fortnight on the neap tides, when the water movements are relatively sluggish; the young worms, which have a very brief swimming stage, then have a good chance of remaining within the most favorable zone of the shore.

There are other tidal effects, mysterious and intangible. Sometimes spawning is synchronized with the tides in a way that suggests response to change of pressure or to the difference between still and flowing water. A primitive mollusk called the chiton spawns in Bermuda when the low tide occurs early in the morning, with the return flow of water setting in just after sunrise. As soon as the chitons are covered with water they shed their spawn. One of the Japanese nereid worms spawns only on the strongest tides of the year, near the new- and full-moon tides of October and November, presumably stirred in some obscure way by the amplitude of the water movements.

Many other animals, belonging to quite unrelated groups throughout the whole range of sea life, spawn according to a definitely fixed rhythm that may coincide with the full moon or the new moon or its quarters, but whether the effect is produced by the altered pressure of the tides or the changing light of the moon is by no means clear. For example, there is a sea urchin in Tortugas that spawns on the night of the full moon, and apparently only then. Whatever the stimulus may be, all the individuals of the species respond to it, assuring the simultaneous release of immense numbers of reproductive cells. On the coast of England one of the hydroids, an animal of plantlike appearance that produces tiny medusae or jellyfish, releases these medusae during the moon's third quarter. At Woods Hole on the Massachusetts coast a clamlike mollusk spawns heavily between the full and the new moon but avoids the first quarter. And a nereid worm at Naples gathers in its nuptial swarms during the quarters of the moon but never when the moon is new or full; a related worm at Woods Hole shows no such correlation although exposed to the same moon and to stronger tides.

In none of these examples can we be sure whether the animal is responding to the tides or, as the tides themselves do, to the influence of the moon. With plants, however, the situation is different, and here and there we find scientific confirmation of the ancient and world-wide belief in the effect of moonlight on vegetation. Various bits of evidence suggest that the rapid multiplication of diatoms and other members of the plant plankton is related to the phases of the moon. Certain algae in river plankton reach the peak of their abundance at the full moon. One of the brown seaweeds on the coast of North Carolina releases its reproductive cells only on the full moon, and similar behavior has been reported for other seaweeds in Japan and other parts of the world. These responses are generally explained as the effect of varying intensities of polarized light on protoplasm.

Other observations suggest some connection between plants and the reproduction and growth of animals. Rapidly maturing herring collect around the edge of concentrations of plant plankton, although the fully adult herring may avoid them. Spawning adults, eggs, and young of various other marine creatures are reported to occur more often in dense phytoplankton than in sparse patches. In significant experiments, a Japanese scientist discovered he could induce oysters to spawn with an extract obtained from sea lettuce. The same seaweed produces a substance that influences growth and multiplication of diatoms, and is itself stimulated by water taken from the vicinity of a heavy growth of rockweeds.

The whole subject of the presence in sea water of the so-called "cctocrines" (external secretions or products of metabolism) has so recently become one of the frontiers of science that actual information is fragmentary and tantalizing. It appears, however, that we may be on the verge of solving some of the riddles that have plagued men's minds for centuries. Though the subject lies in the misty borderlands of advancing knowledge, almost everything that in the past has been taken for granted, as well as problems considercd insoluble, bear renewed thought in the light of the discovery of these substances.

In the sea there are mysterious comings and goings, both in space and time: the movements of migratory species, the strange phenomenon of succession by which, in one and the same area, one species appears in profusion, flourishes for a time, and then dies out, only to have its place taken by another and then another, like actors in a pageant passing before our eyes. And there are other mysteries. The phenomenon of "red tides" has been known from early days, recurring again and again down to the present time — a phenomenon in which the sea becomes discolored because of the extraordinary multiplication of some minute form, often a dinoflagellate, and in which there are disastrous side effects in the shape of mass mortalities among fish and some of the invertebrates. Then there is the problem of curious and seemingly erratic movements of fish, into or away from certain areas, often with sharp economic consequences. When the so-called "Atlantic water" floods the south coast of England, herring become abundant within the range of the Plymouth fisheries, certain characteristic plankton animals occur in profusion, and certain species of invertebrates flourish in the intertidal zone. When, however, this water mass is replaced by Channel water, the cast of characters undergoes many changes.

In the discovery of the biological role played by the sea water and all it contains, we may be about to reach an understanding of these old mysteries. For it is now clear that in the sea nothing lives to itself. The very water is altered, in its chemical nature and in its capacity for influencing life processes, by the fact that certain forms have lived within it and have passed on to it new substances capable of inducing far-reaching effects. So the present is linked with past and future, and each living thing with all that surrounds it.

CHAPTER 14

SKY, A CHILD'S WORLD,
AND A DREAM

THE YEARS 1956 and 1957, between publication of *The Edge of the Sea* and commencement of work on *Silent Spring*, represent a breathing space — or at least a change of pace — in Rachel Carson's writing career. Not for some seven years had she been without a book in some stage of production. In the academic world, she would have been due for a sabbatical. But as she had said, "No writer can stand still." While she was not ready to start in on another major book, she threw herself almost immediately into two short-term projects among the many from which, as a best-selling author in constant demand, she had to choose.

The first of these, already discussed in late 1955, was a television program sponsored by *Omnibus* magazine on the subject of clouds. The film was the work of Dr. Vincent J. Schaefer of the Munitalp Foundation, one of the country's leading meteorologists and experts on clouds and cloud photography. Rachel Carson was to write the accompanying text. She hesitated, but the idea was appealing. All her life she had been fascinated by clouds and the other phenomena of the earth's atmosphere; at one point she had seriously considered writing a book on "The Air Around Us," but nothing ever came of it. Now she had a chance to express some of her ideas in a different medium. She wrote to Marie Rodell: "As yet I haven't heard whether the man from *Omnibus* called you. I do not know whether his idea about Clouds makes sense for me or not; that I could decide better after seeing their film and discovering what expert consultants they had on hand to keep me from going astray as to facts. What I sensed from the conversation I had was chiefly that they want me to do some thing — no matter what — and if their proposed price makes any sense at all, I should be inclined to consider it.

"My feelings about it are rather nebulous but I shall try to state them. Regardless of my own indifference to television, it is probably the medium that reaches the largest audience. I should therefore be open-minded about opportunities to present certain facts, or to foster certain attitudes, that I consider important. As far as I know, this program is the only one that offers an opportunity to have an important hand in it without actually appearing on the program, which, as you know, I am reluctant to do.

"At the moment, I don't know what it is that I am groping for, but I seem to sense an opportunity to have some tremendously worth-while ideas presented to the television audience. Perhaps the present inquiry may serve as a means of getting to know these people, so that the projects I dimly sense, but can't now describe, might come into being."

After some further investigation, she decided to go ahead. "Something About the Sky" was broadcast on March 11, 1956. Though her script was written to accompany the film, not to stand alone, a brief passage will show how the drama of the sky stimulated her imagination:

Hidden in the beauty of the moving clouds is a story that is as old as the earth itself. The clouds are the writing of the wind on the sky. They carry the signature of masses of air drifting across sea and land. They are the aviator's promise of good flying weather, or an omen of furious turbulence hidden within their calm exterior. But most of all they are cosmic symbols, representing an age-old process that is linked with life itself.

Our world has two oceans — an ocean of water and an ocean of air. In the sea the greatest depths lie about 7 miles down. Life exists everywhere. Corals — sponges — waving sea whips inhabit the bottom. Fish glide through the sea, carrying lightly the weight of all the overlying water.

We, too, live on the floor of an ocean — the vast atmospheric sea that surrounds our planet. From airless space down to where it touches earth its depth is some 600 miles, but only in the lowermost layers, some 6 or 7 miles deep, is the atmosphere dense enough to support life. Here, close to the earth in the zone of living things, clouds are born and die.

Like the sea, the atmosphere is a place of movement and turbulence, stirred by gigantic waves, torn by the swift passage of winds that are like ocean currents. These movements of the air are dramatized and made visible by the pattern of the clouds. Look up at these parallel bands of high clouds: like foaming whitecaps at sea, they mark the crests of waves, while the clear areas of sky between the clouds are the troughs of these vast, aerial surges . . .

Rachel Carson found her first encounter with television "quite an experience — educational, no doubt, but I'm not at all sure I'd do it again." One happy result was the friendship of Vincent and Lois Schaefer, who visited her in Southport the following September. Dr. Schaefer gave her expert advice in the pursuit of a new interest: microscopic photography. He sent her an adapter for holding the camera on the microscope. "Now one of my major ambitions," she wrote to him, "will be to learn how to make effective use of it to immortalize on film some of our tiny neighbors on the shore." This interest in microphotography was more than just a hobby. She was already exploring the motion picture possibilities of *The Edge of the Sea,* as a means of reaching a wider audience for some of the things that she wanted to say. In a memo on the subject, she wrote: "While I was writing *The Edge of the Sea*, I used to spend hours at my microscope, sometimes for a whole evening watching the activities of minute sea creatures — feeding, capturing prey, caring for their young — creatures so small that their very existence would be unknown without the use of a microscope. Yet here they were, living their lives under my lens, by their very strangeness capturing my fascinated attention and firing my imagination, and yet forcing me to realize that they faced and solved the same basic problems as more familiar land animals, even as we ourselves . . .

"The creatures of the world between the tide lines are known to only a handful of people. Because they are so different from familiar land animals, it is almost impossible to recreate them in words alone . . . Fortunately, the animals of the sea's edge — both the easily seen and those of microscopic size — are perfect material for photographic purposes. I can think of no part of the earth inhabited by animals of equal beauty, or by creatures whose habits are more fascinating, and whose adaptations to the world about them are more significant. It is part of the paradox of the sea that, while its creatures are so strangely unfamiliar, they present a demonstration of the essential nature and meaning of life that is unequaled in simple perfection and clarity."

The clouds evoked by Vincent Schaefer and Rachel Carson had barely drifted off the TV screen before she was embarked on her second and more lasting project for 1956. The day after the *Omnibus* Sky broadcast, she wrote: "Clouds are now past history. Next, I'm committed to write an article for the *Woman's Home Companion*. It's about encouraging awareness of nature in children, the working title being 'Teach Your Child to Wonder.' I have had a bit of experience through a very young nephew who has visited me at Southport each summer since he was 18 months old, and the *Companion* editors, true to editorial habits of thought, wish me to 'personalize' (horrid word!) the piece as much as possible in terms of Roger. The text is due the end of March. The editors may use some of my own Koda-chromes but may also wish to do some photography of their own with Roger as the subject."

Two days later she wrote to me: "I think the piece I'm doing for the *Companion* will further the impression that, like that old scorpionlike thing in the Silurian, I have come out on land. I'm trying to finish it this month, so that it may appear in August."

She finished on time, and the article appeared under the title "Help Your Child to Wonder." Among the many letters of congratulation that she received was one from Bob Hines, to whom she replied: "Thanks for your nice comments on the *Companion* article. Certain publishers think that I should expand it into a book. Well, maybe." She had, in fact, planned to do so from the outset, but never got around to it. A year after her death the text was reprinted in book form, with handsome photographs by Charles Pratt and others. The book title is *The Sense of Wonder*. The following passages express the central theme, about which she felt very deeply:

A child's world is fresh and new and beautiful, full of wonder and excitement. It is our misfortune that for most of us that clear-eyed vision, that true instinct for what is beautiful and awe-inspiring, is dimmed and even lost before we reach adulthood. If I had influence with the good fairy who is supposed to preside over the christening of all children I should ask that her gift to each child in the world be a sense of wonder so indestructible that it would last throughout life, as an unfailing antidote against the boredom and disenchantments of later years, the sterile preoccupation with things that are artificial, the alienation from the sources of our strength.

If a child is to keep alive his inborn sense of wonder without any such gift from the fairies, he needs the companionship of at least one adult who can share it, rediscovering with him the joy, excitement and mystery of the world we live in. Parents often have a sense of inadequacy when confronted on the one hand with the eager, sensitive mind of a child and on the other with a world of complex physical nature, inhabited by a life so various and unfamiliar that it seems hopeless to reduce it to order and knowledge. In a mood of self-defeat, they exclaim, "How can I possibly teach my child about nature — why, I don't even know one bird from another!"

I sincerely believe that for the child, and for the parent seeking to guide him, it is not half so important to *know* as to *feel*. If facts are the seeds that later produce knowledge and wisdom, then the emotions and the impressions of the senses are the fertile soil in which the seeds must grow. The years of early childhood are the time to prepare the soil. Once the emotions have been aroused — a sense of the beautiful, the excitement of the new and the unknown, a feeling of sympathy, pity, admiration or love — then we wish for knowledge about the object of our emotional response. Once found, it has lasting meaning. It is more important to pave the way for the child to want to know than to put him on a diet of facts he is not ready to assimilate.

The year 1956 saw the flowering of another and extraordinary friendship that brought Rachel Carson both the joy of shared enthusiasms and the sort of wise counsel and humorous comment on life that was particularly helpful at this moment in her career. Curtis Bok, author, and deep-water sailor, soon to be associate justice of the Supreme Court of Pennsylvania, had written to her on publication of *The Edge of the Sea*: "I truly do not go on the prowl for lions. But I do feel that friendly compatibility can shine through paper, and hence I hope that the Carsons (is that right?) and we might sometime foregather over the common interests of the sea and Maine and good writing." He recalled the scene of his "roughest time at sea," when he was caught in a storm close to the site of her cottage on Southport Island.

I am delighted that you know Southport [she replied]. All the places you mention have magical connotation for me — Seguin,

The Sisters, The Cuckolds. We are a little north of Henricks Head and look directly across to Five Islands, but from various places nearby we can look out to Seguin on a clear day or night, and in the heavy fogs that sometimes enclose us we can hear the groan of its fog horn if the atmospheric conditions are right. Somehow there is a world of meaning in that sound. In fact, that is what I was hearing when I wrote the last chapter of *The Edge of the Sea*.

Unfortunately, I do not have your seafaring experience of all this, for as to sailing I can speak only as a fascinated passenger — no earthly good to have aboard in a tight place! You see, I have never quite overcome the handicap of growing up inland, although just possibly the long unsatisfied interest in the sea is what makes me write books about it now!

When *The Sea Around Us* acquired enough readers to make it possible I bought a piece of shore property on Sheepscot Bay (in 1952) and built a cottage to which my mother, a black cat named Geoffrey, and I go each summer in June, remaining until late in October. If you and Mrs. Bok should ever be in that area in summer, we should be so happy to have you come to see us.

I bought the place for its beauty, and only later discovered that it is rarely necessary for me to go elsewhere to observe shore life, for between my own tide lines there are communities of almost all the common Maine shore animals. In fact, one long section from my chapter, "The Rocky Shores," derives its details from my own shore.

She went on to discuss H. M. Tomlinson and other literary favorites, and thus began a correspondence initially about books and the sea, but soon (on Judge Bok's part in particular) branching out in all directions. They exchanged copies of their own works. She wrote to him:

I want to tell you that I have looked up both of your books *The Backbone of the Herring* and *Passage* and have spent some delightful hours sampling them; the page-by-page reading will come later when the days are less crowded. It has been a revealing experience, too, for I know so little of the legal or judicial world and have never been privileged to know anything of how a judge's mind (or at least a very fine judge's mind) might view his problems. In other parts of both books, as you will realize, I feel completely at home, for your Bay is so unmistakably the Maine Coast that I feel I have made an unexpected trip there. Your writing is of that rare kind that charms and delights not only through the whole impression it creates, but in little ways, by a phrase or even a single word so telling that it evokes a flood of memories or imaginings in the reader. I hope there are more books to come.

As for myself, there are two ideas germinating simultaneously, one for a rather small book that must be done first and can, I think, be handled in relatively short time (although three or four years is my usual requirement); the other a subject of much broader scope that will require a long period of conscious and unconscious thought before I even begin to write. Meanwhile, I am about to have a first try at a television script, via *Omnibus* and some unusual film on clouds.

Have you begun your journey with Mr. Tomlinson? For some reason I feel impelled to write to him and I should do it soon, for he is an old man. I feel that I owe him so much that I should like to tell him so. Will you tell me sometime how you liked *The Sea and the Jungle?*

I simply must shout out to you [he replied], what a great find is Tomlinson. And what a real debt of gratitude I am under to you for putting me on to him. He has magic indeed, and a very rare mind. Always the inward eye, and on and on it goes, with apparently inexhaustible material . . .

By this time Judge Bok was writing her at approximately the rate of two letters a week. "I have, as you may have observed, an undisciplined pen. When something to say occurs to it, it says it. This keeps my correspondents at times a bit breathless." They finally met in late April, when she spent a weekend with the Boks at their home in Radnor, outside Philadelphia. He had considered inviting also the winner of that year's National Book Award, but detected a reluctance on her part to meet any literary "lions," and dropped the idea. "Really, it's much better this way . . . No Lions. I have my own definition of what is a Lion.

They are People of Purpose: they are the Fierce, the Wild, the Free, and the Brave. They sit next to me at dinner and with gleaming eyes ask my opinion of transubstantiation, and really want to know, what's more. Or they lay down rigid opinions about the Social Consequences of Desegregation, or what's up at the moment, and do so with violence. I simply dissolve. They are All For the Jews or All For theArabs, and I find them utterly ghastly and appalling.

"May the Lord preserve us from the gleaming eye — it's the sure sign of conversational paranoia."

The visit, which both had anticipated with a certain shyness, was a huge success. "I'm not at all sure," she wrote to Curtis and Nellie Lee Bok, "I can find words for what I really want to say. I had looked forward to the weekend with such pleasure and with all confidence that I would be a happy influence. But then I discovered that the expectation hadn't even approached the reality. All the time I was with you there was such a warm glow — such a sense of understanding and communication, of having found real friends — that this weekend getting acquainted became one of those unforgettable milestones of life. All the way home I kept thinking how wealthy my books have made me — and of course I'm not referring to material things but to the far more precious intangibles. For already they have brought me not only cherished professional associations but friendships that are among the most delightful and rewarding ones of my life — to which are now added the Boks." *

Two months later she was consulting him about the book on evolution that she had agreed some time before to write for a Harper series, but which was looking increasingly impossible.

---

* Curtis Bok died on May 22, 1962. Some months later, Rachel Carson wrote to Dorothy Freeman: "I have now found time to read *Maria* — the book Curtis Bok finished just before his death. You will love it, I know. Full of beauty and elemental things, the sea, sailing lore, lovely descriptions, the apt phrases that seemed to come so readily from his pen. It is very revealing of the kind of man he was. It was a privilege to know him even as well as I did."

"The awful truth is, Curtis, that I myself don't quite know 'the scope of my thrust for the new book.' At present I am just feeling my way. Having contributed nothing to the subject myself, I had intended merely to present and interpret the current thinking, but I suppose that inevitably my own thinking must have a place in the book. This is indeed boggy ground that you point out, and I hope I can find a path that skirts around it on firmer ground. As a biologist, I shall indeed try to stick to what we can observe and test — always realizing, of course, that what we do know now is only a tiny fragment of what Really Is! As you may remember, I spent my years of graduate work at Johns Hopkins. Whatever else I may have learned there, this was the unforgettable lesson: we do not really know anything. What we think we know today is replaced by something else tomorrow . . ."

Curtis Bok's counsel was invariably delivered with a light touch. His penetrating analysis of the difficulties in writing about such a subject as evolution and the origins of life concludes: "Yes, Rachel, face up to it like a big brave girl: what are you going to do about God?"

Late in the summer of 1956 the Boks paid a visit to Rachel in Southport; before the year was out, she was drawing on his legal and business experience in connection with an ambitious conservation project.

Meanwhile summer at the Maine cottage had been unusually hectic. Mrs. Carson, now eighty-seven, was crippled with arthritis and needed constant attention. Rachel's niece Marjorie, who had come to Maine with her four-year-old son Roger, was suffering from the same ailment. (Arthritis ran in the family; Rachel's father also had it, and she was later to be bedridden by it herself.) At the end of August Rachel wrote to Marie Rodell: "For the past three weeks I have been making daily trips to the clinic, where Mamma has been having treatment for her knee and Marjie for her shoulder, which was fast approaching the "frozen" state. Both are somewhat improved, and having at least a temporary respite from treatment. Marjie and Roger were here for three weeks, and now are in the little pink cottage over the hill. Otherwise the summer has brought an extraordinary parade of visitors, some planned for, some not. I don't mean staying here overnight, but requiring entertaining for meals, tide-pooling, etc. Paul and Susie Brooks were here this past weekend. The Boks sailed down from Camden last week; I went aboard the night they arrived and they were here all the next day. The Teales and the Poughs both came recently, plus assorted others you don't know. All pleasant enough, but I'm weary and think of putting a chain across the road with a sign, 'Rachel Carson will return from the antarctic in November.' "

Fortunately she could enjoy the world of nature without going far afield; exciting events occurred within a few yards of her doorstep. She described a perhaps unique experience in a letter to her close friends and summer neighbors, Dorothy and Stanley Freeman, who were not in Maine at the time. "This morning I achieved the difficult feat of getting up without disturbing anyone but Jeffie [her cat]; so maybe I can write a letter before breakfast . . . I *have* to tell you about something strange and wonderful.

"We are now having the spring tides of the new moon, you know, and they have traced their advance well over my beach the past several nights. Roger's raft has to be secured by a line to the old stump, so Marjie and I have an added excuse to go down at high tide. There had been lots of swell and surf and noise all day, so it was most exciting down there toward midnight — all my rocks crowned with foam and long white crests running from my beach to Nahards. To get the full wildness, we turned off our flashlights — and then the real excitement began. Of course you can guess — the surf was full of diamonds and emeralds, and was throwing them on the wet sand by the dozen. It was the night we were there all over, but with everything intensified: a wilder accompaniment of noise and movement, and a great deal more phosphorescence. The individual sparks were so large — we'd see them glowing in the sand, or sometimes caught in the in-and-out play of water, just riding back and forth. And several times I was able to scoop one up in my hand in shells and gravel, and think surely it was big enough to see — but no such luck.

"Now here is where my story becomes different. Once, glancing up, I said to Marjie jokingly, 'Look — one of them has taken to the air!' A firefly was going by, his lamp blinking. We thought nothing special of it, but in a few minutes one of us said, 'There's that firefly again.' The next time he really got a reaction from us, for he was flying so low over the water that his light cast a long surface reflection, like a little headlight. Then the truth dawned on me. He 'thought' the flashes in the water were other fireflies, signaling to him in the age-old manner of fireflies! Sure enough, he was soon in trouble and we saw his light flashing urgently as he was rolled around in the wet sand — no question this time which was insect and which the unidentified little sea will-o'-the-wisps!

"You can guess the rest: I waded in and rescued him (the will-o'-the-wisps had already had me in icy water to my knees so a new wetting didn't matter) and put him in Roger's bucket to dry his wings. When we came up we brought him as far as the porch — out of reach of temptation, we hoped.

"It was one of those experiences that gives an odd and hard-to-describe feeling, with so many overtones beyond the facts themselves. I have never seen any account, scientifically, of fireflies responding to other phosphorescence. I suppose I should write it up briefly for some journal if it actually isn't known.* Imagine

---

* Rachel Carson wrote to her friend Dr. E. Newton Harvey, an expert on luminescence, describing what she saw. He replied: "The observation is most interesting and should be published — perhaps in *Science* — as a short note. I know of no previous account of fireflies attracted to the light of a marine organism but it is undoubtedly the case from your experience."

putting that in scientific language! And I've already thought of a child's story based on it — but maybe that will never get written."

Another memorable moment occurred at the beginning of October. Again she described it in a letter to the Freemans. "I must tell you what happened Friday evening. It had been one of those bright, clear days with a piercing wind from the northwest, and at sunset there was not a cloud in the sky. There had been a thought in my mind all day, and shortly after sunset I went into the living room and began to scan the horizon. Almost instantly I saw a faint line like a wisp of smoke above the Kennebec — then more and more until I knew that one of those great migrations of waterfowl was moving toward Merrymeeting Bay. All, as far as I saw, were far away in the western sky, but with the glasses their formations and even the individual birds stood out clearly. And the flights continued until dusk made the drifting ribbons invisible. One more detail: I had also had in mind that on the evening I should see the new moon — the moon of the month in which I must leave here for another season. But when I looked into that clear, after-sunset sky I couldn't see it. Behind the spruces on the far shore of the bay the sky was a pale orange, fading above into yellow and then a cold, gray-blue. When the ducks appeared, and as I was searching the sky with my glasses, suddenly I saw the moon just above the horizon, a thin sickle, but so enormous that at first I could hardly believe it actually was the moon! Its color was so close to that of the sky that without the glasses I couldn't see it. Last night it was clear in the evening sky, and soon, I suppose, I can begin to watch for its reflection in the Bay."

This same letter touches on the local conservation project in which Rachel Carson became deeply involved emotionally, and about which she was later to seek Judge Bok's expert advice. "The day of the high wind I explored the shore and adjacent woods from Daniel's place north for a short distance. If only

that could be kept always just as it is! If ever I wish for money —
lots of it — it is when I see something like that. How many
acres would you guess are in the land from Daniel's road north to
where the Head cottages begin, between the Dogfish Head Road
and the Bay? Just for fun, tell me what you think, and let's pre-
tend we could somehow create a sanctuary there, where people
like us could go, as my friend said of the Bok Tower and grounds,
'and walk about, and get what they need.' Well, if no one ever
thinks of it, it certainly won't happen; if someone does think
hard enough, it just might. Of course I am just thinking aloud,
and quite confidentially, to two dear kindred spirits. But it's fun
to dream of such things, isn't it?"

From the moment she became a successful author, Rachel
Carson had hoped to devote part of her earnings to just such
conservation projects. As she wrote to Curtis and Nellie Lee
Bok: "I think you understand this in me, even though we've had
little chance to talk about it — my feeling for whatever beautiful
and untouched oases of natural beauty remain in the world, my
belief that such places can bring those who visit them the peace
and spiritual refreshment that our 'civilization' makes so difficult
to achieve, and consequently my conviction that whenever and
wherever possible, such places must be preserved . . .

"When, a few years back and for the first time in my life,
money somewhat beyond actual needs began to come to me
through *The Sea Around Us*, I felt that, almost above all else, I
wished some of the money might go, even in a modest way, to
furthering these things I so deeply believe in."

She went on to describe the strip of coastline she hoped to
save:

> Its charm for me lies in its combination of rugged shore
> rising in rather steep cliffs for the most part, and cut in several
> places by deep chasms where the storm surf must create a mag-
> nificent scene. Even the peaceful high tides explore them and
> leave a watermark of rockweeds, barnacles and periwinkles.

There is one unexpected, tiny beach where the shore makes a sharp curve and there is a protective jutting out of rocks. At another place, something about the angle of the shore and the set of the currents must have produced just the right conditions to trap the driftwood that comes down the bay, and there is an exciting jumble of logs and treetrunks and stumps of fantastic shape. I suppose there is about a mile of shoreline. Behind this is the wonderful, deep, dark woodland — a cathedral of stillness and peace. Spruce and fir, some hemlock, some pine, and hardwoods along the edges where a fire once destroyed what was there and set in action the restorative forces of nature. It is a living museum of mosses and lichens, which in some places form a carpet many inches deep. Rocks jut out here and there, as a flat floor where only lichens may grow, or rising in shadowed walls. For the most part the woods are dark and silent, but here and there one comes out into open areas of sunshine filled with woods smells. It is a treasure of a place to which I have lost my heart, completely . . .

I have had many precious moments in these woods, and this past fall as I walked there the feeling became overwhelming that something must be done. I had just played a small part in helping to organize a Maine chapter of the Nature Conservancy. My rather nebulous plans of last fall had to do with trying to enlist aid from that quarter. But while the Conservancy can help, the real job has to be pretty well provided for.

Unfortunately, her growing family obligations — the support of her mother and her two nieces — had hitherto made any large personal investment impossible. But before the end of 1956, two book projects appeared on the horizon that promised to improve her financial position to the point where she might have some money to spare. The first — to be published two years later — was an illustrated edition of *The Sea Around Us* in Simon and Schuster's Golden Book series. In the negotiations with the two publishers involved, conducted on her behalf by Marie Rodell, she showed that she had developed a keen business sense. "I am being mercenary about it because I think I have to," she wrote Mrs. Rodell. "I need the money to free me to do something more important." The other project, grander but more nebulous, was to be an "enormous, practically encyclopedic" anthology of nature writing, the royalties from which would be used to preserve for all time as a public trust that strip of Maine coast. The anticipated financial returns from this enterprise were such that, in her own words, it "completely transformed my thinking."

The scope of the anthology itself grew wider the more she thought about it, until it became in her mind a vast work presenting the whole story of life on earth. "This, of course, is a project involving Herculean and heartbreaking labors, but considering the good, who cares?" She was aware that the world at large might think she was commercializing her art by devoting herself to a moneymaking anthology instead of to works of her own creation. Soon, however, she had convinced herself that the project possessed "enormous creative possibilities, the end result probably more valuable than anything I could do myself."

Perhaps so. Yet one cannot escape the feeling that there is some wishful thinking here, that the noble objective of "The Dream" — or "The Lost Wood" as she sometimes called it after Tomlinson — had temporarily clouded her literary judgment. In any case the Dream collapsed when the land turned out to be unavailable for purchase at a feasible price. In the light of this effort, however, it seems singularly appropriate that Rachel Carson should have made the Nature Conservancy one of the principal beneficiaries under her will, that the Conservancy is preserving choice bits of land along the Maine coast known as the "Rachel Carson Seashore," and that the Department of the Interior has named a wildlife refuge there in her honor.

෨෨෨

At the very moment that Rachel Carson was dreaming of devoting future royalties to "furthering these things I so deeply believe in," a family tragedy increased her domestic responsibilities to the point where her writing came virtually to a halt. In February

1957, her niece Marjorie died of pneumonia and complications related to her always frail health. And while suffering from the emotional shock of Marjorie's death, Rachel had to take on a new role — that of the mother of a five-year-old boy. Her own mother was now eighty-eight. A letter written to me in early April, though characteristically matter-of-fact, gives some understanding of her situation:

"As I think you know, my mother's convalescence from pneumonia extended almost to the holidays. Then I was confined for the first half of January with a sort of flu; on my first day out Marjorie went to the hospital and died two weeks later. Roger, also sick with flu, came to us the night she was taken to the hospital, and was himself convalescent for another month. Marjorie and I were very close all her life, and of course I miss her dreadfully. Among the many changes this has brought is the fact that I shall now adopt Roger as my own; he had lost his father before he could remember him, and in our small family I am the logical one to care for him and, I'm sure, the one who is really closest to him. He does not fully realize the finality of his loss, and seems quite happy with us. But it is not an easy undertaking — I should be 15 to 20 years younger! [She was then just short of fifty.]

"I had been house-hunting anyway, and now am glad I hadn't bought before our family circle was changed in this way. Being unable to find a house that met my requirements — now rather unusual ones — I am now in the midst of a building venture that I'm very happy about. We shall have somewhat more than an acre of land in suburban Silver Spring, with a house that gives me everything I need. Completion is promised by July 1. I am keeping my fingers crossed, and realize that I may have to curtail my usual season in Maine, for I want to stay here until the house is completed. And as if one building project weren't enough, I'm adding to the Maine cottage."

At the end of May she wrote again: "I have been in the throes of house building since March, with all the attendant chores and headaches related to selecting every scrap of material and equipment. The worst is probably over — I'm delighted with the prospective house — and we expect to move in shortly after the first of July. Then as soon as we can tear ourselves away, we go to Maine . . .

"From all this you will know I am not being a writer at present."

During the summer she worked when she could on the juvenile edition of *The Sea Around Us*, checking the editing and the layout. And before the end of the year she had an assignment from *Holiday* magazine to write an article about the seashore for a special issue devoted to "Nature's America." I discussed with her the possibility of expanding this into a small book, aimed specifically at saving the rapidly disappearing remnant of unspoiled shoreline. She found it "an appealing idea, as giving me a chance to *do* something and a place to say what I want to say, for certainly I can give only a small part of the *Holiday* piece to being a Cassandra." This was one more book that never got written; by the time the article was published in July 1958, Rachel Carson had already plunged into work on *Silent Spring*. However, the article has permanent value, both for its own sake and as showing — in its concluding paragraphs — Rachel Carson's growing concern that man, in this "space-age universe," should save some of the wild places of the earth.

A letter written to Marie Rodell when she was first considering the assignment from *Holiday* clearly expresses this concern. "While I shall certainly be happiest describing a wild shore 'in all its pristine beauty' as Mr. Field requests, no one could write with sincerity of such a shore today without also leaving in his readers' minds the thought that very few such places remain. The undisturbed shore is one of the best places to see Nature at work: in the geologic cycles by which the relation of sea and land is undergoing constant change, and in the flow of life by which species come and go, new forms are evolved, and only those that can adjust to a difficult environment can survive. Yet when man takes over all this is changed. Within the long cycles of the earth what we do probably makes little difference; yet within the restricted cycle that is completed within one person's life the shore can never again be itself once man has 'developed' it.

"The dismal truth is that shores such as we are proposing to describe are fast disappearing, and may well do so completely within the life of some of us. This is not alarmist speculation, but a conclusion based on recent factual surveys and predictions by those qualified to know. Only vision, understanding, and bold action can better the situation. Feeling this so deeply as I do, I cannot write about the shores I love without pointing out their peril, even though briefly. For it is only as people are informed of dangers that threaten such priceless regions that they can be saved."

There could be no better introduction to "Our Ever-Changing Shore" than Judge Bok's instant response, in a letter to the author:

"Oh what a *lovely* piece — yours in July's *Holiday!* Only since going to Greece and reading about it have I come upon a satisfying key to your expression — the spare Greek line, with the etched beauty of a few words selected just right. Wonderful, wonderful: I read it and at once gathered all family and guests and read it aloud to them. You take people right to the shore so that they walk there and feel it and understand it."

CHAPTER 15

"Our Ever-Changing Shore"

From *Holiday*, July 1958

ALONG MILE AFTER MILE of coastline, the land presents a changing face to the sea. Now it is a sheer rock cliff; now a smooth beach; now the frayed edge of a mangrove swamp, dark and full of mystery. Each is the seacoast, yet each is itself, like no other in time or place. In every outthrust headland, in every curving beach, in every grain of sand there is a story of the earth.

Even in the statistics of its length the American shoreline is impressive. The outer coasts of the Atlantic, Gulf of Mexico, and Pacific — from Maine to Texas and from California to Washington — total nearly 5000 miles. But this is a minimum measure, taken as a bird might fly or a fish swim if it were in a hurry to reach its destination, and did not wait to explore the indentations that carry the sea inland in tentative invasions of the continent. If our imagined traveler entered the bays and sounds to a point where they narrow to 3 miles across, the figure would increase to nearly 13,000 miles; and if it ascended the rivers as far as the tides ebb and flow the length of the American shoreline would be found to be 53,677 miles, or twice the distance around the earth.

This coastline plays endless variations on the basic theme of sea and land. On the coastal rocks of northern New England the sea is an immediate presence, compelling, impossible to ignore. Its tides rise and fall on their appointed schedule, draining coves and refilling them, lifting boats even with their wharfs or dropping away to leave them stranded and useless. On the broad beaches of the south the feeling is different. The ocean seems far away as one stands at the edge of the dunes, when the tide is out. Under the push of a rising tide it advances a little, reducing the width of the buffer strip of sand. Storms bring it still further in. But compared with its overwhelming presence on northern shores it seems remote, a shining immensity related to far horizons. The sound of the waves on such a day, when the heated air shimmers above the sand and the sky is without clouds, is a muted whisper. In this quiet there is a tentativeness that suggests that something is about to happen. And indeed we may be sure the present stand of the sea here is only temporary, for many times in the past million years or so it has risen and flowed across all of the coastal plain, paused for perhaps a few thousand years, and returned again to its basin.

For the shore is always changing, and today's sand beach may become the sheer rock coast of a distant tomorrow. This is precisely what happened in northern New England, where the beaches and the coastal plain of a geologically recent time lie far offshore and many fathoms deep, inhabited by fishes instead of by land animals. Only a few thousands of years ago the earth's crust sank and the sea came in, covering the beaches and the plain, running up the river valleys and rising about the hills. So, on the young Maine coast, evergreen forests meet the granite threshold of the sea.

Everywhere the wind and the sea have shaped the coast, sculpturing it into forms that are often beautiful, sometimes bizarre. Along the Oregon coast the rocky cliffs and headlands speak of the age-long battle with the sea. Here and there a lonely tower of rock rises offshore, one of the formations known as stacks or needles. Each of these began as a narrow headland isolated from the main body of the coastal rock. Then a weak spot in its connection with the mainland was found and battered through.

Here and there the assaults of surf have blasted out caves in the sea cliffs. Anemone Cave in Acadia National Park is one. In the famous Sea Lion Caves on the southern Oregon coast a herd of several hundred sea lions gathers each autumn, living in the tumultuous surge of the surf, mingling its roars with the sound of the sea, still at work to break through the roof of the cave.

Back from the surf line, the winds have here and there piled up majestic dunes. At Kitty Hawk in North Carolina perhaps the highest dunes of the American coast rise abruptly from the sea. I have stood on the summit of one of these dunes on a windy day when all the crest appeared to be smoking. Then the winds seemed bent on destroying the very dunes they had created. Clouds and streamers of sand grains were seized in the strong flow of air and carried away. Far below, in the surf line, I could see the source of the dune sand, where the waves are forever cutting and grinding and polishing the fragments of rock and shell that compose the coastal sands.

The curving slopes, the gullies, the ridged surfaces of the dunes all carry the impress of the sea winds. So, in many places, do living things. The westerly winds that sweep across thousands of miles of open ocean at times pile up on our northern Pacific shores the heaviest surf of the whole western hemisphere. They are also the sculptors of the famous Monterey cypresses, the branches of which stream landward as though straining to escape the sea, though rooted near it. Actually the cutting edge that prunes such coastal vegetation is the sea salt with which the wind is armed, for the salt kills the growing buds on the exposed side.

The shore means many things to many people. Of its varied moods the one usually considered typical is not so at all. The true spirit of the sea does not reside in the gentle surf that laps a sun-drenched bathing beach on a summer day. Instead, it is on a lonely shore at dawn or twilight, or in storm or midnight darkness that we sense a mysterious something we recognize as the reality of the sea. For the ocean has nothing to do with humanity. It is supremely unaware of man, and when we carry too many of the trappings of human existence with us to the threshold of the sea world our ears are dulled and we do not hear the accents of sublimity in which it speaks.

Sometimes the shore speaks of the earth and its own creation; sometimes it speaks of life. If we are lucky in choosing our time and place, we may witness a spectacle that echoes of vast and elemental things. On a summer night when the moon is full, the sea and the swelling tide and a creature of the ancient shore conspire to work primeval magic on many of the beaches from Maine to Florida. On such a night the horseshoe crabs move in, just as they did under a Paleozoic moon — just as they have been doing through all the hundreds of millions of years since then — coming out of the sea to dig their nests in the wet sand and deposit their spawn.

As the tide nears its flood dark shapes appear in the surf line. They gleam with the wetness of the sea as the moon shines on the smooth curves of their massive shells. The first to arrive linger in the foaming water below the advancing front of the tide. These are the waiting males. At last other forms emerge out of the darkness offshore, swimming easily in the deeper water but crawling awkwardly and hesitantly as the sea shallows beneath them. They make their way to the beach through the crowd of jostling males. In thinning water each female digs her nest and sheds her burden of eggs, hundreds of tiny balls of potential life. An attending male fertilizes them. Then the pair moves on, leaving the eggs to the sea, which gently stirs them and packs the sand about them, grain by grain.

Not all of the high tides of the next moon cycle will reach this spot, for the water movements vary in strength and at the moon's quarters are weakest of all. A month after the egg laying the embryos will be ready for life; then the high tides of another full moon will wash away the sand of the nest. The turbulence of the rising tide will cause the egg membranes to split, releasing the young crabs to a life of their own over the shallow shores of bays and sounds.

But how do the parent crabs foresee these events? What is there in this primitive, lumbering creature that tells it that the moon is full and the tides are running high? And what tells it that the security of its eggs will somehow be enhanced if the nests are dug and the eggs deposited on these stronger tides of the moon's cycle?

Tonight, in this setting of full moon and pressing tide, the shore speaks of life in a mysterious and magical way. Here is the sea and the land's edge. Here is a creature that has known such seas and shores for eons of time, while the stream of evolution swept on, leaving it almost untouched since the days of the trilobites. The horseshoe crabs in their being obliterate the barrier of time. Our thoughts become uncertain: is it really today? or is it a million — or a hundred million years ago?

Or sometimes when the place and mood are right, and time is of no account, it is the early sea itself that we glimpse. I remember feeling, once, that I had actually sensed what the young earth was like. We had come down through spruce woods to the sea — woods that were dim with drifting mists and the first light of day. As we passed beyond the last line of trees onto the rocks of the shore a curtain of fog dropped silently but instantly behind us, shutting out all sights and sounds of the land. Suddenly our world was only the dripping rocks and the gray sea that swirled against them and occasionally exploded in a muted roar. These, and the gray mists — nothing more. For all one could tell the time might have been Paleozoic, when the world was in very fact only rocks and sea.

We stood quietly, speaking few words. There was nothing, really, for human words to say in the presence of something so vast, mysterious, and immensely powerful. Perhaps only in music of deep inspiration and grandeur could the message of that morning be translated by the human spirit, as in the opening bars of Beethoven's Ninth Symphony — music that echoes across vast distances and down long corridors of time, bringing the sense of what was and of what is to come — music of swelling power that swirls and explodes even as the sea surged against the rocks below us.

But that morning all that was worth saying was being said by the sea. It is only in wild and solitary places that it speaks so clearly. Another such place that I like to remember is that wilderness of beach and high dunes where Cape Cod, after its thirty-mile thrust into the Atlantic, bends back toward the mainland. Over the thousands of years the sea and the wind have worked together to build this world out of sand. The wide beach is serene, like the ocean that stretches away to a far-off horizon. Offshore the dangerous shoals of Peaked Hill Bars lie just beneath the surface, holding within themselves the remains of many ships. Behind the beach the dunes begin to rise, moving inland like a vast sea of sand waves caught in a moment of immobility as they sweep over the land.

The dunes are a place of silence, to which even the sound of the sea comes as a distant whisper; a place where, if you listen closely, you can hear the hissing of the ever mobile sand grains that leap and slide in every breath of wind, or the dry swish of the beach grass writing, writing its endless symbols in the sand.

Few people come out through that solitude of dune and sky into the vaster solitude of beach and sea. A bird could fly from the highway to the beach in a matter of minutes, its shadow gliding easily and swiftly up one great desert ridge and down another. But such easy passage is not for the human traveler, who must make his slow way on foot. The thin line of his footprints, toiling up slopes and plunging down into valleys, is soon erased by the shifting, sliding sands. So indifferent are these dunes to man, so quickly do they obliterate the signs of his presence, that they might never have known him at all.

I remember my own first visit to the beach at Peaked Hill Bars. From the highway a sandy track led off through thickets of pine. The horizon lay high on the crest of a near dune. Soon the track was lost, the trees thinned out, the world was all sand and sky.

From the crest of the first hill I hoped for a view of the sea. Instead there was another hill, across a wide valley. Everything in this dune world spoke of the forces that had created it, of the wind that had shifted and molded the materials it received from the sea, here throwing the surface of a dune into firm ridges, there smoothing it into swelling curves. At last I came to a break in the seaward line of dunes and saw before me the beach and the sea.

On the shore below me there was at first no sign of any living thing. Then perhaps half a mile down the beach I saw a party of gulls resting near the water's edge. They were silent and intent, facing the wind. Whatever communion they had at that moment was with the sea rather than with each other. They seemed almost to have forgotten their own kind and the ways of gulls. When once a white, feathered form drifted down from the dunes and dropped to the sand beside them none of the group challenged him. I approached them slowly. Each time I crossed that invisible line beyond which no human trespasser might come, the gulls rose in a silent flock and moved to a more distant part of the sands. Everything in that scene caused me to feel apart, remembering that the relation of birds to the sea is rooted in millions of years, that man came but yesterday.

And there have been other shores where time stood still. On Buzzards Bay there is a beach studded with rocks left by the glaciers. Barnacles grow on them now, and a curtain of rockweeds drapes them below the tide line. The bay shore of mud and sand is crossed by the winding trails of many periwinkles. On the beach at every high tide are cast the shells and empty husks of all that live offshore: the gold and silver shells of the rock oysters or jingles, the curious little half decks or slipper shells, the brown, fernlike remains of Bugula, the moss animal, the bones of fishes and the egg strings of whelks.

Behind the beach is a narrow rim of low dunes, then a wide salt marsh. This marsh, when I visited it on an evening toward the end of summer, had filled with shore birds since the previous night; and their voices were a faint, continuous twittering. Green herons fished along the creek banks, creeping at the edge of the tall grasses, placing one foot at a time with infinite care, then with a quick forward lunge attempting to seize some small fish or other prey. Farther back in the marsh a score of night herons stood motionless. From the bordering woods across the marsh a mother deer and her two fawns came down to drink silently, then melted back into their forest world.

The salt marsh that evening was like a calm, green sea — only a little calmer, a little greener than the wide sheet of the bay on the other side of the dunes. The same breeze that rippled the surface of the bay set the tips of the marsh grasses to swaying in long undulations. Within its depths the marsh concealed the lurking bittern, the foraging heron, the meadow mouse running down long trails of overarching grass stems, even as the watery sea concealed the lurking squids and fishes and their prey. Like the foam on the beach when the wind had whipped the surface waters into a light froth, the even more delicate foam of the sea lavender flecked the dune barrier and ran to the edge of the marsh. Already the fiery red of the glasswort or marsh samphire flickered over the higher ground of the marsh, while offshore mysterious lights flared in the waters of the bay at night. These were signs of approaching autumn, which may be found at the sea's edge before even the first leaf shows a splash of red or yellow.

The sea's phosphorescence is never so striking alongshore as in

late summer. Then some of the chief light producers of the
water world have their fall gatherings in bays and coves. Just
where and when their constellations will form no one can predict. And the identity of these wheeling stars of the night sea
varies. Usually the tiny glittering sparks are exceedingly minute,
one-celled creatures, called dinoflagellates. Larger forms, flaring
with a ghostly blue-white phosphorescence, may be comb jellies,
crystal clear and about the size of a small plum.

On beach and dune and over the flat vistas of salt marsh, too,
the advancing seasons cast their shadows; the time of change is
at hand. Mornings, a light mist lies over the marshes and rises
from the creeks. The nights begin to hint of frost; the stars take
on a wintry sparkle; Orion and his dogs hunt in the sky. It is a
time, too, of color — red of berries in the dune thickets, rich yellow of the goldenrod, purple and lacy white of the wild asters in
the fields. In the dunes and on the ocean beach the colors are
softer, more subtle. There may be a curious purple shading over
the sand. It shifts with the wind, piles up in little ridges of
deeper color like the ripple marks of waves. When first I saw this
sand on the northern Massachusetts coast, I wondered about it.
According to local belief the purple color comes from some seaweed, left on the shore, dried, and reduced to a thin film of
powder over the coarser particles of sand. Years later I found the
answer. I discovered drifts of the same purple color amid the
coarse sand of my own shore in Maine — sand largely made up
of broken shell and rock, fragments of sea urchin spines, opercula
of snails. I brought some of the purple sand to the house. When
I put a pinch of it under the microscope I knew at once that this
came from no plant — what I saw was an array of gems, clear as
crystal, returning a lovely amethyst light to my eyes. It was pure
garnet.

The sand grains scattered on the stage of my microscope spoke
in their own way of the timeless, unhurried spirit of earth and
sea. They were the end product of a process that began eons ago

deep inside the earth, continued when the buried mineral was brought at last to the surface, and went on through millennia of time and, it may be, through thousands of miles of transport over land and sea until, tiny, exquisite gems of purest color, they came temporarily to rest at the foot of a glacier-scarred rock.

Perhaps something of the strength and serenity and endurance of the sea — of this spirit beyond time and place — transfers itself to us of the land world as we confront its vast and lonely expanse from the shore, our last outpost.

The shore might seem beyond the power of man to change, to corrupt. But this is not so. Unhappily, some of the places of which I have written no longer remain wild and unspoiled. Instead, they have been tainted by the sordid transformation of "development" — cluttered with amusement concessions, refreshment stands, fishing shacks — all the untidy litter of what passes under the name of civilization. And so noisy are these attributes of man that the sea cannot be heard. On all coasts it is the same. The wild seacoast is vanishing.

Five thousand miles of true ocean beach may seem inexhaustible wealth, but it is not. The National Park Service has recently published a survey of the remaining undeveloped areas on the Atlantic and Gulf coasts. (The results of a Pacific survey are yet to be released.) It described the situation it discovered as "foreboding," for "almost every attractive seashore area from Maine to Mexico that is accessible by road has been acquired for development purposes, or is being considered for its development possibilities. The seashore is rapidly vanishing from public use."

The Service urged that public-minded citizens and local, state, and federal governments take the necessary steps, before it is too late, "to preserve this priceless heritage." Of the open shoreline of the Atlantic and Gulf coasts only 6½ percent is now in federal or state ownership. The Park Service urged that at least 15 percent of the general shoreline of the Atlantic and Gulf coasts be publicly acquired at once. This must be done if we are to insure that we ourselves, and generations to follow, may know what the shore is like, may read the meaning and message of this strip between land and sea.

In its current effort to awaken the public to the threatened loss of all natural seashore, the Park Service is echoing a recommendation made following a survey in 1935. Then, a human generation ago (a mere second in earth history) the situation was very different. At that time the Park Service urged that 12 major strips, comprising 437 miles of beach, be preserved for public use. Only one of these was actually acquired. All the rest, except one, have since gone into private or commercial development. One of the areas then recommended could have been bought at that time for $9000 per mile. Now, thanks to the post–World War II boom in seashore property, its price tag is $110,000 per mile.

To convert some of the wild areas that remain into state and national parks is only part of the answer, however. Even public parks are not what Nature created over the eons of time, working with wind and wave and sand. Somewhere we should know what was Nature's way; we should know what the earth would have been had not man interfered. And so, besides public parks for recreation, we should set aside some wilderness areas of seashore where the relations of sea and wind and shore — of living things and their physical world — remain as they have been over the long vistas of time in which man did not exist. For there remains, in this space-age universe, the possibility that man's way is not always best.

CHAPTER 16

THE GENESIS OF *SILENT SPRING*

THE HISTORY of *Silent Spring*, the controversy it aroused, and its still growing influence provides more than enough material for a book in itself. In *Since Silent Spring*, Frank Graham, Jr., has told the story admirably. My purpose here is somewhat different. I should like to show as best I can (when possible in Rachel Carson's own words) how she came to write *Silent Spring*, how it developed in the writing, what sort of research went into it, how she reacted to the chorus of praise and the storm of abuse that followed its publication.

Within a decade of its publication *Silent Spring* has been recognized throughout the world as one of those rare books that change the course of history — not through incitement to war or violent revolution, but by altering the direction of man's thinking. In retrospect its success and its lasting impact may seem easy to explain. The time was ripe, we say, for such a book; the author already had an international reputation, she had the scientific training to deal with the subject and she wrote superbly. But this is only a partial explanation, based on hindsight. At the outset, the answers were far less clear. Was it possible — even for Rachel Carson — to write a best seller on such a dreary theme as pesticides? Many of her strongest admirers thought not; she herself shared their doubts. She went ahead because she had to. "There would be no peace for me," she declared, "if I kept silent." The book she published four years later was effective beyond her wildest dreams. The secret of its success lies not merely in her fitness for the task, her boldness in speaking out, her superb command of the English language. It lies also in her fundamental attitude toward life, which came through most clearly when her deepest beliefs were at stake.

Rachel Carson's moral as well as scientific convictions were to give a prophetic quality to *Silent Spring* that would make it something more than a popular exposition of a technical crisis. A departure from the mainstream of her previous books, it would also involve a very different kind of research: no longer the delights of the laboratory at Woods Hole or the Maine rocks at low tide; no more the piles of books on the sea's mysteries, the exploration of the coral reefs, the rugged trip to the Grand Banks. Joy in the subject itself had to be replaced by a sense of almost religious dedication, and exhilaration in searching out the truth which sustained the author through extraordinary trials.

Rachel was not given to talking about her own work, once it was finished and in print. But occasionally in a speech or in a newspaper interview, after *Silent Spring* had become world-famous, she reminisced briefly about its origins. Typically, she never claimed that the ideas behind the book were uniquely her own. "The time had come," she said, "when it must be written. We have already gone very far in our abuse of this planet. Some awareness of this problem has been in the air, but the ideas had to be crystallized, the facts had to be brought together in one place. If I had not written the book I am sure these ideas would have found another outlet. But knowing the facts as I did, I could not rest until I had brought them to public attention."

The roots of her concern go back many years. She had become aware of the dangers of DDT while she was working for the Fish and Wildlife Service, whose "control" programs she viewed with alarm. On July 15, 1945 — seventeen years before the publication of *Silent Spring* — she wrote a short but prophetic letter to the *Reader's Digest*. This, it will be recalled, was during the period when she was trying to supplement her government salary by free-lance writing nights and weekends. She had just achieved her first substantial success, the article on bats and their use of "radar" which had been published in *Collier's* the previous November and was about to appear in the *Digest*. When they sent her a check for the article, the editors expressed the hope that they might publish her again. She replied by return mail:

> Many thanks for your letter of the 12th, and for your gracious settlement of our problems.
>
> And now here is a query for your consideration — Practically at my back door here in Maryland, an experiment of more than ordinary interest and importance is going on. We have all heard a lot about what DDT will soon do for us by wiping out insect pests. The experiments at Patuxent have been planned to show what other effects DDT may have if applied to wide areas: what it will do to insects that are beneficial or even essential; how it may affect waterfowl, or birds that depend on insect food; whether it may upset the whole delicate balance of nature if unwisely used.
>
> I believe there is a timely story in these tests. The incredible amount of painstaking work involved in setting up the test areas, the methods, results, and the interpretation from the biologist's point of view should add up to a pretty good article. It's something that really does affect everybody.
>
> I am in a position to cover the progress of the thing at first hand during the coming weeks, and with a little encouragement from you, I should do so with a view to turning out an article aimed for the pages of the *Digest*. The background is pretty well sketched in the enclosed release. Does the idea interest you?

This letter is characteristic of her approach to any writing project: a scientist's approach, based on firsthand knowledge of the latest technical research in the field. Apparently the response, if any, was negative.

Even then Rachel Carson was not alone in her concern about

what effect this newly discovered miracle poison, so useful in wartime for emergency control of insect pests, might have on the postwar world. It is sometimes forgotten that many biologists and ecologists were well aware of the danger long before DDT became a household word, before this and other synthetic pesticides began to be produced by the chemical industry on a massive scale. For example, the American Association of Economic Entomologists, following their meeting in New York in December 1944, issued a statement to correct "misunderstanding, overoptimism and distorted impressions" about the new chemical. After pointing out its value in control of malarial mosquitoes and other pests, the report continues: "DDT will not kill all important insect pests. It will kill many beneficial insects which are allies of mankind against the destructive species. Because of its toxicity to a wide variety of insects, its large-scale use might create problems which do not now exist." Such views also won a hearing in the more enlightened corners of the popular press. During 1945, both *Harper's* and *The Atlantic Monthly* published articles by scientific authorities about the danger of DDT upsetting the balance of nature. Ironically in the light of later events, the *Harper's* article was written by a member of the Department of Agriculture. The author was a better scientist than he was a prophet. Indiscriminate use of DDT, he felt, might well be disastrous. Entomologists "do not view DDT as an unmixed blessing and they will not go off the deep end in recommending its use in agriculture until they know a lot more about it."

During the same year *The New Yorker*, which was to play such a prominent part in the publication of *Silent Spring*, ran an editorial about the decision of the War Production Board to release small quantities of DDT for use by civilians. It quoted Edwin Way Teale, the author and former president of the New York Entomological Society, who was to become one of Rachel Carson's closest friends: "A spray as indiscriminate as DDT," said Teale, "can upset the economy of nature as much as a revolution upsets social economy. Ninety per cent of all insects are good, and if they are killed, things go out of kilter right away." At the Fish and Wildlife Service, Clarence Cottam and Elmer Higgins, with whom Rachel was then closely associated, were writing scientific papers pointing out that DDT could have serious long-term consequences, even though controlled use might show few direct and immediate effects on wildlife.

Having failed to interest the *Reader's Digest*, Rachel dropped the subject for the time being. The years immediately following the end of the war were particularly busy, as she took on further responsibilities, including the welcome job of writing and editing the Conservation in Action series on the national wildlife refuges. No sooner were those done (the series was completed in 1948) than she was at work on *The Sea Around Us*; before it was published, she had already begun *The Edge of the Sea*. Finally, in late 1957 an incident occurred that brought her back to the subject about which she had been concerned for so long. *Silent Spring*, she later recalled, had its genesis in an inquiry from her friend, Mrs. Olga Owens Huckins, a former writer for the Boston *Post*. Mr. and Mrs. Huckins had a small place in Duxbury, Massachusetts, just north of Cape Cod, which they had made into a private bird sanctuary. Heedless of the effect on birds and other wildlife, the state sprayed the whole area heavily from the air for mosquito control; insect life was wiped out, and many birds were killed. In January 1958, Olga Huckins wrote a letter to the Boston *Herald*:

To the Editor of *The Herald*:
    Mr. R. C. Codman, who wrote that he "is actively associated" with the Commonwealth of Mass. aerial spraying programs for alleged mosquito control, also says that state tests have proved that the mixture used — fuel oil with DDT — last summer over Plymouth and Barnstable Counties was entirely harmless.

These testers must have used black glasses, and the trout that did not feel the poison were super-fish.

Dr. Robert Cushman Murphy, distinguished scientist, observed after New York State sprayed Long Island in the same way, that no fish in still waters survived. All bees in a large section of the state were killed. Indeed, evidence of the havoc wrought by all air spraying of DDT is accumulating so rapidly that Mr. Codman's placid assurance becomes absurd.

The mosquito control plane flew over our small town last summer. Since we live close to the marshes, we were treated to several lethal doses as the pilot crisscrossed our place. And we consider the spraying of active poison over private land to be a serious aerial intrusion.

The "harmless" shower bath killed seven of our lovely songbirds outright. We picked up three dead bodies the next morning right by the door. They were birds that had lived close to us, trusted us, and built their nests in our trees year after year. The next day three were scattered around the bird bath. (I had emptied it and scrubbed it after the spraying but YOU CAN NEVER KILL DDT.) On the following day one robin dropped suddenly from a branch in our woods. We were too heartsick to hunt for other corpses. All of these birds died horribly, and in the same way. Their bills were gaping open, and their splayed claws were drawn up to their breasts in agony.

Mr. Codman also says that between DDT and mosquitoes, he prefers DDT. We had no choice; we have had both. All summer long, every time we went into the garden, we were attacked by the most voracious mosquitoes that had ever appeared there. But the grasshoppers, visiting bees, and other harmless insects, were all gone.

The remedy of this situation is not to double the strength of the spray and come again. It is to STOP THE SPRAYING OF POISONS FROM THE AIR everywhere until all the evidence, biological and scientific, immediate and long run, of the effects upon wild life and human beings are known.

Air spraying where it is not needed or wanted is inhuman, undemocratic, and probably unconstitutional. For those of us who stand helplessly on the tortured earth, it is intolerable.

— Olga Owens Huckins
Duxbury

Since mass spraying was being proposed next, Mrs. Huckins sent a copy of the letter to Rachel, inquiring about persons in Washington who might be consulted for help . . . "I began to ask around for the information she wanted," Rachel Carson recalled later, "and the more I learned about the use of pesticides the more appalled I became. I realized that here was the material for a book. What I discovered was that everything which meant most to me as a naturalist was being threatened, and that nothing I could do would be more important. However, I wanted to do more than merely express concern: I wanted to demonstrate that that concern was well founded."

When *Silent Spring* was published four and a half years later, Rachel wrote to Mrs. Huckins:

> I think even you have forgotten, however, that it was not just the copy of your letter to the newspaper but your personal letter to me that started it all. In it you told what had happened and your feelings about the prospect of a new and bigger spraying and begged me to find someone in Washington who could help. It was in the source of finding that "someone" that I realized that I must write the book.

However, she reached that conclusion reluctantly. Her first move was to call her agent, Marie Rodell, urging her to get one of her other clients to write an article on the subject. Then a few days later she decided that she would have to do it herself. She wrote to DeWitt Wallace, editor of the *Reader's Digest* (for which she had offered to write the DDT article thirteen years earlier), when she head that the *Digest* was considering an article on the benefits of aerial spraying for gypsy moth control: "If this is true, I cannot refrain from calling your attention to the enormous danger — both to wildlife and, more frighteningly, to public health — in these rapidly growing projects for insect control by poisons, especially as widely and randomly distributed by airplanes." She hoped that the *Digest* might be interested in having her do an article; if not, she was determined to try else-

where. The more she learned, the more she realized the seriousness of the situation; she was prepared to do anything in her
power to give it maximum exposure. She wrote to Marie Rodell:

> Following our telephone conversation, I am sending along a
> somewhat haphazard memorandum which nevertheless does in-
> corporate a few of the horrifying facts about what is happening
> through the mass application of insecticides.
> Having spent a substantial part of two weeks in phone calls,
> correspondence and searching through references, and having
> finally struck what appears to be "pay dirt" — I naturally feel I
> should like to do an article myself. In the course of all this, I
> have made certain valuable contacts and discovered many leads
> still to be followed up; this in its full value would be difficult to
> transfer to another writer. I don't see, however, why more than
> one article might not be written to good advantage — if you can
> find editors willing to listen.
> If the *Digest* is about to publish an article on the horrors of
> clinical X-rays, I still don't see why this subject wouldn't be ap-
> pealing — given the documentation, which I now know exists
> in plenty.
> If you could get an expression of real interest from the *Ladies'
> Home Journal*, I might be willing to gamble, provided they
> would give a prompt decision.

The enclosed memorandum documented, in quite horrifying
detail, the already known toxic effect not only of DDT, but of far
more powerful poisons such as dieldrin (twenty times as toxic as
DDT) and parathion. "So dangerous is this substance that
physicians or first aid workers handling victims of parathion poisoning are cautioned to wear rubber gloves while removing the
patient's clothing." She realized that, as insects developed strains
resistant to DDT, stronger and stronger poisons would be used:

> The effect of these chemical poisons — some of great toxicity
> — is only beginning to be assessed in its relation to the lives and
> welfare, not only of the whole community of animals in the
> area subjected to ground and aerial sprays, but of the human

population as well. There exists already, however, a large body of well-documented evidence that these highly toxic poisons, as presently used, represent an alarming threat to human welfare, and also the basic balance of nature on which human survival ultimately depends.

Neither the *Reader's Digest* nor the *Ladies' Home Journal* took up the suggestion for an article. Nor did the two other magazines that Marie Rodell approached, the *Woman's Home Companion* and *Good Housekeeping*. The reaction of the latter shows what Rachel Carson and her agent were up against. The editor was "very dubious"; he referred the question to the *Good Housekeeping* chemical analysis laboratory, which reported: "It is our feeling that the article proposed by Miss Rodell is something which we should under no circumstances consider. We doubt whether many of the things outlined in this letter could be substantiated." The report quoted the research director of one of the principal manufacturers of baby foods to the effect that "no single case of human poisoning from DDT has been documented" and went on to suggest that such an article would bring "unwarranted fear" to mothers who use these products. The utterly negative response of these magazines finally persuaded Rachel Carson that the subject would have to be treated in a book. But she still did not see her way clear to undertaking the whole job herself.

Meanwhile a shocking case of misuse of pesticides was receiving wide publicity through a trial in the courts: a trial that would provide a hard core of scientific material for any author to draw upon. In late May 1957, parts of Nassau and Suffolk counties in Long Island were drenched with DDT from the air by state and federal authorities for the ostensible purpose of eradicating the gypsy moth.

In what seems the height of absurdity [Rachel Carson wrote later in *Silent Spring*], the "threat of infestation of the New

York City area" has been cited as an important justification of the program. The gypsy moth is a forest insect, certainly not an inhabitant of cities. Nor does it live in meadows, cultivated fields, gardens, or marshes. Nevertheless, the planes hired by the United States Department of Agriculture and the New York Department of Agriculture and Markets in 1957 showered down the prescribed DDT-in-fuel-oil with impartiality. They sprayed truck gardens and dairy farms, fish ponds and salt marshes. They sprayed the quarter-acre lots of suburbia, drenching a housewife making a desperate effort to cover her garden before the roaring plane reached her, and showering insecticide over children at play and commuters at railway stations. At Setauket a fine quarter horse drank from a trough in a field which the planes had sprayed; ten hours later it was dead. Automobiles were spotted with the oily mixture; flowers and shrubs were ruined. Birds, fish, crabs, and useful insects were killed.

A group of Long Island citizens led by the world-famous ornithologist Robert Cushman Murphy had sought a court injunction to prevent the 1957 spraying. Denied a preliminary injunction, the protesting citizens had to suffer the prescribed drenching with DDT, but thereafter persisted in efforts to obtain a permanent injunction. But because the act had already been performed the courts held that the petition for an injunction was "moot." The case was carried all the way to the Supreme Court, which declined to hear it. Justice William O. Douglas, strongly dissenting from the decision not to review the case, held that "the alarms that many experts and responsible officials have raised about the perils of DDT underline the public importance of this case."

When Rachel first heard that the case was coming to trial, she wrote to E. B. White, whose editorials in *The New Yorker* had frequently been concerned with man's arrogant attitude toward the natural world and who, she felt, had "almost prophetic vision" regarding the problems with which she was concerned. She suggested that he cover the trial for his magazine. "It would delight me beyond measure if you should be moved to take up your pen against this nonsense — though that is far too mild a

word! There is an enormous body of fact waiting to support anyone who will speak out to the public — and I shall be happy to
supply the references."

White replied from his home in Maine on February 7, 1958.
"Your letter was forwarded here, where I am living year round
now. I am sending it off in the mail to Mr. Shawn, the editor of
The New Yorker, in the hope that he will want to assign a reporter to cover the court proceedings. I can't undertake it — for
a number of reasons that I won't bother you with.

"I think the whole vast subject of pollution, of which this
gypsy moth business is just a small part, is of the utmost interest and concern to everybody. It starts in the kitchen and ex-
tends to Jupiter and Mars. Always some special group or interest
is presented, never the earth itself.

"This letter is written in haste, in order to catch the mail. It
occurs to me that you might want to cover the federal court
case yourself. I cannot suggest any such thing officially, as I do
not operate in an executive capacity with *The New Yorker*; but if
you should have such a desire, I think you should get in touch
with Mr. Shawn."

Two weeks later Rachel Carson wrote an almost identical letter to Mr. Shawn and myself:

"I don't know what I should do about this . . . as you know,
I had various other plans, to be carried out as speedily as my
rather difficult personal situation allows. I feel I should do something on this, however. If I can do a magazine article that would
also serve as a chapter of a book on this subject, then also perhaps an introduction and some general editorial work, this would
probably be all I should undertake. But let's discuss it as soon as
you hear more."

She already had, in her own words, "mountains of material."
One useful if obscure source of technical information was the
several volumes of testimony before a no longer existent House
Select Committee to Investigate the Use of Chemicals in Foods

and Cosmetics. These were not easy to track down. "At such times," she wrote, "I find authorship pays off. I gave only my name [to the official in charge], but presently the question came: 'Are you the author of *The Sea Around Us?*' He and his wife had read all of that — and such parts of *The Edge* as pertained to their summer place on Fire Island. 'We would do anything for you —' he said. So, I should soon have another source of evidence." More immediately important was the mass of medical and other professional evidence gathered by the plaintiffs in the Long Island trial, which was now in its final stages. Marjorie Spock who, with the encouragement and financial backing of Mary Richards, had organized the suit from the beginning, had invited Rachel Carson to testify. She replied that family illness made this impossible, but that she hoped to advance the cause in other ways and wanted to see the full transcript of the experts' testimony. This proved of great value in the early stages of her research. And thus began a fruitful exchange of information that continued throughout the writing of *Silent Spring,* and which Rachel found (in her own words) "enormously helpful." It led to many contacts in the medical and agricultural fields, which supplemented the professional knowledge that Rachel had already accumulated over the years in laboratory study and through her work with other biologists in the field of wildlife ecology.

Miss Spock and Miss Richards expressed the sense of urgency with which the project was begun. "Time pressed. Rachel went into high gear at once. Every few days came a new letter discussing an article or clipping, inquiring into the background of some fact we had called to her attention, or asking to be put in touch with this or that witness from our lawsuit. She began to correspond with every independent scientist who knew some facet of pesticides. When she got dizzy writing, she telephoned. Every item of interest led to a new train of inquiry as she checked and double-checked, to new contacts, to an enormously

Silent Spring

Hugh Haynie in *The Louisville Courier Journal*

Gordon Brooks in *Yankee Magazine*, May, 1963

"Not so silent spring"

"Just say the blow was inflicted
by a blunt instrument"

J. W. Taylor in *Punch*. Copyright © Punch Publicatio

"This is the dog that bit the cat that killed the rat that ate the malt
that came from the grain that Jack sprayed"

Art Bimrose in *The Oregonian*

"Another such victory and
I am undone"

The one we wonder about

Shirley A. Briggs

Shirley Briggs's painting of Rachel as her readers seemed
to imagine her

Richard Q. Yardley

"We're not sure you know what you're doing!"

"After we read *Silent Spring*, we
decided to live and let live"

"But if I bribe them to eat
vegetables, I'll have to bribe them
not to read Rachel Carson!"

Herblock. From *Straight Herblock* (Simon & Schuster, 1964)

"Ain't it a beaut?"

"Now, don't sell me anything Rachel Carson wouldn't buy"

swelling stack of notes and papers. Yet so orderly and punctilious was she, no material we ever sent her failed to be returned eventually, more often than not with some interesting comment."

It is sometimes assumed that the lawsuit failed because, in 1958, there was not yet enough solid evidence of the harmful effects of DDT. On the contrary, the facts were already well known in professional circles, if not to the general public. During the trial no less than seventy-five findings of fact (unchallenged statements by plaintiff's witnesses or statements conceded by the defendants) were not allowed in evidence by the judge. When the case reached the Supreme Court, the refusal to hear it was based not on the merits of the case, but (as Rachel Carson pointed out) on a technicality.

Though the raw material was piling up, the plan for the book itself had not yet crystallized. In line with Rachel's original thought that she would be able to contribute only one chapter and perhaps an introduction, a search was begun for an editor who could work with her. However, as it became clear that she would do most of the writing, the position became that of a research assistant. Houghton Mifflin briefly employed a magazine writer in this capacity, but the agreement was terminated when he failed to produce any original material. Meanwhile *The New Yorker* had decided that they would like to have twenty or thirty thousand words. This could obviously be the core of what she still thought of as a "short book," with perhaps a chapter summarizing the evidence of the Long Island trial. The hope was to have a complete manuscript by approximately July 1, for publication in January 1959. A book contract was signed with Houghton Mifflin on May 22, 1958, using the working title "The Control of Nature." But Rachel soon realized that the phrase was far too inclusive to apply to this particular book. Her comment in this connection is interesting in showing the breadth of her thinking:

For months (or perhaps years) before I suddenly felt called upon to write about insecticides, I have been considering the problem of what living things do to change or even control their environment. It has many aspects (including the vital one of weather control) and this pollution of soil and vegetation is only one of them. We shall therefore have to limit the title; just what it should be I have not the faintest idea at the moment.

As the spring wore on, it became obvious that the manuscript would not be finished for many months to come. Work in the libraries kept her from her beloved Maine cottage until mid-July. Her past record as an editor and as an author had already shown her to be an expert researcher. Now in reply to her inquiries about pesticides, information came pouring in from all parts of the world. One of her best sources was Dr. C. J. Briejèr, of the Plant Protection Service in Holland. Again her literary reputation helped to open doors. *The Sea Around Us* had sold widely in the Dutch edition and her name was well known throughout the country. Dr. Briejèr was working in the same field, and glad to help her in any way he could. *Atlantic Naturalist,* with which Rachel Carson was closely associated, printed at her suggestion Marjorie Spock's translation of an article by Dr. Briejèr that showed he had a fundamental reverence for life not unlike Rachel's own:

> We are going to have to do some very energetic research on other control measures, measures that will have to be biological not chemical. Our aim should be to guide natural processes as cautiously as possible in the desired direction rather than to use brute force . . .
>
> We need a more high-minded orientation and a deeper insight, which I miss in many researchers. Life is a miracle beyond our comprehension, and we should reverence it even where we have to struggle against it. It is a fact that the resort to weapons such as insecticides to control it is a proof of insufficient knowledge and an incapacity so to guide the processes of nature that brute force becomes unnecessary. Humbleness is in order; there is no excuse for scientific conceit here.

Rachel was pleased but astonished at the amount of comment this article aroused among the "birdmen" and the entomologists in Washington's scientific community. Her reaction shows her awareness of the central intellectual conflict that lay at the heart of the problem: the conflict between those scientists who are willing to extrapolate possibilities from the known facts, and the "positivists" who say there can be no damage because damage has not been demonstrated.

"To my great surprise, the idea of biological control as something workable seemed new to them, and they were vastly intrigued with the idea of something positive that they could support, instead of just being 'agin sprays.' (Incidentally, I'm convinced there is a psychological angle in all this: that people, especially professional men, are uncomfortable about coming out against something, especially if they haven't absolute proof the 'something' is wrong, but only a good suspicion. So they will go along with a program about which they privately have acute misgivings. So I think it is most important [in the book, that is] to build up the positive alternatives.)"

The book kept growing. On Columbus Day, 1958, Rachel wrote to Edwin Way Teale, who was nearing completion of *Journey into Summer,* the third volume in his classic series:

"Twenty-one chapters sounds like a very impressive achievement — how did you do it? With a great deal of luck, I might be through in time for publication in the fall of '59, too, but it will take some doing, for this job gets bigger and more complex all the time. I have already covered about as many references as for *The Sea Around Us,* which I thought was my limit as a research job. However, it has some fascinating aspects, and the correspondence involved is most rewarding. The right people are so glad I'm doing the job."

A few weeks later she wrote to Marjorie Spock: "I am working like mad, of course; and equally of course, the material to be covered keeps piling up ahead of me. There are so many ramifications; but then that is what makes it fascinating to me, and I trust will do the same for future readers!"

But as the job grew, so did the obstacles, many of them related to her family situation. Rachel was suffering from a sinus infection, Roger was ill and out of school, and — in early December — her mother died. It was a severe shock, since they had always been very close. "Some time I want to tell you more of her," Rachel wrote to a friend. "Her love of life and of all living things was her outstanding quality, of which everyone speaks. More than anyone else I know, she embodied Albert Schweitzer's 'reverence for life.' And while gentle and compassionate, she could fight fiercely against anything she believed wrong, as in our present Crusade! Knowing how she felt about that will help me to return to it soon, and to carry it through to completion."

Maria Carson was undoubtedly the strongest single influence in her daughter's life. Her love of nature went along with a love of books, and she fostered Rachel's literary ambitions from the start. When the daughter became famous, the mother helped with the correspondence and basked in the reflected limelight. Her influence on Rachel's personal life — which cannot be wholly separated from her writing career — is more difficult to measure. It was she who, two decades earlier, had encouraged Rachel to take on the two nieces when their mother died; and this led eventually to Rachel's adopting a five-year-old boy when she herself was fifty. These family responsibilities, whatever their rewards and satisfactions, kept Rachel from enjoying what Thoreau called a broad margin to her life. And it is probably an understatement to say that Maria Carson never urged Rachel to marry.

By mid-February 1959, Rachel was again hard at work. I had written her inquiring about progress and quoting a remark of Roger Tory Peterson to the effect that our present use of poisons was the greatest threat to wildlife since time began. "What he says," she replied, "is virtually what Professor George Wallace of

Michigan told the National Audubon Society, with very effective documentation, at its annual meeting. If you do not have those papers, be sure to let me know."

I had also asked her opinion about the spraying from helicopters of the swamps in my hometown of Lincoln, Massachusetts.

> I hate to advise you on your helicopter problem. Of course it is better than airplane spraying, and I know it is not realistic to take a flat position against any spraying at all. I am afraid there have to be compromises, much as I hate any part of it. Have your local people taken into consideration, however, that by spraying they may be producing a race of fiercely resistant mosquitoes that will in the future be untouchable by any chemical means? A man from McGill gave a paper at the recent science meetings in Washington about the control of mosquitoes (and other insects important from the public health standpoint) by biological methods. I want to get this and other work of his and will let you know if it proves as important as it seems.

In the same mail she sent me a long-anticipated report of progress. It is such lucid exposition of her line of thought (and of the clarity with which she viewed her work) that it seems worth quoting almost in its entirety:

A Report of Progress

I have wanted for a very long time to write you and bring you up-to-date on the progress of the book. I am sure it must seem a long time in the making, but in the end I believe you will feel, as I do, that my long and thorough preparation is indispensable to doing an effective job. I can see clearly now that a book I might have written last summer would have been half-baked, at best. Now it is as though all the pieces of an extremely complex jigsaw puzzle are at last falling into place.

As you know, it has always been my intention to give principal emphasis to the menace to human health, even though setting this within the general framework of disturbances of the basic ecology of all living things. As I look over my reference material now, I am impressed by the fact that the evidence on this particular point outweighs by far, in sheer bulk and also significance, any other aspect of the problem.

I have a comforting feeling that what I shall now be able to achieve is a synthesis of widely scattered facts, that have not heretofore been considered in relation to each other. It is now possible to build up, step by step, a really damning case against the use of these chemicals as they are now inflicted upon us.

It is an amusing fact that although the American Medical Association and the Public Health Service, when asked to take a stand, are rather on the fence, their various published statements constitute quite an indictment. Of course, I plan to quote them so as to take due advantage of the weight of their authority.

I shall be concerned less with acute poisoning, which occurs usually through accident or carelessness, than with the slow, cumulative and hard-to-identify long-term effects. It is chiefly when life-span experiments are conducted with animals that the real damage shows up. No one now can honestly say what the effects of lifetime exposure in man will be, because not enough time has elapsed since these chemicals came into use. But we do know that every child born today carries his load of poison even at birth, for studies prove that these chemicals pass through the placenta. And after birth, whether breast-fed or bottle-fed, the child continues to accumulate poisons, for checks of mothers' milk, as well as of the dairy product, always show some content of DDT or other chlorinated hydrocarbons. There is also a body of evidence to show that young, rapidly growing animals are more seriously affected than adults.

Besides the effects on liver and nervous system, which are generally recognized by professional men if not by the public, I think I shall be able to support a claim to even more serious and insidious effects, which include the most basic functions of every living cell. This has been an extremely interesting line of research, and, to me, a terrifying one. One of its aspects has led me to the fundamental recent research of Otto Warburg, of the Max Planck Institute for Cell Physiology in Germany, on the physiological changes that may lead cells into the wild proliferation of cancer. Besides and beyond this vitally important fact, I shall be able to show that the chemicals used as insecticides interfere with many of the enzymes that control the most basic functions of the body. There is also scattered evidence, needing additional research, indicating that some of these chemicals interfere with normal cell division and may actually disturb the hereditary pattern.

If you receive the releases of the National Audubon Society and the Conservation Foundation, you are up to date on the far-reaching, inadvertent effects of the fire ant spraying in the south. This will probably be my "Exhibit A" among examples of ill-advised, irresponsible Governmental actions. I am told by friends in the National Wildlife Federation that the reaction in the south is so strong that there is hope funds may be shut off, at least for the fiscal year 1960! If you do not have these comprehensive reports of the two organizations let me know — I may have extra copies.

On the positive side, there are many new lines of thought. It is encouraging to find that many different people are working on alternatives to chemical sprays. A great deal of publicity was given a few weeks ago (in part through an article in *Life*) to the possibility of controlling insects through hormones, which would interfere with their normal metamorphosis. I have corresponded with the scientists chiefly involved, and get the impression that this Utopia, if it ever materialized, is a long way off insofar as practical application is concerned. However, the very attempt is a fascinating story.

Personally, I am much more impressed with attempts at control through man-induced insect diseases. The Japanese beetle problem is already on the way to solution by this means. I gather the Dean of this whole school of research is Dr. Steinhaus of California, with whom I have had some interesting correspondence. One of his former graduate students is now in charge of a Department of Agriculture unit concerned with such research. I am to see him soon and get the whole story. It is a very live thing, for recently it has been announced that two chemical firms are producing agents for microbial control — whether on a large scale or merely experimentally was not made clear. Also, Food and Drug has given its approval of such attempts in a list of some sixteen states. The bacteria or viruses used are specific for the insect and have further advantages, such as leaving no residues.

There is also a new Agriculture unit dealing with Insect Physiology. One of its staff told me that the real purpose is to develop alternatives to spraying. This, again, is a story I shall cover by visiting the laboratory. An example of practical application is the recent attempt to control screwworms and, even more recently, mosquitoes, by releasing males rendered sterile by radioactive cobalt.

I am really happy about these new developments. The older forms of biological control, depending on introduction of parasites and predators, had their values but also their limitations. One difficulty about pointing to them as the sole alternative was that they seemed to belong to an earlier age — whereas radioactive cobalt can firmly assert its place in 1959.

This will give you a general idea of the direction the book is taking. For myself, I feel happy about it, although I would not be so rash as to predict when you will have the manuscript. In another month, I should be better able to guess.

CHAPTER 17

MARSHALING THE EXPERTS

As with *The Sea Around Us,* so with the book to be known as *Silent Spring:* the subject was far too complex for any writer, however skilled in research, to handle alone. Though Rachel Carson tracked down every available published source, she relied heavily on personal correspondence with countless experts who were currently working in various corners of her broad field. Behind every chapter of *Silent Spring* lies reams of such correspondence, often of a highly technical nature, the substance of which only a trained biologist could appreciate. But even the layman can see here the creative process at work: the mutual fortification that results when a number of concerned persons, each with his contribution to make, share their knowledge to a common purpose.

Among the many distinguished scientists with whom Rachel Carson corresponded during the writing of *Silent Spring,* none was more helpful in providing source material, more wise in his advice, or more staunch in his support when the storm broke, than her old friend from the Fish and Wildlife Service, Dr. Clarence Cottam. A distinguished biologist, since 1955 director of the Welder Wildlife Foundation in Sinton, Texas, Dr. Cottam had been assistant director of the Service when Rachel was editor in chief of their publications. They had always worked well together. He had encouraged her in the production of the series of booklets on the federal wildlife refuges; they shared the same view of conservation, including a deep-seated opposition to wholesale predator control. He had been a pioneer in studying the harmful effects of DDT and other poisons used by the Service. Now, after a chance meeting in Washington in the fall of 1958, she turned to him for further information about the mass-poisoning program for control of the fire ant which the Department of Agriculture had recently launched with "one of the most remarkable publicity campaigns in its history." (The disastrous results are described in Chapter 10 of *Silent Spring*.) Her letter to Dr. Cottam of November 18, 1958, marks the beginning of a voluminous and creative correspondence, which lasted until shortly before Rachel's death:

> It seemed quite like "old times" to see you at the National Museum in September, and I regretted very much there was no opportunity to sit down for a good talk with you. I have regretted it all the more since learning, recently, that you have been concerned about the fire ant program in the south and have taken what I consider an admirable stand in opposition to what has been done.
>
> The news seems to be out on the grapevine, so possibly you have heard, that my current writing project is a book dealing with the basic problem of the effect of chemical insecticides in present use on all living things and on their fundamental ecological relationships. This was something I had not expected to do, but facts that came to my attention last winter disturbed me so deeply that I made the decision to postpone all other commitments and devote myself to what I consider a tremendously important problem.
>
> Of course I have assembled an enormous amount of literature and have talked to many people, but much is still to be done — in fact, the subject seems to have endless ramifications.

Dr. Cottam replied by return mail:

I am immensely pleased and honored to receive your delightful letter of November 18, regarding the controversial fire ant problem. It does seem like old times to hear from you and to know something of your activity . . .

I am delighted to know that you are devoting your energies for the time being in preparing a book on this broad control problem. I hope you include both insecticides, herbicides, rodenticides, and fungicides. The whole gamut of poisons should be considered, and I know of no one who is more able to summarize this situation than you. I am sure you will render a great public service, although I shall predict that your book will not be the best seller that *The Sea Around Us* has been. The total effect, however, might be infinitely more important to our national economy and well-being.

Shortly after this, Rachel was invited by the National Audubon Society to take part in a panel discussion on pesticides, of which Dr. Cottam was to be the moderator. "I considered the matter," she wrote him, "but regretfully gave a negative decision. My material will not be ready for publication before summer, and my publishers and I feel that a premature disclosure of even part of the material would do more harm than good to our cause. As a matter of fact, I have said just as little as possible about my project, although inevitably many people have had to be told what I am doing. But, as you know, the whole thing is so explosive, and the pressures on the other side so powerful and enormous, that I feel it far wiser to keep my own council insofar as I can until I am ready to launch my attack as a whole."

It would be hard to find a happier symbiotic relationship than that between Clarence Cottam and Rachel Carson during this period. Each contributed valuable support to the work of the other. While he spoke out publicly and vigorously against misuse of pesticides at various meetings through the country, she was quietly amassing the evidence which would shake the nation when it finally appeared in print. Throughout 1959 they regularly exchanged information about the latest developments in the field. From the sheaf of technical correspondence between them, I should like to print one letter as an example of the breadth and depth of her research:

Dear Clarence: According to the notes I made during our luncheon conversation the other day, I am to send you information on three different subjects.

The recent paper which showed that the toxicity of malathion may be increased or "potentiated" by a chemical which is not an insecticide was published in the Proceedings of the Society of Experimental Biology, 100; 3, pp. 483–487, March 1959 (Potentiation of Toxicity of Malathion by Triorthotolyl Phosphate [24668]), Murphy, S. D., Anderson, R. L. and Dubois, K. P. It was found that quantities of the chemical, which I shall abbreviate as TOTP, which produced no apparent harmful effects in themselves, greatly increased susceptibility to malathion. The potentiation actually was greatest when exposure to TOTP occurred before exposure to malathion. The authors say that the potentiation then was greater than any observed between combinations of insecticides (you will remember that the FDA investigators got a 50-fold potentiation with malathion and EPN). The authors comment that we must now consider not merely potentiation of one insecticide by another, but the possible potentiation by drugs, food additives, and all other chemical agents to which we are commonly exposed. TOTP is a chemical used industrially as a plasticizer.

As to the increase in the arsenic content of American cigarette tobacco, Dr. Henry Satterlee reported in the *New England Journal of Medicine* for June 21, 1956, that the arsenic content of American-tobacco cigarettes increased more than 300 percent from 1932 to 1951. A later paper by R. N. Holland, published in *Cancer*, 2, No. 6, p. 1115, stated that the increase during the past 25 years had ranged from 200 to 600 percent. This increase has occurred, of course, during a period when organic insecticides were being substituted to a large extent for arsenic. But the point is that the soils of tobacco plantations have been so heavily impregnated by a relatively insoluble poison that their contamination is for all practical purposes, a permanent one.

On the matter of the damages sustained by the hop growers

in Washington and Idaho, I find I have an extra copy of a letter that was written by Mr. Lloyd Kelley, Jr., of Yakima, Washington, to Robert Strother of the *Reader's Digest*. Since receiving this letter I have corresponded with Mr. Kelley, myself, and I am sure he would be glad to give you any supplemental information you need. He sent me a copy of a publication that I think you might want to have from the Washington Agricultural Experiment Stations at the State College of Washington. The title is "Pesticide Chemicals as a Factor in Hop Die-out," Stations Circular 362, published in July 1959.

You were interested, also, in the suit being brought by the sugar cane growers in Louisiana and I am enclosing an excerpt from a letter written to Mr. Strother on that subject.

As always, it was very good to see you the other day. I am tremendously inspired and encouraged by all you are doing to bring out the facts in this critically important situation.

In his reply, Dr. Cottam wrote: "It seems to me you have gone deeper into this subject than anyone else with whom I have had correspondence or contact. I certainly will be looking forward to your book on this subject. Because of the controversy I doubt that it will ever be a best seller regardless of how beautifully it is written and how valuable it might become. I can predict, however, that in years to come the value of it will increase." Dr. Cottam was right about its value but wrong about the effect of the controversy; the extravagance of the attacks on *Silent Spring* by the agricultural chemical industry undoubtedly helped rather than hindered its sale.

As she sought expert advice in various technical fields, Rachel invariably found that the specialists were interested in what she was doing, and more than ready to give her the help she needed. The chapter on herbicides, for example, owes much to the pioneer work by Frank E. Egler and others in the field of vegetation management. For firsthand information about the effect of pesti-

cides on birds and other wild life, Rachel turned to such experts as
Harold S. Peters, field biologist for the National Audubon Society in Atlanta, Georgia, and George J. Wallace, professor of zoology at Michigan State University. Professor Wallace and one of
his graduate students had been making detailed observations of
the spectacular decline in bird populations on the campus of the
university, as a result of intensive spraying for control of Dutch
elm disease. (See *Silent Spring*, Chapter 8). "The sprayers and
their allies," she wrote to him, "adopt such a loftily scornful attitude about birds (a man very high in Food and Drug said to me:
'What if a few meadowlarks have stepped in this poison dieldrin
for fire ants and died?') that I want to build up this part of my
material with every bit of factual evidence available." Dr. Wallace not only provided her with detailed surveys of bird mortality
in many parts of the country from use of DDT, he also put her
in direct touch with various amateur observers who were adding
to the growing pile of evidence.

Meanwhile she was already putting some of her material to
use. In early April she wrote a letter to the Washington *Post*:

> Your excellent March 30 editorial, "Vanishing Americans," is
> a timely reminder that in our modern world nothing may be
> taken for granted — not even the spring songs that herald the
> return of the birds. Snow, ice and cold, especially when visited
> upon usually temperate regions leave destruction behind them, as
> was clearly brought out in the report of the National Audubon
> Society you quote.
>
> But although the recent severe winters in the south have taken
> their toll of bird life, this is not the whole story, nor even the
> most important part of the story. Such severe winters are by no
> means rare in the long history of the earth. The natural resilience
> of birds and other forms of life allows them to take these adverse
> conditions in their stride and so to recover from temporary re-
> duction of their populations.
>
> It is not so with the second factor, of which you make passing
> mention — the spraying of poisonous insecticides and herbicides.
> Unlike climatic variations, spraying is now a continuing and un-
> remitting factor.

During the past 15 years, the use of highly poisonous hydro-carbons and of organic phosphates allied to the nerve gases of chemical warfare has built up from small beginnings to what a noted British ecologist recently called "an amazing rain of death upon the surface of the earth." Most of these chemicals have long-persisting residues on vegetation, in soils, and even in the bodies of earthworms and other organisms on which birds depend for food . . .

The death of the robins is not mere speculation. The leading authority on this problem, Professor George Wallace of Michigan State University, has recently reported that "Dead and dying robins, the latter most often found in a state of violent convulsions, are most common in the spring, when warm rains bring up the earthworms, but birds that survive are apparently sterile or at least experience nearly complete reproductive failure."

The fact that doses that are sub-lethal may yet induce sterility is one of the most alarming aspects of the problem of insecticides. The evidence on this point, from many highly competent scientists, is too strong to question. It should be weighed by all who use the modern insecticides, or condone their use . . .

To many of us, this sudden silencing of the song of birds, this obliteration of the color and beauty and interest of bird life, is sufficient cause for sharp regret. To those who have never known such rewarding enjoyment of nature, there should yet remain a nagging and insistent question: If this "rain of death" has produced so disastrous an effect on birds, what of other lives, including our own?

Mrs. Eugene Meyer, the *Post's* owner, was delighted: "I want to thank you for writing the excellent letter about the poisoning of the birds through spraying of the trees. There was another letter in the paper yesterday. I am sure you started all the nature lovers on an important campaign. At this moment the ginkgo trees in front of my house all have a sign to motorists to beware because the trees are going to be sprayed within a few days. I wish the birds could read!"

The fatal impact of pesticides on birdlife, particularly on the reproductive capacity of the predators at the top of the "food chain," has since been proved beyond reasonable doubt — not only by observations in the field, but by painstaking laboratory experiments which have revealed the physiological effects of chlorinated hydrocarbons on the living bird and its reproductive system. Yet the disappearance of birds was but one obvious indicator of an underlying peril of greater dimensions: the slow poisoning of the entire environment, of which man himself is a part.

Evidence of the effect of these poisons on the human body was abundant, yet "pure histories" in the medical sense of the term were hard to obtain, since in most cases a multiplicity of possible agents was involved, often over an extended period of time. Nor can human beings be subjected to laboratory experiments. In obtaining her evidence, Rachel Carson had the cooperation of many distinguished physicians, such as Dr. M. M. Hargraves of the Mayo Clinic, who had testified at the Long Island trial. "To me," he wrote Rachel, "the implications of this entire problem are tremendous, and I am sure that you see them also or you couldn't be engaged in writing a book. From my standpoint, I feel almost that I could write such a book from the medical aspect of the problem. I wish you luck with yours . . ."

Another physician who gave Rachel strong professional support was Dr. Morton S. Biskind of Westport, Connecticut. He had, she felt, been most clear-thinking and articulate in pointing out the hazards of contamination by these newly developed poisons. She carried on a highly technical correspondence with him during the entire period that *Silent Spring* was being written, concerned principally with the effect of pesticides on the body cells, including a possible relationship with cancer. Early in the discussion she wrote to him on the subject of cancer hazards related to pesticides:

. . . Through your guidance into this field, I have been pursuing all the evidence about the disturbance of enzyme systems, uncoupling of phosphorylation, etc. I have been fascinated to discover recently that, according to Greenstein, von Euler, and others, defective operation of the cytochrome system is "the main characteristic of the respiratory mechanism of the cancerous cell." Now that I have tabulated all the pesticidal chemicals that disturb cytochrome oxidase, a great light is breaking in my mind. I have never seen this connection fully pursued. Perhaps I shall be "a fool rushing in" where angels would not tread, but I think this possible mechanism should be suggested as one means by which the cell may be converted to the cancerous way of life.

A month later she wrote again: "Since writing you, I have done a vast amount of reading concerning the subject matter of your letter [he had pointed out that the question of carcinogenesis was simply one facet of the much larger picture of anoxia, or oxygen deficiency] and I am convinced that this is the basic problem underlying the whole matter of pesticides. It seems strange that these effects on cellular metabolism have been mentioned so seldom except by you and a very few others."

One of these "others," whose work is referred to at some length in *Silent Spring*, is Dr. Wilhelm C. Hueper of the National Cancer Institute. "Dr. Hueper," she concluded, "now gives DDT the definite rating of a 'chemical carcinogen.'" As the manuscript progressed, she sent portions of it to Dr. Hueper for review, especially those sections dealing with cancer hazards related to pesticides. During the personal interviews that followed, he found her (as he recalls later) "a sincere, unusually well informed scientist possessing not only an unusual degree of social responsibility but also having the courage and ability to express and fight for her convictions and principles . . . When the storm of abuse and denunciation broke, Rachel Carson stood up well against her accusers because her scientific facts were sound and valid and her interpretations were reasonable."

During the 1958 Long Island trial, medical witnesses for the defense had insisted that there were no scientific data to indicate that DDT causes leukemia or other blood changes. In that connection it is interesting to read a letter from a sportsman that

Rachel kept in her file of source material: "On a hunting trip in Northern British Columbia the latter part of August 1957, we sprayed a tent for twenty-one nights with DDT. We did not sufficiently aerate the tent. When I got back home in September, my marrow and white and red corpuscles were terribly impaired. I nearly lost my life. I have had forty-one infusions in my arm, each lasting from four to six to eight hours, in Philadelphia, and I am slowly coming back." At the bottom of the letter is a note in Rachel's hand: "Died of leukemia, May 1959."

The research file on *Silent Spring* clearly gives the lie to those who claimed, after the book was published, that Rachel Carson's concern with the cancer hazards in pesticides was exaggerated because she knew that she had cancer herself. She had reached her conclusions long before that tragic discovery.

CHAPTER 18

THE END AND THE BEGINNING

As the summer of 1959 approached, the book manuscript had reached the point where completion by the fall appeared to be possible, for publication early in 1960. "It seems advisable by all means to announce the book for February," Rachel wrote me on June 3, "and hope for the best . . . I am pressing ahead just as fast as I can, driven by the knowledge that the book is desperately needed. Unquestionably, what it has to say will come as news to 99 out of 100 people."

Considering the nature of the subject, she was quite properly concerned with the exact wording of any public announcement: "It is a very difficult book to describe — even I find it so — and because of the rather violent controversies that have raged around this subject we shall, of course, have to choose our words very carefully. It would be so easy to imply inadvertently a sensationalism that really has no place in my approach to the problem. I do want to give you all the help I can on this for only someone who is up to his ears in this material as I am could possibly know all the pitfalls."

Alas, any announcement of early publication turned out to be premature. Rachel was plagued with sinus trouble, then her adopted son Roger came down with a respiratory infection that kept him out of camp and on his mother's hands. The summer proved far less productive than she had hoped. Late in 1959, she wrote to me with a sense of frustration yet faith in the final outcome: "I guess all that sustains me is a serene inner conviction that when, at last, the book is done, it is going to be built on an unshakable foundation. That is so terribly important. Too many people — with the best possible motives — have rushed out statements without adequate support, furnishing the best possible targets for the opposition. That we shall not have to worry about . . . I know you realize as fully as anyone not directly involved could that this is a very big job. But I don't think anyone but myself could know how big. I am very happy deep down inside with what I have been able to dig out and fit together, but I'm also horribly frustrated that it is taking so long . . ."

She also wrote in similar vein to Marjorie Spock, with whom she kept up a steady exchange of scientific and legal information: "My own work goes on at a furious pace but I feel a little like the Red Queen who had to run as fast as she could just to stay where she was. Seriously, however, I am very happy about the basis of all I have to say and continue to feel that the case against the insecticides can be made extremely convincing. I know it has been hard on everyone's nerves to take so long, but I feel in the end it will be very much better to have done so."

A few months later she commented further along the same line: "It is a great problem to know how to penetrate the barrier of public indifference and unwillingness to look at unpleasant facts that might have to be dealt with if one recognized their existence. I have no idea whether I shall be able to do so or not, but knowing what I do, I have no choice but to set it down to be read by those who will. I guess my own principal reliance is in marshaling all the facts and letting them largely speak for themselves." All this required an enormous amount of correspondence and other paperwork. It would have been well nigh impossible to handle had not Rachel employed — on her return from Maine — an unusually talented secretary and general assistant, Mrs. Jeanne Davis. The close friendship that grew up between them endured until Rachel's death some three and a half years later.

One small but encouraging incident had occurred during the summer just past. Learning that there were plans for spraying the area that included her home in Silver Spring, Maryland, she decided to speak to the local community association. "You will be glad to know," she wrote afterward to Marjorie Spock, "that the threat of spraying in our area was removed by a decisive vote at the recent meeting. I spoke to the group but limited myself to fifteen minutes, for it was a fiendishly hot night and I thought a longer talk might have the wrong effect. I really hit hard on the few points I gave and was delighted by the reception of my facts. I felt this was a fair little test of the reception that may be given the book."

The same incident gives us a rare glimpse of this outwardly calm and gentle author when she was aroused. A young research assistant* who was working with her at the time recalls: "One afternoon she was preparing a brief talk to be presented to her local community association . . . trying to persuade them not to spray the area. One of the men of the community called to tell her she was an alarmist, and added patronizingly when she began to cite case histories to him, that she really mustn't believe everything she read in the newspapers. She was furious. Of course, this was, as you know, typical of an attitude of many Americans that she deplored . . . a general unwillingness to look thoughtfully about them lest they interrupt their frenzied rush to an immediate goal. No one, seeing her response that afternoon, could have called her gentle." The comments of her young researcher also provide an interesting sidelight on Rachel Carson's work habits. "Working with Rachel was like seeing the

* Betty Haney, now Mrs. Thomas Duff.

fable of the hare and the tortoise come alive. I honestly thought she would never finish that book. It was not because of all the obvious difficulties; her illness, her mother's death, care of Roger, but more with her pace of work . . . it seemed so slow. As a child of my culture, I had not yet learned to associate progress with that pace . . . and I did not know then the extent of her determination and what a powerful force that kind of determination can be. It was a valuable lesson."

In October of 1959, Rachel took time off from the book to give a talk at a meeting of the Audubon Council in Washington. Her comment is not without humor: "I felt rather as though I were a professor lecturing to an extraordinarily attentive and diligent class. I was surprised to discover they were all equipped with pencil and paper, and from the moment I began, throughout the 30 or 40 minutes I talked, they all scribbled away for dear life, taking notes. (Or so I assumed — could they have been writing letters home? ? ?)"

Though she was pretty well tied to her desk in Silver Spring, and no longer able to get out in the field to observe the fall migration, Rachel found great pleasure in watching the birds from her study window. She would occasionally include some "nature notes" in a letter to a friend.

Yesterday morning — Wednesday October 21, I discovered there had been a perfect eruption of whitethroats into the area. During the night the wind had shifted around to ENE and maybe that had something to do with it. Anyway, as I looked out of the study window toward the group of pines, I saw that the grass was fairly bubbling with whitethroats — scores and scores of them all moving about purposefully, intent on gleaning seeds from the lawn. So when I had sent Roger on his way I took the bird glasses and went out for the half hour just on my own place. There were a good many chickadees, titmice, and downies — hardly enough to suggest any such wave of migration as the whitethroats, but many more than we've been having. But I had one very special reward for going out. A movement in the big pine by the corner of the porch caught my eye — a golden crowned kinglet! First I've seen in years. It must have been a female, for the crown was very golden; Peterson says the male's is orange . . .

After an early morning filled with sunshine the day turned gray and rather bleak, with a sharp wind. In late afternoon, from the study, I could see countless birds pitching down from the sky into my wild corner. While trying to spot some of them from the window, for identification, again I saw the kinglet, her crown visible across the length of the lawn, for she was in a pine down by Apple Grove Road.

Back at work on the book, she at last began to feel happy with her progress: "The other day someone asked Leonard Bernstein about his inexhaustible energy and he said 'I have no more energy than anyone who loves what he is doing.' Well, I'm afraid mine has to be recharged at times, but anyway I do seem just now to be riding the crest of a wave of enthusiasm and creativity, and although I'm going to bed late and often rising in very dim light to get in an hour of thinking and organizing before the household stirs, my weariness seems easily banished."

In November of 1959, shortly before Thanksgiving, occurred the famous "cranberry scandal," when the Food and Drug Administration banned the marketing of cranberries that had been sprayed with aminotriazol. Rachel described the hearing in Washington.

Yesterday I attended the big Cranberry Meeting, which was most interesting. Flemming* certainly went away up in my estimation; he handled the whole thing with such quiet dignity and courtesy, but they didn't ever put anything over on him! At the conclusion of a speaker's statement, he would gently pick up the very thing I'd been hoping he would demolish. I think he's going to stand firm. I was delighted by the support he was given from various independent organizations that had asked to be heard. And I was impressed by the fact that the tone of industry spokesmen was on the whole mild and conciliatory. I had been told privately that industry heads had been shocked when they

* Arthur S. Flemming, Secretary of Health, Education and Welfare.

really began to look into the situation, and their attitude yesterday bore that out. A congressman from Oregon — whom I had
expected to be full of pleas for the industry, took quite a different
line. He said that, sad as this might be for the industry, it has
served to point up the whole enormous problem of contamination of food by pesticides and other chemicals, and called for better laws and more rigid enforcement. I was so impressed that I
called his office later for a copy of the statement. You will laugh,
as I did, at the response. When it became necessary to give my
name for the mailing of the document, there was a sudden brief
silence, then — "You frighten me — could you have written *The
Sea Around Us*"? I assured her that, though I had, I was quite
harmless! As you may have heard, the industry's prize exhibit
was a doctor from Tufts who says he uses the chemical clinically
in treatment of the thyroid and it could not be harmful. Oh
dear — his testimony can be shot so full of holes as to be absolutely worthless, and the disheartening thing is that he must
know this full well, if he is the great specialist they say he is. For
those who might not see the holes, however, it was good that
Consumer's Union had sent a man who gave the opinion of a
leading cancer specialist of the U. of Chicago — exactly the opposite of the man from Tufts. And my files are full of things that
refute the Tufts man!

During the early spring of 1960, Rachel continued to be
plagued with ill health: flu — leading to a sinus infection — and
now for the first time she developed an ulcer. She wrote to me in
exasperation: "I should think it might have waited until the
book is done! I'm sure some people would think the subject
matter I'm dealing with is the cause of the ulcer, but I'm equally
sure it isn't. I am finding it all quite fascinating. Of course, I
have felt under pressure to finish (though certainly not from
you!) and have felt frustrated by the slow progress."

But she kept doggedly on, and by now was sending me chapters in first draft for comment. By the end of the summer
Rachel had a complete draft of one of the most dramatic and
controversial chapters, that on birds. As always, she took the utmost care to make sure that her interpretation of the work of

specialists in the field was fair and accurate. To George Wallace she wrote: "I am enclosing a draft of my chapter dealing with the effect of pesticides on birds which you have kindly offered to read for me . . . My thought in asking you to read it is that you will be able to detect any places in which I may have gone astray in interpreting your data or other situations with which you will be more familiar than I."

One of the amateur observers with whom Professor Wallace had put Rachel in touch was Mrs. F. L. Larkin of Milwaukee (whose letter is quoted in *Silent Spring*). "Like you," Rachel wrote to her, "I have 'bushels' of material on literally every aspect of this problem, so it may seem strange that I want still more. However, in dealing with the subject of the tragic destruction of bird life I find that many people are deeply touched and concerned by it and find that they respond more to the actual experiences and observations of people like yourself, than to laboratory experiments or the findings of professional biologists."

While reading some of these heartbreaking accounts of the silencing of our songbirds, the phrase came to my mind that we eventually used as the title of the book. At first I had thought of it in connection with this one chapter only. "I like your suggestion of 'Silent Spring' as a title for the bird chapter very much," Rachel wrote me in September. However, not until many months later, after we had all agonized over finding something more appealing than "Man Against the Earth," did it occur to me that the image of "silent spring" symbolized the theme of the book as a whole. Rachel was doubtful, until Marie Rodell chose the following appropriate lines from Keats for the motto page:

> The sedge is wither'd from the lake,
> And no birds sing.

And so it was decided.

〜〜〜

Despite ill health and overwork, Rachel Carson managed during this election year to keep an eye on possible federal legislation to do with public health. In June 1960 she was asked to serve on the Natural Resources Committee of the Democratic Advisory Council. In accepting the position she explained: "My participation will have to be limited, because of temporary health problems and especially because of very heavy writing commitments. However, I do sincerely wish to do all I can." She went on to outline what she considered essential planks in the Democratic platform respecting pollution control, radioactive contamination of the sea, and of course particularly chemical poisoning of the environment. She concluded with a strong plea for preservation of natural areas and for passage of the Wilderness Bill, then awaiting action by the Senate. Shortly afterward she collaborated with Pare Lorentz in drafting the section on pollution in the Committee's report. In early October, at the invitation of Jacqueline Kennedy, she attended a meeting of the Women's Committee for the New Frontier.

As if all this was not enough, Rachel had to devote many hours during summer and fall to preparing the new edition of *The Sea Around Us*, which was to be published by Oxford Press the following spring. To attempt to bring the text itself up to date was impractical; as she pointed out, the book "deals with a body of knowledge that is changing from day to day as more and more intensive research programs are carried out." Instead, she added a section of notes that revised the statistical information and incorporated the most important discoveries of the past decade. In her preface she sought "to give some impression of the enormous growth of our knowledge of the sea even in the few years since the book was originally published." The preface also gave an early warning of a danger that in another ten years had become generally recognized: the widespread pollution of the sea by radioactive and other wastes. (Among the worst of these, of course, is pesticides.) "I feel very strongly about the seriousness of this problem," she wrote to her publisher, "and would like to find some way to focus more attention on this portion of the book."

The year 1960 ended on a somber note. Rachel learned that she had not been told the truth about a breast operation she had undergone the previous spring, "even though I asked directly." The tumor had been malignant and there was evidence that it had metastasized. She promptly sought the best medical advice, putting herself in the hands of Dr. George Crile, Jr., of the Cleveland Clinic, whom she had known for some years. (And whose wife Jane, in her own courageous battle against cancer, was later to be such a source of strength and inspiration to Rachel.) "I had admired his little book on cancer greatly when it was published," she wrote to me on December 27, "and had thought then that if ever I had such a diagnosis I would want to consult him. So, after a telephone conversation with him, I flew up to Cleveland a couple of weeks ago for a consultation. Dr. Crile is so much more than a medical man — he is also a biologist with the greatest possible breadth of understanding, with such awareness of what we don't know, and consequent unwillingness to rush in with procedures that may disrupt the little understood but all important ecology of the body cells. He has outlined a plan of treatment that makes sense and reflects his fine understanding, and through him I have gone to a man here who has an outstanding reputation in radiation therapy. So, we have started."

The calm courage with which she faced all this is hard to exaggerate. The recurrent treatments, she wrote, would involve a "pretty serious diversion of time and capacity for work . . . But in the intervals I hope to work hard and productively. Perhaps even more than ever, I am eager to get the book done." Though she never complained, she was sometimes baffled by the mounting obstacles to what she was determined to accomplish. "It rather seems Fate has been otherwise minded these recent years.

Very puzzling, to one who thought there were important things to be done."

The new year brought further trials. In early February, 1961, Rachel wrote to her friends Marjorie Spock and Mary Richards: "I seem always to write of illness and disaster but unfortunately my luck has not changed. Rather severe flu after Thanksgiving and then a persistent intestinal virus early in January apparently lowered my resistance and prepared for the real trouble — a staphylococcus infection that settled in my knees and ankles so that my legs are, and have been for 3 weeks, quite useless. I've been abed all that time, initially of course, quite ill with the infection, but now feeling fairly good if only I could walk! I've had 2 practical nurses all the time, supplementing dear Ida, my housekeeper, who has managed to take beautiful care of me during her hours here.

"It has all been very trying for poor Roger, who looks anything but 'Jolly' at the moment. Of course our various blizzards have added to the trials of getting people and groceries to the house."

Work on the book was temporarily out of the question. "About the only good thing I can see in all this experience," she wrote to me in late March, "is that the long time away from close contact with the book may have given me a broader perspective which I've always struggled for but felt I was not achieving. Now I'm trying to find ways to write it all more simply and perhaps more briefly and with less exhaustive detail. Later, when I have enough in this new vein to make it worth while, I hope you can come down and talk it over."

Virtually bedridden, she nevertheless managed to get a thrill from the early signs of spring. Yet the migrating birds and her reading about far places could not but make her impatient with her confinement. On March 13 she wrote:

This morning began (7 a.m.) with the cries of geese, and I managed to stagger to the window (shouting for Roger to share the excitement) and get it open in time to hear them better and see the dark, shifting column in the gray sky. I don't think I've heard them from this house before. Another "first" yesterday morning — the first robin song of the year. And Saturday we had 2 fox sparrows scratching on the ground under the feeder. They are rare with us. And I thought I heard a Carolina wren . . .

Yesterday's *Times* has a full page ad for R. of B.W. [*Ring of Bright Water* by Gavin Maxwell] using quotes from Edwin Teale and me. Also, it appears in the Best Seller list. I've been looking over Mr. Maxwell's earlier book and between the two have developed a bad case of wanderlust — my old longing to see something of the islands and coastline of Scotland!

By early June she was able to send me a draft of one of the most difficult chapters in the book (difficult, that is, from the point of view of readability), the chapter on poisons. Chlorinated hydrocarbons and organic phosphates are less intrinsically attractive than birds; no small literary skill is required to describe simply yet accurately such forbidding substances as DDT, chlordane, heptachlor, dieldrin, aldrin, endrin, and the rest. I always felt that if the reader could be piloted through chapter 3, the remainder would be comparatively smooth sailing.

About this time, we decided — contrary to our original plan — that the book should have illustrations, partly to aid understanding, partly to break up the solid text and make reading easier. We quickly settled on the perfect illustrator — or rather, illustrators — Louis and Lois Darling, who worked together as a team. The late Louis Darling, who won the John Burroughs Medal in 1966 for *A Gull's Way*, was a professional artist with a lifelong passion for natural history; Lois is a trained zoologist, free-lance illustrator, and conservation leader. Together they had produced a number of successful books, largely for young readers. Rachel was delighted when she saw samples of their work. They welcomed the chance to illustrate *Silent Spring*. As Louis once remarked, the overcoming of "biological illiteracy" was one of his main interests in life.

〰〰〰

Despite the increasing pressures on her, Rachel was always ready to help out in a conservation crisis where her knowledge and her influence might be effective. For instance, when certain city-minded citizens in my hometown (where mosquitoes had been slapped as a matter of course for two hundred years) called for a special town meeting to increase DDT spraying, I once more sought her assistance, in the form of a letter that I could read at the meeting. Her response was immediate. "Enclosed" she wrote, "is your weapon to brandish before the community fathers." A preview of one of the most important points in the book, her letter summarizes the biological facts of life that so many suburban communities still seem unable to grasp:

> You have asked my opinion about chemical spraying on a community basis for the control of mosquitoes. I can say without hesitation that such spraying operations are not only dangerous but they are also largely self-defeating. For the latter reason (as well as for others) they make very little sense.
>
> The reason I say they are self-defeating is that insect populations very quickly develop resistance to chemical sprays. This nullifies all we are trying to accomplish by spraying. In the end we find we have gone to considerable expense and trouble for nothing. We have killed off or endangered fish, birds, and other wildlife, contaminated vegetables and fruits, damaged shrubbery and flowers, and introduced poisonous chemicals into soil and water supplies. After all this, we find the mosquito has the last laugh, for while we have been progressively poisoning our own environment, the mosquito has been breeding a superior race composed of individuals that are immune to chemical attack.
>
> This phenomenon is exactly comparable to what is happening among bacterial populations subjected to antibiotics; it represents the typical ability of living organisms to adapt to unfavorable conditions . . . The common mosquitoes of the genus Culex develop resistance very quickly. DDT resistance among common house mosquitoes was detected in Boston and its suburbs several years ago. From DDT resistance, it is only a step to resistance to dieldrin, chlordane, and all the other available materials. The

irony of the situation is that the harder we spray, the more rapidly we bring on the day when nothing we can use will reduce the mosquito populations.

At the town meeting the motion in favor of spraying was defeated by a four-to-one vote.

It is typical of Rachel Carson that, however serious the personal problems she had to contend with, she never failed to help and encourage other writers whose work she believed in. Notable among these was Lois Crisler, with whom she had struck up a warm friendship following the publication of *Arctic Wild* in the fall of 1958. At that time, before they had personally met, she had written to Mrs. Crisler: "Through your sensitive awareness of the land and its creatures, I think you found the words you longed for, to communicate your experience to others. Of course I felt special sympathy with your thoughts of the 'secret tension between love and despair' so that 'no carefree love of the planet is now possible.' Each day those words become more true!" Now, when Mrs. Crisler was temporarily "blocked" on her new book, Rachel wrote her again. "I understand, as I suppose only another writer can, the agony of longing to write yet being unable to! It is bad enough to be kept from it by tangible things, but worse to sit down to it at last and find that the words will not come . . . I have been through it all many times, and I imagine it is the experience of most writers. Try to have faith that it will change — *for it will* . . . And it has changed for me. I really feel over the hump now — there remain only two new chapters to do, plus, of course, a lot of final revisions. There has been good solid progress this summer and at last it moves with its own momentum."

A few weeks later she was apparently struggling with the final revision of that difficult chapter on poisons. She drove herself hard: "I am working late at night most of the time now. If I can fight off the desire to go to bed around 11:30 I seem to get my second wind and be able to go on. This chapter has been very difficult but by now I understand myself and my way of working well enough to know I'm over the hump and it is now all fitting together about as it should. But with any chapter that presents difficult problems, as this one does, there is first a period when nothing moves and then it is hard not to be discouraged. What lies underneath the most important part of this chapter is a whole field of the most technical and difficult biology-discoveries only recently made. How to reveal enough to give understanding of the most serious effects of the chemicals without being technical, how to simplify without error — these have been problems of rather monumental proportions."

Early in 1962 — the year of publication — Rachel looked back along the rough path over which she had come, and worried over the hurdles that still lay ahead.

Yes, there is quite a story behind *Silent Spring*, isn't there? Such a catalogue of illnesses! If one were superstitious it would be easy to believe in some malevolent influence at work, determined by some means to keep the book from being finished. Some of the earlier things have been more serious, but I don't think anything has been frustrating and maddening in quite the same way as this iritis. And of course having the end in sight when it struck makes it, in a way, all the worse. I just creep along, a few hours a day. And I know that before I can happily let it go to the printer, there is a tremendous lot of work that only my eyes can do. I have always known I am visual minded, and I've certainly been reminded of it now. Having Jeanne [her secretary, Mrs. Jeanne Davis] read is of such limited help. I have to see it, and on revision I have to keep going over and over a page — with my eyes!

Doing so, not swiftly and easily, but draggingly with the impediments of the arthritis and now the iritis, has been rather like those dreams where one tries to run and can't or to drive a car and it won't go. But now that it seems I shall somehow make this goal, of course I'm not satisfied — now I want time for the

Help Your Child to Wonder book, and for the big Man and Nature book. Then I suppose I'll have others — if I live to be 90 still wanting to say something.

Following the step-by-step progress of the manuscript during these final months, one cannot but share Rachel's sense of exhilaration when the end at last came into sight. For more than four years she had wrestled with a book that grew like a living organism, spreading in unforeseen directions, nourished by the mountains of research material that she had amassed. To give shape and beauty to her unpromising subject matter, to keep it down to manageable size, to bring out the clear pattern underlying the complex details, above all to bolster every statement against inevitable attack — this was a feat to be achieved only by a scientist who was also an artist. Rachel was not yet sure that she had succeeded. On January 23, 1962, she wrote again to Lois Crisler:

"A hasty note just to assure you that, if you don't hear, it doesn't mean anything is wrong or that you are forgotten. But it is a *busy* time, with now the added spice of excitement with the knowledge that I have almost reached the end of the long road. I'm on the final chapter, but the rest of the mss is now in the hands of Marie, Paul, Mr. Shawn (*New Yorker*) and the artists. Last night Mr. Shawn telephoned to tell me he had finished reading. His reactions were everything I could have asked or hoped for, and though I had not consciously been waiting to hear them, I felt an enormous surge of relief — as if now I knew the book would accomplish what *I long for it to do*."

She described the same incident at greater length in a letter to Dorothy Freeman: ". . . It was odd. I really had not been waiting breathlessly for Mr. Shawn's reaction, yet once I had it I knew how very much it meant to me. You know I have the highest regard for his judgment, and suddenly I knew from his reaction that my message would get across. After Roger was asleep, I took Jeffie [her cat] into the study and played the Beethoven violin concerto — one of my favorites, you know. And suddenly the tension of four years was broken and I let the tears come. I think I let you see last summer what my deeper feelings are about this when I said I could never again listen happily to a thrush song if I had not done all I could. And last night the thoughts of all the birds and other creatures and all the loveliness that is in nature came to me with such a surge of deep happiness, that now I had done what I could — I had been able to complete it — now it had its own life . . ."

CHAPTER 19

FROM *SILENT SPRING*

"The Obligation to Endure"

THE HISTORY OF LIFE on earth has been a history of interaction between living things and their surroundings. To a large extent, the physical form and the habits of the earth's vegetation and its animal life have been molded by the environment. Considering the whole span of earthly time, the opposite effect, in which life actually modifies its surroundings, has been relatively slight. Only within the moment of time represented by the present century has one species — man — acquired significant power to alter the nature of his world.

During the past quarter century this power has not only increased to one of disturbing magnitude but it has changed in character. The most alarming of all man's assaults upon the environment is the contamination of air, earth, rivers, and sea with dangerous and even lethal materials. This pollution is for the most part irrecoverable; the chain of evil it initiates not only in the world that must support life but in living tissues is for the most part irreversible. In this now universal contamination of the environment, chemicals are the sinister and little-recognized partners of radiation in changing the very nature of the world — the very nature of its life. Strontium 90, released through nuclear explosions into the air, comes to earth in rain or drifts down as fallout, lodges in soil, enters into the grass or corn or wheat grown there, and in time takes up its abode in the bones of a human being, there to remain until his death. Similarly, chemicals sprayed on croplands or forests or gardens lie long in soil, entering into living organisms, passing from one to another in a chain of poisoning and death. Or they pass mysteriously by underground streams until they emerge and, through the alchemy of air and sunlight, combine into new forms that kill vegetation, sicken cattle, and work unknown harm on those who drink from once pure wells. As Albert Schweitzer has said, "Man can hardly even recognize the devils of his own creation."

It took hundreds of millions of years to produce the life that now inhabits the earth — eons of time in which that developing and evolving and diversifying life reached a state of adjustment and balance with its surroundings. The environment, rigorously shaping and directing the life it supported, contained elements that were hostile as well as supporting. Certain rocks gave out dangerous radiation; even within the light of the sun, from which all life draws its energy, there were short-wave radiations with power to injure. Given time — time not in years but in millennia — life adjusts, and a balance has been reached. For time is the essential ingredient; but in the modern world there is no time.

The rapidity of change and the speed with which new situations are created follow the impetuous and heedless pace of man rather than the deliberate pace of nature. Radiation is no longer merely the background radiation of rocks, the bombardment of cosmic rays, the ultraviolet of the sun that have existed before there was any life on earth; radiation is now the unnatural creation of man's tampering with the atom. The chemicals to which life is asked to make its adjustment are no longer merely the calcium and silica and copper and all the rest of the minerals washed out of the rocks and carried in rivers to the sea; they are the synthetic creations of man's inventive mind, brewed in his laboratories, and having no counterparts in nature.

To adjust to these chemicals would require time on the scale that is nature's; it would require not merely the years of a man's life but the life of generations. And even this, were it by some miracle possible, would be futile, for the new chemicals come from our laboratories in an endless stream; almost five hundred annually find their way into actual use in the United States alone. The figure is staggering and its implications are not easily grasped — 500 new chemicals to which the bodies of men and animals are required somehow to adapt each year, chemicals totally outside the limits of biologic experience.

Among them are many that are used in man's war against nature. Since the mid-1940s over 200 basic chemicals have been created for use in killing insects, weeds, rodents, and other organisms described in the modern vernacular as "pests"; and they are sold under several thousand different brand names.

These sprays, dusts, and aerosols are now applied almost universally to farms, gardens, forests, and homes — nonselective chemicals that have the power to kill every insect, the "good" and the "bad," to still the song of birds and the leaping of fish in the streams, to coat the leaves with a deadly film, and to linger on in soil — all this though the intended target may be only a few weeds or insects. Can anyone believe it is possible to lay down such a barrage of poisons on the surface of the earth without making it unfit for all life? They should not be called "insecticides," but "biocides."

The whole process of spraying seems caught up in an endless spiral. Since DDT was released for civilian use, a process of escalation has been going on in which ever more toxic materials must be found. This has happened because insects, in a triumphant vindication of Darwin's principle of the survival of the fittest, have evolved super races immune to the particular insecticide used, hence a deadlier one has always to be developed — and then a deadlier one than that. It has happened also because, for reasons to be described later, destructive insects often undergo a "flareback," or resurgence, after spraying, in numbers greater than before. Thus the chemical war is never won, and all life is caught in its violent crossfire.

Along with the possibility of the extinction of mankind by nuclear war, the central problem of our age has therefore become the contamination of man's total environment with such substances of incredible potential for harm — substances that accumulate in the tissues of plants and animals and even penetrate the germ cells to shatter or alter the very material of heredity upon which the shape of the future depends . . . All this is not to say there is no insect problem and no need of control. I am saying, rather, that control must be geared to realities, not to mythical situations, and that the methods employed must be such that they do not destroy us along with the insects . . .

It is not my contention that chemical insecticides must never be used. I do contend that we have put poisonous and biologically potent chemicals indiscriminately into the hands of persons largely or wholly ignorant of their potentials for harm. We have subjected enormous numbers of people to contact with these poisons, without their consent and often without their knowledge. If the Bill of Rights contains no guarantee that a citizen shall be secure against lethal poisons distributed either by private individuals or by public officials, it is surely only because our forefathers, despite their considerable wisdom and foresight, could conceive of no such problem.

I contend, furthermore, that we have allowed these chemicals to be used with little or no advance investigation of their effect on soil, water, wildlife, and man himself. Future generations are unlikely to condone our lack of prudent concern for the integrity of the natural world that supports all life.

There is still very limited awareness of the nature of the threat. This is an era of specialists, each of whom sees his own problem and is unaware of or intolerant of the larger frame into which it fits. It is also an era dominated by industry, in which the right to make a dollar at whatever cost is seldom challenged.

When the public protests, confronted with some obvious evidence of damaging results of pesticide applications, it is fed little tranquilizing pills of half truth. We urgently need an end to these false assurances, to the sugar coating of unpalatable facts. It is the public that is being asked to assume the risks that the insect controllers calculate. The public must decide whether it wishes to continue on the present road, and it can do so only when in full possession of the facts. In the words of Jean Rostand, "The obligation to endure gives us the right to know."

"The Story of Clear Lake"

WATER MUST ALSO be thought of in terms of the chains of life it supports — from the small-as-dust green cells of the drifting plant plankton, through the minute water fleas to the fishes that strain plankton from the water and are in turn eaten by other fishes or by birds, mink, raccoons — in an endless cyclic transfer of materials from life to life. We know that the necessary minerals in the water are so passed from link to link of the food chains. Can we suppose that poisons we introduce into water will not also enter into these cycles of nature?

The answer is to be found in the amazing history of Clear Lake, California. Clear Lake lies in mountainous country some 90 miles north of San Francisco and has long been popular with anglers. The name is inappropriate, for actually it is a rather turbid lake because of the soft black ooze that covers its shallow bottom. Unfortunately for the fishermen and the resort dwellers on its shores, its waters have provided an ideal habitat for a small

gnat, *Chaoborus astictopus*. Although closely related to mosquitoes, the gnat is not a bloodsucker and probably does not feed at
all as an adult. However, human beings who shared its habitat
found it annoying because of its sheer numbers. Efforts were
made to control it but they were largely fruitless until, in the late
1940s, the chlorinated hydrocarbon insecticides offered new
weapons. The chemical chosen for a fresh attack was DDD, a
close relative of DDT but apparently offering fewer threats to
fish life.

The new control measures undertaken in 1949 were carefully
planned and few people would have supposed any harm could
result. The lake was surveyed, its volume determined, and the
insecticide applied in such great dilution that for every part of
chemical there would be 70 million parts of water. Control of
the gnats was at first good, but by 1954 the treatment had to be
repeated, this time at the rate of 1 part of insecticide in 50
million parts of water. The destruction of the gnats was thought
to be virtually complete.

The following winter months brought the first intimation that
other life was affected: the western grebes on the lake began to
die, and soon more than a hundred of them were reported dead.
At Clear Lake the western grebe is a breeding bird and also a
winter visitant, attracted by the abundant fish of the lake. It is a
bird of spectacular appearance and beguiling habits, building its
floating nests in shallow lakes of western United States and
Canada. It is called the "swan grebe" with reason, for it glides
with scarcely a ripple across the lake surface, the body riding low,
white neck and shining black head held high. The newly
hatched chick is clothed in soft gray down; in only a few hours it
takes to the water and rides on the back of the father or mother,
nestled under the parental wing coverts.

Following a third assault on the ever-resilient gnat population,
in 1957, more grebes died. As had been true in 1954, no evidence of infectious disease could be discovered on examination

of the dead birds. But when some thought to analyze the fatty tissues of the grebes, they were found to be loaded with DDD in the extraordinary concentration of 1600 parts per million.

The maximum concentration applied to the water was $\frac{1}{50}$ part per million. How could the chemical have built up to such prodigious levels in the grebes? These birds, of course, are fish eaters. When the fish of Clear Lake also were analyzed the picture began to take form — the poison being picked up by the smallest organisms, concentrated and passed on to the larger predators. Plankton organisms were found to contain about 5 parts per million of the insecticide (about 25 times the maximum concentration ever reached in the water itself); plant-eating fishes had built up accumulations ranging from 40 to 300 parts per million; carnivorous species had stored the most of all. One, a brown bullhead, had the astounding concentration of 2500 parts per million. It was a house-that-Jack-built sequence, in which the large carnivores had eaten the smaller carnivores, that had eaten the herbivores, that had eaten the plankton, that had absorbed the poison from the water.

Even more extraordinary discoveries were made later. No trace of DDD could be found in the water shortly after the last application of the chemical. But the poison had not really left the lake; it had merely gone into the fabric of the life the lake supports. Twenty-three months after the chemical treatment had ceased, the plankton still contained as much as 5.3 parts per million. In that interval of nearly two years, successive crops of plankton had flowered and faded away, but the poison, although no longer present in the water, had somehow passed from generation to generation. And it lived on in the animal life of the lake as well. All fish, birds, and frogs examined a year after the chemical applications had ceased still contained DDD. The amount found in the flesh always exceeded by many times the original concentration in the water. Among these living carriers were fish that had hatched nine months after the last DDD application, grebes, and California gulls that had built up concentrations of more than 2000 parts per million. Meanwhile, the nesting colonies of the grebes dwindled — from more than 1000 pairs before the first insecticide treatment to about 30 pairs in 1960. And even the thirty seem to have nested in vain, for no young grebes have been observed on the lake since the last DDD application.

This whole chain of poisoning, then, seems to rest on a base of minute plants which must have been the original concentrators. But what of the opposite end of the food chain — the human being who, in probable ignorance of all this sequence of events, has rigged his fishing tackle, caught a string of fish from the waters of Clear Lake, and taken them home to fry for his supper? What could a heavy dose of DDD, or perhaps repeated doses, do to him?

Although the California Department of Public Health professed to see no hazard, nevertheless in 1959 it required that the use of DDD in the lake be stopped. In view of the scientific evidence of the vast biological potency of this chemical, the action seems a minimum safety measure. The physiological effect of DDD is probably unique among insecticides, for it destroys part of the adrenal gland — the cells of the outer layer known as the adrenal cortex, which secretes the hormone cortin. This destructive effect, known since 1948, was at first believed to be confined to dogs, because it was not revealed in such experimental animals as monkeys, rats, or rabbits. It seemed suggestive, however, that DDD produced in dogs a condition very similar to that occurring in man in the presence of Addison's disease. Recent medical research has revealed that DDD does strongly suppress the function of the human adrenal cortex. Its cell-destroying capacity is now clinically utilized in the treatment of a rare type of cancer which develops in the adrenal gland.

"Earth's Green Mantle"

WATER, SOIL, and the earth's green mantle of plants make up the world that supports the animal life of the earth. Although modern man seldom remembers the fact, he could not exist without the plants that harness the sun's energy and manufacture the basic foodstuffs he depends upon for life. Our attitude toward plants is a singularly narrow one. If we see any immediate utility in a plant we foster it. If for any reason we find its presence undesirable or merely a matter of indifference, we may condemn it to destruction forthwith. Besides the various plants that are poisonous to man or his livestock, or crowd out food plants, many are marked for destruction merely because, according to our narrow view, they happen to be in the wrong place at the wrong time. Many others are destroyed merely because they happen to be associates of the unwanted plants.

The earth's vegetation is part of a web of life in which there are intimate and essential relations between plants and the earth, between plants and other plants, between plants and animals. Sometimes we have no choice but to disturb these relationships, but we should do so thoughtfully, with full awareness that what we do may have consequences remote in time and place. But no such humility marks the booming "weed killer" business of the present day, in which soaring sales and expanding uses mark the production of plant-killing chemicals . . .

I know well a stretch of road where nature's own landscaping has provided a border of alder, viburnum, sweet fern, and juniper with seasonally changing accents of bright flowers, or of fruits hanging in jeweled clusters in the fall. The road had no heavy load of traffic to support; there were few sharp curves or intersections where brush could obstruct the driver's vision. But the sprayers took over and the miles along that road became something to be traversed quickly, a sight to be endured with one's mind closed to thoughts of the sterile and hideous world we are letting our technicians make. But here and there authority had somehow faltered and by an unaccountable oversight there were oases of beauty in the midst of austere and regimented control — oases that made the desecration of the greater part of the road the more unbearable. In such places my spirit lifted to the sight of the drifts of white clover or the clouds of purple vetch with here and there the flaming cup of a wood lily.

Such plants are "weeds" only to those who make a business of selling and applying chemicals. In a volume of *Proceedings* of one of the weed-control conferences that are now regular institutions, I once read an extraordinary statement of a weed killer's philosophy. The author defended the killing of good plants "simply because they are in bad company." Those who complain about killing wildflowers along roadsides reminded him, he said, of antivivisectionists "to whom, if one were to judge by their actions, the life of a stray dog is more sacred than the lives of children."

To the author of this paper, many of us would unquestionably be suspect, convicted of some deep perversion of character because we prefer the sight of the vetch and the clover and the wood lily in all their delicate and transient beauty to that of roadsides scorched as by fire, the shrubs brown and brittle, the bracken that once lifted high its proud lacework now withered and drooping. We would seem deplorably weak that we can tolerate the sight of such "weeds," that we do not rejoice in their eradication, that we are not filled with exultation that man has once more triumphed over miscreant nature.

"Through a Narrow Window"

THE BIOLOGIST George Wald once compared his work on an exceedingly specialized subject, the visual pigments of the eye, to "a very narrow window through which at a distance one can see only a crack of light. As one comes closer the view grows wider and wider, until finally through this same narrow window one is looking at the universe."

So it is that only when we bring our focus to bear, first on the individual cells of the body, then on the minute structures within the cells, and finally on the ultimate reactions of molecules within these structures — only when we do this can we comprehend the most serious and far-reaching effects of the haphazard introduction of foreign chemicals into our internal environment. Medical research has only rather recently turned to the functioning of the individual cell in producing the energy that is the indispensable quality of life. The extraordinary energy-producing mechanism of the body is basic not only to health but to life; it transcends in importance even the most vital organs, for without the smooth and effective functioning of energy-yielding oxidation none of the body's functions can be performed. Yet the nature of many of the chemicals used against insects, rodents, and weeds is such that they may strike directly at this system, disrupting its beautifully functioning mechanism.

The research that led to our present understanding of cellular oxidation is one of the most impressive accomplishments in all biology and biochemistry. The roster of contributors to this work includes many Nobel Prize winners. Step by step it has been going on for a quarter of a century, drawing on even earlier

284 THE HOUSE OF LIFE

work for some of its foundation stones. Even yet it is not complete in all details. And only within the past decade have all the varied pieces of research come to form a whole so that biological oxidation could become part of the common knowledge of biologists. Even more important is the fact that medical men who received their basic training before 1950 have had little opportunity to realize the critical importance of the process and the hazards of disrupting it.

The ultimate work of energy production is accomplished not in any specialized organ but in every cell of the body. A living cell, like a flame, burns fuel to produce the energy on which life depends. The analogy is more poetic than precise, for the cell accomplishes its "burning" with only the moderate heat of the body's normal temperature. Yet all these billions of gently burning little fires spark the energy of life. Should they cease to burn, "no heart could beat, no plant could grow upward defying gravity, no amoeba could swim, no sensation could speed along a nerve, no thought could flash in the human brain," said the chemist Eugene Rabinowitch.

The transformation of matter into energy in the cell is an everflowing process, one of nature's cycles of renewal, like a wheel endlessly turning. Grain by grain, molecule by molecule, carbohydrate fuel in the form of glucose is fed into this wheel; in its cyclic passage the fuel molecule undergoes fragmentation and a series of minute chemical changes. The changes are made in orderly fashion, step by step, each step directed and controlled by an enzyme of so specialized a function that it does this one thing and nothing else. At each step energy is produced, waste products (carbon dioxide and water) are given off, and the altered molecule of fuel is passed on to the next stage. When the turning wheel comes full cycle the fuel molecule has been stripped down to a form in which it is ready to combine with a new molecule coming in and to start the cycle anew.

This process by which the cell functions as a chemical factory is one of the wonders of the living world. The fact that all the functioning parts are of infinitesimal size adds to the miracle. With few exceptions cells themselves are minute, seen only with the aid of a microscope. Yet the greater part of the work of oxidation is performed in a theater far smaller, in tiny granules within the cell called mitochondria. Although known for more than 60 years, these were formerly dismissed as cellular elements of unknown and probably unimportant function. Only in the 1950s did their study become an exciting and fruitful field of research; suddenly they began to engage so much attention that 1000 papers on this subject alone appeared within a five-year period.

Again one stands in awe at the marvelous ingenuity and patience by which the mystery of the mitochondria has been solved. Imagine a particle so small that you can barely see it even though a microscope has enlarged it for you 300 times. Then imagine the skill required to isolate this particle, to take it apart and analyze its components and determine their highly complex functioning. Yet this has been done with the aid of the electron microscope and the techniques of the biochemist.

It is now known that the mitochondria are tiny packets of enzymes, a varied assortment including all the enzymes necessary for the oxidative cycle, arranged in precise and orderly array on walls and partitions. The mitochondria are the "powerhouses" in which most of the energy-producing reactions occur. After the first, preliminary steps of oxidation have been performed in the cytoplasm the fuel molecule is taken into the mitochondria. It is here that oxidation is completed; it is here that enormous amounts of energy are released . . .

When any of these enzymes — even a single one of them — is destroyed or weakened, the cycle of oxidation within the cell comes to a halt. It makes no difference which enzyme is affected. Oxidation progresses in a cycle like a turning wheel. If we thrust a crowbar between the spokes of a wheel it makes no difference where we do it, the wheel stops turning. In the same way, if we destroy an enzyme that functions at any point in the cycle, oxidation ceases. There is then no further energy production, so the end effect is very similar to uncoupling.

The crowbar to wreck the wheels of oxidation can be supplied by any of a number of chemicals commonly used as pesticides. DDT, methoxychlor, malathion, phenothiazine, and various dinitro compounds are among the numerous pesticides that have been found to inhibit one or more of the enzymes concerned in the cycle of oxidation. They thus appear as agents potentially capable of blocking the whole process of energy production and depriving the cells of utilizable oxygen. This is an injury with most disastrous consequences . . .

"The Balance of Nature"

FROM ALL OVER THE WORLD come reports that make it clear we are in a serious predicament. At the end of a decade or more of intensive chemical control, entomologists were finding that problems they had considered solved a few years earlier had returned to plague them. And new problems had arisen as insects once present only in insignificant numbers had increased to the status of serious pests. By their very nature chemical controls are self-defeating, for they have been devised and applied without taking into account the complex biological systems against which they have been blindly hurled. The chemicals may have been pretested against a few individual species, but not against living communities.

In some quarters nowadays it is fashionable to dismiss the balance of nature as a state of affairs that prevailed in an earlier, simpler world — a state that has now been so thoroughly upset that we might as well forget it. Some find this a convenient assumption, but as a chart for a course of action it is highly dangerous. The balance of nature is not the same today as in Pleistocene times, but it is still there: a complex, precise, and highly integrated system of relationships between living things which cannot safely be ignored any more than the law of gravity can be defied with impunity by a man perched on the edge of a cliff. The balance of nature is not a *status quo*; it is fluid, ever shifting, in a constant state of adjustment. Man, too, is part of this balance. Sometimes the balance is in his favor; sometimes — and all too often through his own activities — it is shifted to his disadvantage.

Two critically important facts have been overlooked in designing the modern insect control programs. The first is that the really effective control of insects is that applied by nature, not by man. Populations are kept in check by something the ecologists call the resistance of the environment, and this has been so since the first life was created. The amount of food available, conditions of weather and climate, the presence of competing or predatory species, all are critically important. "The greatest single factor in preventing insects from overwhelming the rest of the world is the internecine warfare which they carry out among themselves," said the entomologist Robert Metcalf. Yet most of the chemicals now used kill all insects, our friends and enemies alike.

The second neglected fact is the truly explosive power of a species to reproduce once the resistance of the environment has been weakened. The fecundity of many forms of life is almost beyond our power to imagine, though now and then we have suggestive glimpses. I remember from student days the miracle that could be wrought in a jar containing a simple mixture of hay and water merely by adding to it a few drops of material from a mature culture of protozoa. Within a few days the jar would contain a whole galaxy of whirling, darting life — uncountable trillions of the slipper animalcule, *Paramecium*, each small as a dust grain, all multiplying without restraint in their temporary Eden of favorable temperatures, abundant food, absence of enemies. Or I think of shore rocks white with barnacles as far as the eye can see, or of the spectacle of passing through an immense school of jellyfish, mile after mile, with seemingly no end to the pulsing, ghostly forms scarcely more substantial than the water itself.

We see the miracle of nature's control at work when the cod move through winter seas to their spawning grounds, where each female deposits several millions of eggs. The sea does not become a solid mass of cod as it would surely do if all the progeny of all the cod were to survive. The checks that exist in nature are such that out of the millions of young produced by each pair only enough, on the average, survive to adulthood to replace the parent fish . . .

No one knows how many species of insects inhabit the earth because so many are yet to be identified. But more than 700,000 have already been described. This means that in terms of the number of species, 70 to 80 per cent of the earth's creatures are insects. The vast majority of these insects are held in check by natural forces, without any intervention by man. If this were not so, it is doubtful that any conceivable volume of chemicals — or any other methods — could possibly keep down their populations.

The trouble is that we are seldom aware of the protection afforded by natural enemies until it fails. Most of us walk unseeing through the world, unaware alike of its beauties, its wonders, and the strange and sometimes terrible intensity of the lives that are being lived about us. So it is that the activities of the insect predators and parasites are known to few. Perhaps we may have noticed an oddly shaped insect of ferocious mien on a bush in the garden and been dimly aware that the praying mantis lives at the expense of other insects. But we see with understanding eye only if we have walked in the garden at night and here and there with a flashlight have glimpsed the mantis stealthily creeping upon her prey. Then we sense something of the drama of the hunter and the hunted. Then we begin to feel something of that relentlessly pressing force by which nature controls her own . . .

Everywhere, in field and hedgerow and garden and forest, the insect predators and parasites are at work. Here, above a pond, the dragonflies dart and the sun strikes fire from their wings. So their ancestors sped through swamps where huge reptiles lived. Now, as in those ancient times, the sharp-eyed dragonflies capture mosquitoes in the air, scooping them in with basket-shaped legs. In the waters below, their young, the dragonfly nymphs, or naiads, prey on the aquatic stages of mosquitoes and other insects.

Or there, almost invisible against a leaf, is the lacewing, with green gauze wings and golden eyes, shy and secretive, descendant of an ancient race that lived in Permian times. The adult lacewing feeds mostly on plant nectars and the honeydew of aphids, and in time she lays her eggs, each on the end of a long stalk which she fastens to a leaf. From these emerge her children — strange, bristled larvae called aphis lions, which live by preying on aphids, scales, or mites, which they capture and suck dry of fluid. Each may consume several hundred aphids before the ceaseless turning of the cycle of its life brings the time when it will spin a white silken cocoon in which to pass the pupal stage.

And there are many wasps, and flies as well, whose very existence depends on the destruction of the eggs or larvae of other insects through parasitism. Some of the egg parasites are exceedingly minute wasps, yet by their numbers and their great activity they hold down the abundance of many crop-destroying species.

All these small creatures are working — working in sun and

rain, during the hours of darkness, even when winter's grip has damped down the fires of life to mere embers. Then this vital force is merely smoldering, awaiting the time to flare again into activity when spring awakens the insect world. Meanwhile, under the white blanket of snow, below the frost-hardened soil, in crevices in the bark of trees, and in sheltered caves, the parasites and the predators have found ways to tide themselves over the season of cold.

The eggs of the mantis are secure in little cases of thin parchment attached to the branch of a shrub by the mother who lived her life span with the summer that is gone.

The female *Polistes* wasp, taking shelter in a forgotten corner of some attic, carries in her body the fertilized eggs, the heritage on which the whole future of her colony depends. She, the lone survivor, will start a small paper nest in the spring, lay a few eggs in its cells, and carefully rear a small force of workers. With their help she will then enlarge the nest and develop the colony. Then the workers, foraging ceaselessly through the hot days of summer, will destroy countless caterpillars.

Thus, through the circumstances of their lives, and the nature of our own wants, all these have been our allies in keeping the balance of nature tilted in our favor. Yet we have turned our artillery against our friends. The terrible danger is that we have grossly underestimated their value in keeping at bay a dark tide of enemies that, without their help, can overrun us.

"The Other Road"

WE STAND NOW where two roads diverge. But unlike the roads in Robert Frost's familiar poem, they are not equally fair. The road we have long been traveling is deceptively easy, a smooth superhighway on which we progress with great speed, but at its end lies disaster. The other fork of the road — the one "less traveled by" — offers our last, our only chance to reach a destination that assures the preservation of our earth.

The choice, after all, is ours to make. If, having endured much, we have at last asserted our "right to know," and if, knowing, we have concluded that we are being asked to take senseless and frightening risks, then we should no longer accept the counsel of those who tell us that we must fill our world with poisonous chemicals; we should look about and see what other course is open to us.

A truly extraordinary variety of alternatives to the chemical control of insects is available. Some are already in use and have achieved brilliant success. Others are in the stage of laboratory testing. Still others are little more than ideas in the minds of imaginative scientists, waiting for the opportunity to put them to the test. All have this in common: they are *biological* solutions, based on understanding of the living organisms they seek to control, and of the whole fabric of life to which these organisms belong. Specialists representing various areas of the vast field of biology are contributing — entomologists, pathologists, geneticists, physiologists, biochemists, ecologists — all pouring their knowledge and their creative inspirations into the formation of a new science of biotic controls.

Through all these new, imaginative, and creative approaches

to the problem of sharing our earth with other creatures there runs a constant theme, the awareness that we are dealing with life — with living populations and all their pressures and counter-pressures, their surges and recessions. Only by taking account of such life forces and by cautiously seeking to guide them into channels favorable to ourselves can we hope to achieve a reasonable accommodation between the insect hordes and ourselves.

The current vogue for poisons has failed utterly to take into account these most fundamental considerations. As crude a weapon as the cave man's club, the chemical barrage has been hurled against the fabric of life — a fabric on the one hand delicate and destructible, on the other miraculously tough and resilient, and capable of striking back in unexpected ways. These extraordinary capacities of life have been ignored by the practitioners of chemical control who have brought to their task no "high-minded orientation," no humility before the vast forces with which they tamper.

The "control of nature" is a phrase conceived in arrogance, born of the Neanderthal age of biology and philosophy, when it was supposed that nature exists for the convenience of man. The concepts and practices of applied entomology for the most part date from that Stone Age of science. It is our alarming misfortune that so primitive a science has armed itself with the most modern and terrible weapons, and that in turning them against the insects it has also turned them against the earth.

CHAPTER 20

THE STORM

SILENT SPRING was serialized in *The New Yorker* beginning
June 16, 1962, and instantly created a sensation throughout the
country. The complete book was published on September 27.
Perhaps not since the classic controversy over Charles Darwin's
The Origin of Species just over a century earlier had a single
book been more bitterly attacked by those who felt their interests threatened. Darwin's study challenged the entrenched
power of the established church. By comparison, *Silent Spring*
initially offended a relatively small (though very rich) segment
of society, the chemical and other related industries (such as
food-processing), and — in the federal government — the immensely powerful Department of Agriculture. But the fury with
which it was attacked, the attempts to discredit that "hysterical
woman" as she was called, have, I believe, deeper roots than a
simple concern for profits or power on the part of special interest
groups. Her opponents must have realized — as was indeed the
case — that she was questioning not only the indiscriminate use
of poisons but the basic irresponsibility of an industrialized, technological society toward the natural world: She refused to accept
the premise that damage to nature was the inevitable cost of
"progress." The facts she revealed were bad enough, but it was

the point of view behind them that was really dangerous, and must be suppressed.

The first attempt at suppression was made while *Silent Spring* was still at the printer's. Velsicol Corporation of Chicago claimed (on the basis of the *New Yorker* serialization) that an inaccurate statement had been made about one of their principal products, chlordane. They threatened suit if the text was published as it stood. However, when the publishers, convinced that the statement was correct, declined to change it, no more was heard of the matter.*

Though publication could not be stopped and the *New Yorker* serial extracts had already been the subject of over fifty newspaper editorials and some twenty columns, there remained the possibility of discrediting *Silent Spring* before it appeared in book form. Most of the individual companies left this task to the trade associations, such as the National Agricultural Chemicals Association, which took the lead by appropriating approximately a quarter of a million dollars "to improve the image of the industry." Its first effort was a publication entitled *Fact and Fancy*, which quoted from *Silent Spring* (without either credit or copyright permission) and supplied so-called "facts" to refute its statements. Monsanto Chemical Company, however, made its own unique contribution. Ignoring facts altogether, it ridiculed the book in a parody called *The Desolate Year*, depicting the horrors of a world without pesticides: something that Rachel Carson had specifically not recommended. "It is not my contention that chemical insecticides must never be used. I do contend that we have put poisonous and biologically potent chemicals indiscriminately into the hands of persons largely or wholly ignorant of their potentials for harm." (*Silent Spring*, page 12.)

* But more was heard about Velsicol. Just before she died, Rachel Carson learned that the enormous fish kills in the Mississippi, which had reached a climax in 1963, had been definitely traced by the Public Health Service to endrin, and specifically to the sewers of Memphis, where this poison — thirty times more deadly to fish than DDT — was found caked three feet thick. Since the only manufacturer of endrin in Memphis was Velsicol, their denials of responsibility were unconvincing.

The *New Yorker* series was barely on the newsstands before the trade journal *Chemical and Engineering News* launched a counterattack, without specifically referring to Rachel Carson. Under the headline "Pesticides Sales Pick Up" the editor wrote: "Federal-state spraying continues, but it has been hampered by the adverse publicity from conservationists who claim residues of the insecticide, dieldrin, kill birds and wild animals." The article quoted the director of New Jersey's Department of Agriculture, in connection with aerial spraying for gypsy moth control: "In any large scale pest control program in this area, we are immediately confronted with the objection of a vociferous, misinformed group of nature-balancing, organic-gardening, bird-loving, unreasonable citizenry that has not been convinced of the important place of agricultural chemicals in our economy."

Some of the least temperate reactions came from the agricultural journals and the state institutions whose agricultural research was heavily financed by the chemical industry. An editorial in the *American Agriculturist* presented a parody of the future in which a young boy and his grandfather "sat on opposite ends of a log in a forest clearing, cracking acorns and eating them greedily." Gramps explained that a book had come out called *Quiet Summer* expressing the views of "a number of people who believed that no chemical material should be used in agriculture . . . So now we live naturally. Your mother died naturally from malaria that mosquitoes gave her; your Dad passed away naturally in that terrible famine when the grasshoppers ate up everything; now we are starving naturally, because the blight killed those potatoes we planted last spring. I only wish the author of that book had stayed around to share the joys of living 'naturally' — but she made so much money as an author that she moved to a country where her book was banned. Farming there is still 'unnatural.' Please pass the acorns!"

Another magazine, *County Agent and Vo-Ag Teacher*, ran an article entitled, "How to Answer Rachel Carson." "We hope," wrote the editor, "you will use this information in talks before groups on TV or radio, or in newspaper articles." The article refers the reader to "a kit of valuable information from the National Agricultural Chemicals Association" and "a devastating satire, written in the manner of Rachel Carson's book, describing a world in which no pesticides were allowed, titled *The Desolate Year*." On conclusion, it quotes the "chief horticulturist at Michigan State University" as saying: "Her book is more poisonous than the pesticides she condemns."

In short, the pesticide industry treated the challenge of *Silent Spring* as a problem in public relations, to be met by any means at hand. Yet not all the trade papers ignored the substance of the book while searching for clever ways to discredit it. For instance, *Agricultural Chemicals*, despite its orientation toward the industry, quoted Professor Moody Trevett of the University of Maine: "Miss Carson has posed some unanswerable questions as to what may happen to us in the next twenty years and this may be the time to sit down and do some serious thinking about the answers."

Of course, the organized opposition to *Silent Spring* was not confined to the chemical industry. Paradoxical as it might seem (since the problem of pesticides in prepared foods had been known for at least a decade), one of the most violent attacks came from the Nutrition Foundation, Inc., of New York City, which, in collaboration with the Manufacturing Chemists Association, reprinted and distributed a collection of the most unfavorable reviews. These included condemnations by Frederick T. Stare of the School of Public Health, Harvard University, and William J. Darby of Vanderbilt University. In the words of Paul Knight, a member of the staff of Secretary of the Interior Stewart L. Udall, who kept the Secretary informed on the continuing controversy over the book, they "reviewed *Silent Spring* in terms some of their fellow-chemists have characterized as polemical rather than scientific, prompting one nutritionist to remark that 'where the shot hit, the feathers fly.' This remark was made in reference to the fact that research on nutrition and processing in many university laboratories is heavily supported by the food industry." In his review, Dr. Darby wrote: "This book should be ignored." Dr. Stare described it as "baloney."

The position of the American Medical Association in the controversy also seems surprising when one considers that some of Rachel Carson's strongest support came from specialists in public health, and that the largest number of letters she received, in cases where occupation was identifiable, were from physicians. Yet the *AMA News* for November 26, 1962, referred its readers to an "information kit," compiled by the National Agricultural Chemicals Association!

What of the popular press? On the whole, the reviews of *Silent Spring*, like the mail received by the author, were overwhelmingly favorable. There were, however, notable exceptions. *Time* magazine accused the author of trying to frighten the public by "using emotion-fanning words" and referred to her "oversimplifications and downright errors." Scientists, physicians and other technically informed people — according to *Time* — considered her case "unfair, one-sided, and hysterically overemphatic. Many of the scary generalizations — and there are lots of them — are patently unsound. 'It is not possible,' says Miss Carson, 'to add pesticides to water anywhere without threatening the purity of water everywhere.' It takes only a moment of reflection to show that this is nonsense." Today one may reflect for a moment on the fact that DDT is found hundreds of miles out to sea, even in the polar ice. The review concluded: "Many scientists sympathize with Miss Carson's love of wildlife, and even with her mystical attachment to the balance of nature. But they fear that her emotional and inaccurate outburst in *Silent Spring* may do harm by alarming the nontechnical public, while doing no good for the things that she loves." *

* On April 18, 1969, *Time* printed a photograph of Rachel Carson at the head of their new section entitled "The Environment." The accompanying article began as follows: "Pesticides such as DDT, parathion, aldrin and dieldrin are both ally and enemy to man. The chemicals annihilate predators: the aphids that plague

The *Reader's Digest* followed suit. An option contract with Houghton Mifflin for a 20,000-word condensation of *Silent Spring*, signed two months prior to book publication, was canceled. Instead, the *Digest* ran an abridgment of the *Time* article. It is interesting to note that the view of the *Digest*, like that of *Time*, proved subject to change; some years later it was pointing with pride to the articles it had published on the dangers of pesticides.

This is but a small sampling of the opposition to *Silent Spring* that appeared in print. At the same time, TV, radio and the lecture platform were not neglected by the industry and its allies. For at least one individual, refutation of the book became a full-time job. In the words of *Croplife: A Businesspaper for the Farm Chemical Industry*, "Perhaps the most eloquent champion of the pesticide industry and its most indefatigable defender is Dr. Robert White-Stevens of the Research and Development Department of American Cyanamid Co. For many months he has been appearing before all types of groups in many parts of the nation, reminding his listeners of the continuing need for pesticides . . ." *Croplife* printed a picture of a clock with the "pressing schedule kept by Robert White-Stevens to silence *Silent Spring*." From the sample given, attacks apparently came on the average of one every forty minutes during waking hours. His theme was repetitious but clear: "If man were to faithfully follow the teachings of Miss Carson, we would return to the Dark Ages, and the insects and diseases and vermin would once again inherit the earth."

Rachel Carson's reaction to all this was predictable. Even had

---

rose fanciers, disease-bearing mosquitoes, beetles that spread Dutch elm disease, insects that devour crops. As a farmer's helper, pesticides increase crop yields, hence profits. But poison is blind. Loosed annually by the ton from planes, boats, trucks, tractors and handy spray cans, it cannot isolate its target. Since Rachel Carson exposed the pesticides' threat seven years ago, in *Silent Spring*, evidence of the chemicals' pernicious effects on birds, plants, fish, animals and occasionally man has continued to grow. Yet little in the way of effective control has been attempted — until now." The article went on to cite recent evidence completely supporting the statements made in *Silent Spring*.

her health permitted it, she had no desire to take an active part in the controversy. She did make one appearance — with White-Stevens and others — on the televised CBS Report, "The Silent Spring of Rachel Carson." From the multitude of invitations to speak, frequently in connection with some award, she accepted only the most essential. She stuck to the belief that the facts in her book spoke for themselves.

Though the controversy aroused by *Silent Spring* came as no surprise to the author, its instantaneous success, beginning with the *New Yorker* series, definitely did. "I never predicted the book would have a smashing success. I doubted it would, so all this is unexpected and wonderful to me . . ." Even better, it promised to get results: "The tremendous response that has come in letters to me and to the *New Yorker* Editor has been beyond all expectations and seems to indicate a strong desire on the part of the public to bring about some improvement in the situation." Once again, as in the case of *The Sea Around Us*, she was deluged with fan mail beyond her capacity to reply. It was a burden, yet it was also a great source of inner strength and satisfaction. Sometimes she would send a copy of a particularly moving letter to a friend. Such as this:

Dear Miss Carson:
I have a city boy's attraction to nature: this is, ignorant and undiscriminating, but reverential. And I must say thank you for the brilliant beginning to your series in *The New Yorker*. Not since I read *The Sea Around Us* years ago have I breathed so deep indoors.
I'm sure that you have been told many times that you are a poet as well as a scientist, but I wanted to say it to you myself. You are a poet not only because you use words so well, but because by describing non-human life without pathetic fallacies you make us readers understand our place on earth so much better. As I drive home along the Hudson tonight I'll feel more human for having read your lovely, loving words today. I know, too, that your great quiet eloquence will open many eyes and close many bottles.

Across the top of the letter is a note in her own hand: "This alone makes the long travail worth while."

On October 2, 1962, Rachel Carson was guest speaker at the annual meeting of the National Parks Association in Washington, whose publication, *National Parks Magazine*, was printing selections from *Silent Spring* in their November and December issues, as *Audubon Magazine* had in September and October. Clarence Cottam, president of the Association, presided. Carl Buchheister, president of the National Audubon Society, made a bold and eloquent address, in keeping with the strong position on pesticides that the Society — whose vice president, Roland C. Clement, was an expert in these matters — had taken from the start. Beneath blinding television lights, Rachel began her talk by recalling Dr. Cottam's pioneering studies, as assistant director of the Fish and Wildlife Service, on the effect of DDT on birds and fishes. "In retrospect," she said, "the problems about which we were disturbed then seem small indeed compared with those of the present. Instead of one chemical, as then, we now worry about scores, if not hundreds of extremely toxic pesticides. Instead of very limited use in crop dusting and forest sprays, we are now confronted with the spraying or dusting of areas ranging in size from a small suburban lawn to several millions of acres of forest or range lands.

"Between 1947 and 1960 the production of synthetic chemicals for use as pesticides increased five-fold. If plans and predictions are realized, this is merely a beginning."

She went on to stress the fact — so familiar today — that the pesticide problem must be understood in context, that it is part of a broader picture: "a picture marred by polluted rivers, by cities half hidden in a murky smog, by a world now visited by rains of radioactive fallout from the skies." She saw one hope for the future. From the mountains of mail she had received "a very striking thing has emerged — the reappearance of a sense of personal responsibility." The environmental revolution, whose full power she never lived to see, was gathering momentum.

On October 11 — two weeks after book publication — she addressed a conference sponsored by the National Council of Women of the United States. By then *Silent Spring* was on the best-seller list, destined to approach the top before the end of the month. She made only one reference to her critics: "There are those who would have you believe I advocate that we abandon all chemicals tomorrow and turn the world over to the insects. Those who say this have not read *Silent Spring* or, if they have, they do not wish to interpret it correctly. It would not be possible to abandon all chemicals tomorrow even if we wanted to. What we can and must do is to begin a determined and purposeful program of substitution, of replacing dangerous chemicals with new and even more efficient methods as rapidly as we can." The burden of her talk had to do with what she termed "perhaps the most important — as it is also the most neglected — aspect of this whole problem," that is, what pesticides may be doing to future generations.

Genetics, or the science of heredity, is a complex subject, studied by relatively few people. Its principles are not always understood in those places where important decisions are made. So I should like to digress briefly to trace the evolution of the idea that what we do today may affect tomorrow's children for good or ill. When I was a graduate student at Johns Hopkins University, studying under the great geneticist H. S. Jennings, the whole biological community was stirring with excitement over the recent discovery of another distinguished geneticist, Professor H. J. Muller, then at the University of Texas. Professor Muller had found that by exposing organisms to radiation he could produce those sudden changes in hereditary characteristics that biologists call mutations.

Before this it had been assumed that the germ cells were immutable — immune to influences in the environment. Muller's discovery meant that it was possible for many, by accident or design, to change the course of heredity, although the nature of the changes could not be controlled.

It was much later that two Scottish investigators discovered that certain chemicals have a similar power to produce mutations and in other ways to imitate radiation. This was before the days of the modern synthetic pesticides, and the chemical used in these experiments was mustard gas. But over the years it has been learned that one after another of the chemicals used as insecticides or as weedkillers has power to produce mutations in the organisms tested or to change or damage the chromosome structure in some other way. These discoveries have not been made as part of a manufacturer's tests of a chemical before it is marketed. They have rather been in the realm of what is sometimes called pure science.

She went on to point out that neither the manufacturers nor the Food and Drug Administration tested pesticides for genetic effects; indeed, the FDA did not even have a geneticist on its staff. This seemed to her "a very deplorable omission . . . There is something more than mere feminine intuition behind my concern about the possibility that our freewheeling use of pesticides may endanger generations yet unborn."

Though she had neither the strength nor the desire to engage in public debate, Rachel Carson did reply briefly to her critics in her speech to the Women's National Press Club on December 5, 1962. Her choice for her text was an item from a Bethlehem, Pennsylvania, newspaper, describing in detail the adverse reactions to *Silent Spring* in two county farm bureaus. The reporter continued: "No one in either county farm office who was talked to today had read the book, but all disapproved of it heartily." Rachel Carson went on to trace the public reaction beginning with the first installment in *The New Yorker*, which stimulated "a tidal wave of letters — letters to congressmen, to newspapers, to government agencies, to the author. These letters continue to come and I am sure represent the most important and lasting reaction." She described the defensive tactics of the chemical industry, which by late summer "had begun to pour out the first of a growing stream of booklets designed to protect and repair the somewhat battered image of pesticides" and which was making a coordinated drive on public opinion through mailings to opinion leaders, through news releases, canned editorials, radio and television programs, and lecturers throughout the country. "It is clear," she said, "that we are all to receive heavy doses of tranquilizing information, designed to lull the public into the sleep from which *Silent Spring* so rudely awakened it." The attack was falling into a definite pattern, in which all the well-known devices were being used. "One obvious way to try to weaken a cause is to discredit the person who champions it. So — the masters of invective and insinuation have been busy: I am a 'bird lover — a cat lover — a fish lover,' a priestess of nature, a devotee of a mystical cult having to do with laws of the universe which my critics consider themselves immune to. Another well-known, and much used, device is to misrepresent my position and attack the things I have never said . . . Another piece in the pattern of attack largely ignores *Silent Spring* and concentrates on what I suppose would be called the soft sell — the soothing reassurances to the public."

She also pointed out that "Inaccurate statements in reviews of *Silent Spring* are a dime a dozen," and went on to list a few easily documented examples, such as *Time* magazine's description of accidental poisoning from pesticides as "very rare" — whereas California alone (the only state to keep complete records) had 900 to 1000 cases a year. "Another reviewer," she said, "was offended because I made the statement that it is customary for pesticide manufacturers to support research on chemicals in the universities . . . I can scarcely believe the reviewer is unaware of it, because his own university is among those receiving such grants . . . Such a liaison between science and industry is a growing phenomenon, seen in other areas as well. The AMA, through its newspaper, has just referred physicians to a pesticide trade association for information to help them answer patients' questions about the effects of pesticides on man. I am sure physicians have a need for information on this subject. But I would like to see them referred to authoritative scientific or medical literature — not to a trade organization whose business it is to promote the sale of pesticides. We see scientific societies acknowledging as 'sustaining associates' a dozen or more giants of a related industry. When the scientific organization speaks, whose voice do we hear — that of science? or of the sustaining industry?"

Throughout the controversy, Rachel Carson's chief concern was that *Silent Spring* should have a lasting effect on government policy. In this area, conservationists suffered a real setback with the publication in 1962 of Parts 1 and 2 of a three-part report of the Committee on Pest Control and Wildlife Relationships of the National Academy of Sciences. Contrary to popular belief, the committee did not consist of members of the Academy, but was composed of representatives of universities, research institutions, the chemical industry, and conservation groups. Both the Departments of Agriculture and Interior were represented; but the latter was in the minority, as were the conservationists. The bitter reaction of many scientists to this report has been described in detail in *Since Silent Spring*. In brief, the industrial and agricultural representatives on the committee and subcommittees overrode protests of the conservationist minority that the report was weighted in industry's favor. Since the ground rules required unanimous approval, the minority view never got a public hearing, and the pesticides and agricultural interests were henceforth able to invoke the prestige of the Academy in defense of their position. The situation was, in fact, so bad that Dr. Clarence Cottam refused to sign Part 3 of the report until it was substantially modified a year later.

Nevertheless, progress was about to be made, at the highest level of government. As Paul Knight has pointed out in an unpublished account of events following *Silent Spring*'s publication, the pesticides controversy was given a new direction at the President's press conference on August 29, 1962.

Question: Mr. President, there appears to be a growing concern among scientists as to the possibility of dangerous long-range side effects from the use of DDT and other pesticides. Have you considered asking the Department of Agriculture or the Public Health Service to take a closer look at this?

Answer: Yes, and I know that they already are. I think particularly, of course, since Miss Carson's book, but they are examining the matter.

As a direct result of the furor over *Silent Spring*, President Kennedy requested Dr. Jerome B. Wiesner, his scientific adviser, to make a study of the whole issue. A Pesticides Committee was set up by the Office of Science and Technology, a Special Panel of the President's Science Advisory Committee. (Rachel Carson met informally with members of the Committee in late January, 1963.) When the report, *Use of Pesticides*, was released on May 15, it criticized both the industry and agencies of the federal government, particularly Agriculture and FDA. It also recognized the service performed by *Silent Spring*: "Public literature and the experiences of Panel Members indicate that, until the publication of *Silent Spring* by Rachel Carson, people were generally unaware of the toxicity of pesticides. The government should present this information to the public in a way that will make it aware of the dangers while recognizing the value of pesticides."

Though the report was not as severe in its recommendations as the industry had feared it might be, it amounted to an official scientific endorsement of Rachel Carson's position. Its whole approach supported her basic argument that we simply do not have enough scientific knowledge to assess accurately the risks we run when we use these poisons, and that they should be certified for safety before their first use. The chemical industry, of course, had taken the opposite view: that it is all right to use them unless the danger has been proved beyond reasonable doubt. This conflict of philosophies — which is not confined to pesticides — remains one of the basic conflicts of our time.

The report itself was widely accepted as a fair and accurate statement, even by some of those who had been the strongest opponents of government regulation. *Science*, the journal of the American Association for the Advancement of Science, had hitherto recognized *Silent Spring* only in one highly critical review. Now it commented: "The long awaited pesticides report of the President's Science Advisory Committee (PSAC) was issued last week, and, though it is a temperate document, even in tone, and carefully balanced in its assessment of risks versus benefits, it adds up to a fairly thorough-going vindication of Rachel Carson's *Silent Spring* thesis."

Rachel herself considered the report one of the most important government documents in many years. "I think no one can read this report and retain a shred of complacency about our situation," she wrote in a feature article for the New York *Herald Tribune*. "I am particularly pleased to see recognition given to what I consider the chief problem for man — the effect of long-continued exposure to small amounts of highly toxic chemicals. The widely publicized fact — if fact it be — that more people die of aspirin overdosage than of acute pesticide poisoning is quite beside the point, as the committee recognizes. Acute poisonings can usually be diagnosed and treated; not so the illness that comes on gradually and with obscure symptoms. The Panel found available clinical studies quite inadequate to predict the long-term effects of exposure even to DDT, the most studied of all the pesticides . . . One of the most refreshing recommendations is the call for full information to the public in the form of prompt reports on the actual effects of spray programs and the candid disclosure of the hazards of pesticides, where formerly only their benefits had been stressed."

But as she pointed out: "This excellent report alone does not solve our problem. It must now be translated into action. This is the task of the government agencies which, given the will, could act quickly. It is also the task of the Congress and state legislatures, where action will inevitably be slower. It is important to remember that pressures which opponents of reform know how to apply will continue unabated. The now awakened public must see that its views are also made known. These are social problems of the greatest public importance. The decisions affect every individual. As the Panel points out: 'In the end society must decide, and to do so it must obtain adequate information on which to base its judgments.' The Panel itself has made a notable contribution to this end."

CHAPTER 21

THE CLOSING JOURNEY

THE PUBLICATION of the President's Science Advisory Committee report had marked a turning point in the controversy aroused by *Silent Spring*. By corroborating Rachel Carson's essential thesis, the report changed the nature of the debate. No one could any longer deny that the problem existed; the question now was what we were willing to do about it — i.e., how the recommendations in the report could be implemented. Rachel Carson lived only long enough to see the beginnings of this second stage. The long, tedious, continuing battle to save the environment — which, in her quiet way, she helped so much to bring about — is beyond the scope of this book. She did, however, play an important role in the initial steps toward legislative action. The day after the report was released, hearings began before a Senate committee on environmental hazards — the so-called "Ribicoff Committee." One of the opening witnesses was Dr. Wiesner, who characterized pesticide hazards from DDT and related compounds as potentially more serious than nuclear fallout. On June 4, 1963, Rachel herself appeared before the committee. Her testimony has a note of urgency.

The problem you have chosen to explore is one that must be solved in our time. I feel strongly that a beginning must be made on it now — in this session of Congress . . . I have pointed out before, and I shall repeat now, that the problem of pesticides can be properly understood only in context, as a part of the general introduction of harmful substances into the environment . . .

She put particular stress on the helplessness of the ordinary citizen who is subjected to personal or other injury by government-sponsored pest control programs, and who generally finds that he has no legal recourse. She emphasized the ignorance of the medical profession — with certain notable exceptions — in respect to this very important health hazard.

The plight of the person affected by these poisons is pitiful. Many case histories have come to me in letters. As a rule these people can find no physician who understands their problem. Indeed, I remember several cases in current medical literature in which the physician, even though told of the patient's exposure to such relatively common insecticides as malathion or lindane, had never heard of the chemical and did not know the appropriate treatment. About ten years ago the American Medical Association had a special committee on pesticides which from time to time published authoritative information on the toxicology of these chemicals. I have seen none of these reports for several years. I do not know whether the committee is still functioning; if it is, it is hard to see why the American Medical Association last fall recommended that physicians seek information to allay their patients' fears, not from unbiased scientific literature, but from one of the pesticide trade organizations.

I should like to emphasize, however, that many individual physicians are aware of the hazard and of the need for research in this field. Some of the most interesting letters I receive are from doctors.

She introduced into the record what she believed to be the first recognition of this problem by a medical organization: the resolution recently passed by the Illinois Medical Society on "Study and Evaluation of Toxicants."

Two days later, Rachel Carson appeared before the Senate Committee on Commerce, which was considering two bills aimed at resolving the conflict between agricultural and wildlife interests. Both she felt needed strengthening. "As perhaps you know," she testified, "I speak not as an outsider, but as one who has had some 16 years' experience as a government biologist. I therefore am aware of the problems, the frustrations, the inevitable conflicts that arise when two or more agencies attempt to carry out their sometimes conflicting mandates. In the course of the more than five years I have spent in intensive study of the pesticide problem, I have arrived at the conclusion that the conflicts inherent in this problem can be resolved only by an independent board or commission to be set up at the level of the Executive Offices." She also emphasized the statement in the President's Science Advisory Committee report that "the Secretary of the Interior should actively participate in decisions concerning the registration of all pesticides for uses that may affect fish and wildlife."

Secretary of the Interior Stewart L. Udall was one of Rachel Carson's staunchest supporters. As Paul Knight remarked later: "At that time Interior stood almost alone among Federal agencies in considering the persistent pesticides as serious and possibly permanent contaminants." Mr. Knight also stressed Rachel Carson's broad interest in policy questions, "especially how government could be made more responsive to the whole problem of environmental pollution, of which she considered the pesticide controversy but one element." (Or as Rachel Carson herself put it at the time: "The problem I dealt with in *Silent Spring* is not an isolated one. It is merely one part of a sorry whole — the reckless pollution of our living world with harmful and dangerous substances. Until very recently, the average citizen assumed that 'someone' was looking after these matters and that some little understood but confidently relied upon safeguards stood like shields between his person and any harm. But now he has experienced a rather rude shattering of these beliefs.")

"In dealing with personalities," continues Mr. Knight, "she did not impugn motives but nevertheless was most forthright in questioning judgments made by them. Here I think she was much too generous . . . But I believe she regarded many of her critics in agriculture and industry as prostitutes and kept scientists, regardless of what her attitude was publicly. As you well know, she approached problems most cautiously but once she had made a judgment would defend it tenaciously against people who were *presumably* better informed. In the end, it became obvious that she was many, many times better informed than her critics although she was a newcomer to the field. Basically, I think this was because she approached the problem from the viewpoint of *basic science,* while the agro-chemical community functioned at the *technician* level."

The political repercussions of *Silent Spring* were not confined to the federal government in Washington, or even to this country. By the spring of 1963 the book had become almost as famous in England as it was in America. It already had the endorsement of Prince Philip: "I strongly recommend Rachel Carson's *Silent Spring* if you want to see what is going on." Published on February 14 by Hamish Hamilton, with a preface by Sir Julian Huxley and an introduction by Lord Shackleton, it had been an immediate success. "Miss Rachel Carson's book, *Silent Spring,*" wrote the *Times Literary Supplement,* "had a profound effect on American opinion when it was launched last year. Its message is no less important for us." Feature articles considered at length the pesticides threat in Britain which, as one writer put it, was as yet less ravaged than America, but where the same class of poisons — particularly in seed dressing — was already causing havoc. "In Britain," wrote W. H. Thorpe, the distinguished zoologist at Cambridge University, "we are not so far advanced along this dangerous path as they are in the U.S., but our long-term risks are the same. How is it that this threat has come about? Largely because of ignorance, insufficient fundamental research, complacency, vested interests and lack of public awareness. Miss Carson's book should remove the last obstacle once and for all."

A month after publication occurred the famous debate in the House of Lords, in which Lord Shackleton referred to "the story of the cannibal in Polynesia who now no longer allows his tribe to eat Americans because their fat is contaminated with chlorinated hydrocarbons." He was speaking, the noble Lord explained, "purely in the interests of the export trade. The figure shows that we are rather more edible than Americans . . . that we have about 2 parts per million of DDT in our bodies, whereas the figure for Americans is about 11 parts per million." Quoted on both sides of the Atlantic, his deadpan humor was worth a good deal of more solemn publicity.

The English edition of *Silent Spring* had instant repercussions as far away as South Africa and Australia. Translations were, of course, already under way. During 1963, *Silent Spring* was published in France, Germany, Italy, Denmark, Sweden, Norway, Finland, and Holland. Shortly thereafter it appeared in Spain, Brazil, Japan, Iceland, Portugal, and Israel. Thus was laid the groundwork for later legislation, such as that in Sweden, which was far in advance of the half measures taken by our own government in the United States.

Rachel could view all this only at long distance. Her English publishers, Hamish Hamilton, had invited her to London to help publicize the launching of their edition. Her Swedish publisher, Tidens förlag, invited her to give a lecture at the University of Upsala. But poor health made such trips out of the question. Meanwhile, at home she continued to use her influence and knowledge wherever it would be effective. She kept on collecting information from all over the country, such for example, as the death of thousands of ducks in the poisoned "industrial lakes" near the Rocky Mountain Arsenal in Denver, Colorado. "I shall be grateful," she wrote to her correspondent, "if you will pass on to me any other information about local happenings. I am trying to collect as much as possible of this sort to counteract the industry campaign to the effect that all untoward happenings related to pesticides occurred some time in the past and that we now have complete and adequate control of the situation." Nearer home, she joined the fight to save from private exploitation wild, windswept Assateague Island off the Maryland coast, site of the Chincoteague National Wildlife Refuge she had described so many years ago in a booklet for the Fish and Wildlife Service. She was deeply concerned with the irresponsible "control" policies of both the Service and the state fish and game departments, such as the ill-conceived poisoning of "trash fish" in Utah's Green River, or the massive "wolf control" in Arkansas where, as Clarence Cottam remarked, "there are more control workers than there are wolves." "I am particularly glad to know," she wrote to Dr. Cottam, "that you and your associates on the committee appointed by Secretary Udall are working on the problem of predator control. This has long seemed to me an area in which the Fish and Wildlife Service is most vulnerable to criticism and one in which I can be least happy with its activities." In this same letter (written only three months before her death), she asked whether he was aware of any extensive use in this country of a deadly chemical called fluoroacetamide, which had been responsible for the notorious "Smarden Affair" — a disaster in which cows and domestic animals had been killed in an English farm village, and which subsequently required dumping two thousand tons of poisoned topsoil into the Atlantic Ocean. In describing the incident, London's *Daily Mail* wrote: "An American woman, Rachel Carson, wrote a book last year that frightened and horrified her countrymen . . . She was, in fact, reinforcing warnings given by British experts. But we were assured that it could not happen here. That it can happen here is shown by the dreadful story from Smarden, Kent, which the Minister of Agriculture told the Commons yesterday."

During the last year of her life, Rachel Carson was showered with honors and awards. Since it was physically impossible for her to receive them all in person — as it was impossible for her to accept countless invitations for public appearances and speaking engagements — she had to choose how best to ration her limited time and strength. "So many ironic things," she wrote to a friend, when a heart attack, on top of her other ailments, had rendered her almost an invalid. "Now all the 'honors' have to be received for me by someone else. And all the opportunities to travel to foreign lands — all expenses paid — have to be passed up." In pain much of the time, she was wearier than ever, probably as a result of heavy radiation treatments. "Sometimes I wish I had nothing to do, but probably it is better to keep my mind occupied. But the never dwindling piles of letters sometimes oppress me — like a treadmill — and I wonder how to get free to think about the book I still have to write." Her reputation was now so great that the mere use of her name gave weight to any cause. "I keep thinking — if only I could have reached this point ten years ago! Now, when there is an opportunity to do so much, my body falters and I know there is little time left. But it is making it all the more necessary to be rid of the tyranny of 'pieces of paper' — to use the months or years that remain to do what I can that is *worth* doing, not remain trapped in trivia."

She had no intention of giving up. As she wrote to Dr. George Crile, Jr., of the Cleveland Clinic (whom she had depended upon as physician and friend ever since her condition had become apparent two and a half years earlier): "I still believe in the old Churchillian determination to fight each battle as it comes ('We shall fight on the beaches' . . . etc.) and I think a determination to win may well postpone the final battle."

One award that Rachel Carson received in person — on January 7, 1963 — was of particular personal significance. *Silent*

Spring had been dedicated to Albert Schweitzer. Now the author was the recipient of the Schweitzer Medal of the Animal Welfare Institute. Her response shows how much it meant to her:

I can think of no award that would have more meaning for me or that would touch me more deeply than this one, coupled as it is with the name of Albert Schweitzer. To me, Dr. Schweitzer is the one truly great individual our modern times have produced. If, during the coming years, we are to find our way through the problems that beset us, it will surely be in large part through a wider understanding and application of his principles.

I often reread his own account of the day when there suddenly dawned in his mind the concept of Reverence for Life. In few words, yet so vividly, he describes that scene on a remote river in Africa. He had traveled laboriously upstream for three days in a small river steamer, traveling 160 miles to treat the ailing wife of a missionary. On the way he had been deep in thought, struggling to formulate that universal concept he had been unable to find in any philosophy.

At sunset on the third day the steamer came upon a herd of hippopotami. Suddenly there flashed into his mind the phrase, "Reverence for Life," which all the world now knows.

He gives us few details — just that sand-choked river at sunset, the herd of great beasts — but there it was, that flash of deep insight, that sudden awareness.

In his various writings, we may read Dr. Schweitzer's philosophical interpretation of that phrase. But to many of us, the truest understanding of Reverence for Life comes, as it did to him, from some personal experience, perhaps the sudden, unexpected sight of a wild creature, perhaps some experience with a pet. Whatever it may be, it is something that takes us out of ourselves, that makes us aware of other life.

From my own store of memories, I think of the sight of a small crab alone on a dark beach at night, a small and fragile being waiting at the edge of the roaring surf, yet so perfectly at home in its world. To me it seemed a symbol of life, and of the way life has adjusted to the forces of its physical environment. Or I think of a morning when I stood in a North Carolina marsh at

sunrise, watching flock after flock of Canada geese rise from resting places at the edge of a lake and pass low overhead. In that
orange light, their plumage was like brown velvet. Or I have
found that deep awareness of life and its meaning in the eyes of
a beloved cat.

Dr. Schweitzer has told us that we are not being truly civilized
if we concern ourselves only with the relation of man to man.
What is important is the relation of man to all life. This has
never been so tragically overlooked as in our present age, when
through our technology we are waging war against the natural
world. It is a valid question whether any civilization can do this
and retain the right to be called civilized. By acquiescing in needless destruction and suffering, our stature as human beings is
diminished.

All the world pays tribute to Dr. Schweitzer, but all too seldom
do we put his philosophy into practice. The Schweitzer Medal is
one means of disseminating the thoughts and ideals of this great
man. I am very proud, and also very humble, to be a recipient
of this award.

A significant aspect of the award to Rachel Carson was
brought out in an article written shortly after her death by the
journalist and author Ann Cottrell Free, who herself received the
Schweitzer Medal the following year — and who was later responsible for getting the Department of the Interior to name
their new Maine coast wildlife reserve the Rachel Carson National Wildlife Refuge. "During the last tragic but triumphant
days of her life," wrote Mrs. Free, "another dimension opened
up for Rachel Carson. Had she lived, not only would she have
continued as nature's most articulate spokesman and the person
to make 'ecology' a household word, she would have done a great
deal more for animals. She had always been humane. She would
pick up the stray cat, rescue the injured dog, return sea specimens to the sea after examination under the microscope. She
did not look at the efforts of the humanitarian groups as unrelated to those of naturalists. Rachel Carson knew that exerting
her strength to end other abuses would not only exhaust her, but

lay her open to attacks by her detractors as a 'do-gooder.' But she did the best she could in the time allowed.

"She sent a message to a Congressional Committee urging federal standards for protection of animals used in research. She wrote a forceful foreword to a 1964 British book, *Animal Machines*, by Ruth Harrison that attacks the intensified methods of raising livestock.

"A short while before she died she became a member of the Board of Directors of the Defenders of Wildlife. Incensed by the cruel predator control programs of wanton poisoning of wildlife by the federal government, Rachel Carson would have been one of the great fighters to eliminate these excesses.

"She looked at abuse of animals this way: 'It is my belief that man will never be at peace with his own kind until he has recognized the Schweitzerian ethic that embraced decent consideration for all creatures — a true reverence for life.' "

Later in January, Rachel Carson spoke in Boston before the New England Wildflower Preservation Society, stressing once more that destruction of wildlife by pesticides "did not stop with the publication of *Silent Spring*," and attacking the policy of roadside spraying with herbicides that was replacing wildflowers and ferns and shrubs with virtually lifeless strips. In the same speech, she anticipated an issue that was soon to become of major concern to the whole conservation movement: the threatened loss of tax-exempt status by nonprofit organizations that devote a "substantial" part of their activities to influencing legislation, while at the same time private firms may deduct the cost of lobbying as a business expense. "It means, to cite a specific example, that the chemical industry may now work at bargain rates to thwart future attempts at regulation."

During the course of the speech, she quoted with amusement a bit of wishful thinking published in one of the chemical trade magazines: "Industry can take heart from the fact that the main impact of the book will occur in the late fall or winter — seasons when consumers are not normally active buyers of insecticides . . . It is fair to hope that by March or April *Silent Spring* no longer will be an interesting conversational subject." "If the tone of my mail from readers is any guide," she commented, "and if the movements that have already been launched gain the expected momentum, this is one prediction that will not come true."

The same week that she spoke in Boston Rachel Carson received a letter that showed a rare understanding of the deeper meaning of her life and work. It was from Thomas Merton, written from the Abbey of Gethsemani, Trappist, Kentucky. He not only found *Silent Spring* exact and persuasive, but also considered it essential evidence in diagnosing the ills of contemporary civilization. Unless we understand the sickness, our remedies will only aggravate it. "I would almost dare to say that the sickness is perhaps a very real and very dreadful hatred of life as such, of course subconscious, buried under our pitiful and superficial optimism about ourselves and our affluent society." In order to survive in that society, we are, in our lack of humility, destroying that on which our survival depends. Her book, Merton felt, sounded a most salutary and important warning.

〰〰〰

In early March 1963, Rachel Carson received the "Conservationist of the Year" award of the National Wildlife Federation. A month later came the major television appearance previously referred to: "The Silent Spring of Rachel Carson," on "CBS Reports," where her principal antagonist was Dr. Robert White-Stevens. When she had read the advance news release from CBS, she got the impression that the show (which was put together from previously taped interviews) would be weighted against her. She was also concerned about her own appearance on the screen. "I just hope I don't look and sound like an utter idiot. When I remember my state of extreme exhaustion those two days, plus the huskiness of voice, I can't be too optimistic." She need not have worried. The contrast between the approach and the appearance of the two chief advocates could scarcely have been sharper, and the documentation spoke for itself. She concluded her testimony: "We still talk in terms of conquest. We still haven't become mature enough to think of ourselves as only a tiny part of a vast and incredible universe. Man's attitude toward nature is today critically important simply because we have now acquired a fateful power to alter and destroy nature. But man is a part of nature and his war against nature is inevitably a war against himself. The rains have become an instrument to bring down from the atmosphere the deadly products of atomic explosions. Water, which is probably our most important natural resource, is now used and re-used with incredible recklessness. Now, I truly believe that we in this generation must come to terms with nature, and I think we're challenged as mankind has never been challenged before to prove our maturity and our mastery, not of nature, but of ourselves."

Throughout these difficult months, Rachel Carson was sustained, as always, by the world of living nature for whose preservation she had fought so boldly and so well. On March 12, while shopping in Silver Spring with her devoted housekeeper Ida Sprow, she had seen a huge V of geese: "I sped on out Colesville Road to try to get closer. They were shifting about, changing formation, and finally headed off almost south, at right angles to their earlier course. When we came near, I stopped to listen, but they were silent. What a thrill just to see them! Cowbirds arrived yesterday. Sunday there were 11 robins on the lawn at sunset." A week later. "Oh — at long last, the first thin bubble of frog song came from the swamp Sunday night, after a warm, sunny day. And last evening I heard the first robin song. So spring is not to be silent!"

Though the Garden Club of America had already given

Rachel Carson their highest conservation award (the Frances Hutchinson Medal), they decided to honor her work on *Silent Spring* with a "Special Commendation" at the annual meeting, to take place in Philadelphia in early May. The long program was an ordeal ("I know now — if never before — why I have never been a clubwoman!") but she felt it important that she put in an appearance. As she wrote to a friend on another occasion: "I have now reached that state of eminence where my sniffles, like the President's, are news. The morning paper explains my failure to appear at the Air Pollution Conference with a fairly conspicuous article carrying the heading, 'Author of *Silent Spring* Silenced by Cold.' What good news in chemical circles!"

In mid-June, she was the recipient of yet another important conservation award, from the Isaak Walton League of America. Finally late in the month, accompanied by her adopted son Roger, now eleven years old, and her two beloved cats, she drove to Maine for what was to be her last summer in her cottage at the edge of the sea. For once she did not take along a new manuscript to work on; to deal with the correspondence arising from *Silent Spring* was in itself a major job. Though she did not look particularly ill, and managed to do the cooking and household chores, the cancer in her bones caused her to move with difficulty; her heart was troubling her and the arthritis in her hands made writing painful. Nevertheless, she worked in her study mornings; on pleasant afternoons, she liked to go to a little clearing in the woods nearby with her dear friend and neighbor, Dorothy Freeman, where she could watch the sky and the clouds, the gulls soaring overhead and the songbirds among the trees. "She liked to be read to," recalls her friend. "One of her favorites was *Wind in the Willows*. Then anything of E. B. White's — also H. M. Tomlinson, Richard Jefferies, Henry Beston . . ." Nor did she lose her interest in the minute creatures of the tide pools, though others had to bring them to her microscope. "It wasn't an unhappy summer for any of us," as Mrs. Freeman remembers it. "All too soon it was over. Rachel never left Maine in the fall without a pang. This time, just as she was about to leave, one of her cats fell ill, and died after two weeks in the hospital — a sad prelude to the long and taxing journey back to Maryland."

In mid-October, Rachel realized a lifelong ambition to see the California redwoods. Despite the fact that she was now virtually confined to a wheelchair, she had determined to carry through with a lecture engagement at the Kaiser Medical Center in San Francisco. Marie Rodell accompanied her. Following the lecture, they visited Muir Woods with the Sierra Club leader and conservationist, David Brower, and his wife Anne. "We had a wonderful morning in the Muir Woods yesterday with the Browers," she wrote to me, "the best part of the trip, really. Now I'm leaving in the morning — really hating to miss seeing more of this lovely country before I go." Brower later summarized the reasons for Rachel Carson's effectiveness in a single sentence: "She did her homework, she minded her English, and she cared."

Just as she was leaving for San Francisco, Rachel had written in response to a telephone call from Lois Crisler, whom she was still helping to get over her "writing block." Rachel urged Lois to take a "sabbatical" as the one way to get her current book written. "But how can one know what is really in the heart of another? My solutions may not be yours."

To the end of Rachel's life, she and Lois had a mutually creative relationship, in which joys as well as problems were shared. And so we have in her own words Rachel's reaction to the three signal honors that came to her all at once at the close of this memorable year. In late November she wrote to Lois: "I go to New York next week for what has turned out to be an extraordinary constellation of events. I know you will enjoy being reminded, and having some news you don't know. You have heard, I am sure, that I receive the Audubon Medal Dec. 3 at the annual dinner of the National Audubon Society. This is the

10th (or maybe 11th) time it has been given in 16 years, and the first to a woman. Then on the 5th I receive the Cullum Medal of the American Geographical Society, also at a formal dinner. They set great store by the award and I am truly pleased to be a recipient.

"But this you *don't* know — because I heard it less than 48 hours ago! A letter from Lewis Mumford, President of the American Academy of Arts and Letters, tells me I have been elected to membership. Really, Lois, this is about the most deeply satisfying thing that has happened in the 'honors department.' As you may know, membership in the Academy is limited to 50 and includes artists, sculptors and musicians as well as writers . . . at present there are only three women in the Academy (Pearl Buck, Marianne Moore, and an artist whose name escapes me). Looking back through the 60-year history of the Academy, there seem never to have been more than about a dozen women. I truly never expected this to happen. For one thing, the writers chosen are usually novelists or poets. The strange thing is that this, too, happens next week. The day after the Geographic dinner, I'm asked to attend a luncheon and annual meeting of the Academy, at which announcements of new members will be made. It is so convenient, but so surprising, that these three unrelated events should all be taking place in New York, within a few days . . . I have written this at the hospital, in waiting intervals while having new X-rays of various bones. Now I can tell you that the pictures for the most part confirm the improvement that has been obvious otherwise. There is one trouble area (new) in the neck vertebrae, and this is causing the numbness in my hand. However, Dr. Caulk is confident a few treatments will help that too, so I'll have them when I return from New York. On the whole, however, things look very good and I feel I have been handed a nice new chunk of borrowed time — enough that some of those 'dreams unrealized' may yet come true.

"And how goes it with you, dear Lois, and with the writing? Let me hear briefly, soon."

The Academy citation read as follows: "Rachel Carson will be the sixth occupant of seat nineteen, that was last occupied by Lee Lawrie. A scientist in the grand literary style of Galileo and Buffon, she has used her scientific knowledge and moral feeling to deepen our consciousness of living nature and to alert us to the calamitous possibility that our short-sighted technological conquests might destroy the very sources of our being. Who could better exemplify the humanist tradition of this Academy?"

As the year 1964 opened, Rachel Carson was aware that her time was running out. Yet she continued to hope. "I am able to feel that another reprieve can perhaps be won," she wrote to Dorothy Freeman. "As perhaps you realized, when I left Southport I didn't expect to return. Now it seems possible that there might be yet another summer. But we do know that now every month, every day, is precious." She maintained an active interest in the "environmental revolution" that had been touched off by *Silent Spring*. In mid-January appeared the paperback edition; two printings totaling 600,000 copies. On March 23, three weeks before her death, a feature article (headed by her photograph) appeared in the New York *Herald Tribune*, on the subject of the massive fish kills in the Mississippi River, which had finally and definitively been traced to pesticides. " 'How does Rachel Carson look now?' a reporter asked a group of Public Health Service officials and scientists last week. 'She looks pretty good,' one answered."

A year earlier, in the spring of 1963, when she already realized that she probably did not have long to live, Rachel wrote: "It is good to know that I shall live on even in the minds of many who do not know me and largely through association with things that are beautiful and lovely." In looking back across Rachel Carson's life work, it is important, I think, not to allow the smoke of battle that lay over the *Silent Spring* controversy to obscure the sunlight that shone through all her writing, even when she was facing up to the "ugly facts" of man's destruction of the world she loved. Not long after *The Sea Around Us* was published, she gave a talk which contained, in its concluding remarks, "A statement of something I believe in very deeply." Much of the statement was to appear in *The Sense of Wonder.*

A Statement of Belief

A large part of my life [she said] has been concerned with some of the beauties and mysteries of this earth about us, and with the even greater mysteries of the life that inhabits it. No one can dwell long among such subjects without thinking rather deep thoughts, without asking himself searching and often unanswerable questions, and without achieving a certain philosophy.

There is one quality that characterizes all of us who deal with the sciences of the earth and its life — we are never bored. We can't be. There is always something new to be investigated. Every mystery solved brings us to the threshold of a greater one.

I like to remember the wonderful old Swedish oceanographer, Otto Petterson. He died a few years ago at the age of ninety-three, in full possession of his keen mental powers. His son, also a distinguished oceanographer, tells us in a recent book how intensely his father enjoyed every new experience, every new discovery concerning the world about him. "He was an incurable romantic," the son wrote, "intensely in love with life and with the mysteries of the Cosmos which, he was firmly convinced, he had been born to unravel." When, past ninety, Otto Petterson realized he had not much longer to enjoy the earthly scene, he said to his son: "What will sustain me in my last moments is an infinite curiosity as to what is to follow." ["To me," she wrote on another occasion, "that sort of feeling is an acceptable substitute for the old fashioned 'certainties' as to heaven and what it must be like. I know that we do not really 'know' and I'm content that it should be so."]

The pleasures [she continued], the values of contact with the natural world are not reserved for the scientists. They are available to anyone who will place himself under the influence of a lonely mountain top — or the sea — or the stillness of a forest; or who will stop to think about so small a thing as the mystery of a growing seed.

I am not afraid of being thought a sentimentalist when I say that I believe natural beauty has a necessary place in the spiritual development of any individual or any society. I believe that whenever we destroy beauty, or whenever we substitute something man-made and artificial for a natural feature of the earth, we have retarded some part of man's spiritual growth . . .

We see the destructive trend on a national scale in proposals to invade the national parks with commercial schemes such as the building of power dams. The parks were placed in trust for all the people, to preserve for them just such recreational and spiritual values as I have mentioned. Is it the right of this, our generation, in its selfish materialism, to destroy these things because we are blinded by the dollar sign? Beauty — and all the values that derive from beauty — are not measured and evaluated in terms of the dollar.

Years ago I discovered in the writings of the British naturalist Richard Jefferies a few lines that so impressed themselves upon my mind that I have never forgotten them.

The exceeding beauty of the earth, in her splendor of life, yields a new thought with every petal. The hours when the mind is absorbed by beauty are the only hours when we really live. All else is illusion, or mere endurance.

Those lines are, in a way, a statement of the creed I have lived by . . . I have had the privilege of receiving many letters from people who, like myself, have been steadied and reassured by contemplating the long history of the earth and sea, and the deeper meanings of the world of nature . . . In contemplating "the exceeding beauty of the earth" these people have found calmness and courage. For there is symbolic as well as actual beauty in the migration of birds; in the ebb and flow of the tides; in the folded bud ready for the spring. There is something infinitely healing in these repeated refrains of nature — the assurance that dawn comes after night, and spring after the winter.

Mankind has gone very far into an artificial world of his own creation . . . But I believe that the more clearly we can focus our attention on the wonders and realities of the universe about us, the less taste we shall have for destruction.

∽∾∽

In early September of that last summer in Maine, Rachel and Dorothy Freeman spent a morning on the rocky point at the tip of the peninsula south of her cottage. Here they witnessed a fall migration of Monarch butterflies. Later in the day, Rachel wrote a note to her friend:

This is a postscript to our morning at Newagen, something I think I can write better than say. For me it was one of the loveliest of the summer's hours, and all the details will remain in my memory: that blue September sky, the sounds of wind in the spruces and surf on the rocks, the gulls busy with their foraging, alighting with deliberate grace, the distant views of Griffiths Head and Todd Point, today so clearly etched, though once seen in swirling fog. But most of all I shall remember the Monarchs, that unhurried drift of one small winged form after another, each drawn by some invisible force. We talked a little about their life history. Did they return? We thought not; for most, at least, this was the closing journey of their lives.

But it occurred to me this afternoon, remembering, that it had been a happy spectacle, that we had felt no sadness when we spoke of the fact that there would be no return. And rightly — for when any living thing has come to the end of its cycle we accept that end as natural. For the Monarch butterfly, that cycle is measured in a known span of months. For ourselves, the measure is something else, the span of which we cannot know. But the thought is the same: when that intangible cycle has run its course it is a natural and not unhappy thing that a life comes to its end.

That is what those brightly fluttering bits of life taught me this morning. I found a deep happiness in it — so, I hope, may you. Thank you for this morning.

Rachel Carson died in Silver Spring, Maryland, on April 14, 1964, at the age of fifty-six. In her own words: "For all at last return to the sea — to Oceanus, the ocean river, like the ever-flowing stream of time, the beginning and the end."

∽∽∽

No better epitaph could be written for Rachel Carson than the final passage in *The Edge of the Sea*, which she also had wished to be read at her funeral service.*

"The Enduring Sea"

Now I hear the sea sounds about me; the night high tide is rising, swirling with a confused rush of waters against the rocks below my study window. Fog has come into the bay from the open sea,

* This was not done. However on the Sunday following Rachel Carson's death, April 19, 1964, her friend Dr. Duncan Howlett read the letter to Dorothy Freeman about the Monarch butterflies as part of the service at All Souls Unitarian Church in Washington. Long an admirer of her work, Dr. Howlett had preached sermons based on both *The Sea Around Us* and *Silent Spring*. He prefaced the reading of the letter — which made a great impact on the congregation — with the following statement:

"Last week one of the true prophets of our time, Rachel Carson, died here in Washington. She had asked me to read at her funeral service certain passages which expressed her philosophy. Her wish was denied. I therefore take this opportunity to do as I promised, and in her memory shall read a passage from her own hand which expresses in a remarkable way the strength, the simplicity and the serenity that marked her character.

"We are already familiar with the extraordinary depth of insight and high poetic quality that marked her published writings. The following passage was not written for publication. It is a letter to a close friend, written but a few months ago when Rachel Carson already knew her time on earth might be short."

and it lies over water and over the land's edge, seeping back into the spruces and stealing softly among the juniper and the bayberry. The restive waters, the cold wet breath of the fog, are of a world in which man is an uneasy trespasser; he punctuates the night with the complaining groan and grunt of a foghorn, sensing the power and menace of the sea.

Hearing the rising tide, I think how it is pressing also against other shores I know — rising on a southern beach where there is no fog, but a moon edging all the waves with silver and touching the wet sands with lambent sheen, and on a still more distant shore sending its streaming currents against the moonlit pinnacles and the dark caves of the coral rock.

Then in my thoughts these shores, so different in their nature and in the inhabitants they support, are made one by the unifying touch of the sea. For the differences I sense in this particular instant of time that is mine are but the differences of a moment, determined by our place in the stream of time and in the long rhythms of the sea. Once this rocky coast beneath me was a plain of sand; then the sea rose and found a new shore line. And again in some shadowy future the surf will have ground these rocks to sand and will have returned the coast to its earlier state. And so in my mind's eye these coastal forms merge and blend in a shifting, kaleidoscopic pattern in which there is no finality, no ultimate and fixed reality — earth becoming fluid as the sea itself.

On all these shores there are echoes of past and future: of the flow of time, obliterating yet containing all that has gone before; of the sea's eternal rhythms — the tides, the beat of surf, the pressing rivers of the currents — shaping, changing, dominating; of the stream of life, flowing as inexorably as any ocean current, from past to unknown future. For as the shore configuration changes in the flow of time, the pattern of life changes, never static, never quite the same from year to year. Whenever the sea builds a new coast, waves of living creatures surge against it, seeking a foothold, establishing their colonies. And so we come to perceive life as a force as tangible as any of the physical realities of the sea, a force strong and purposeful, as incapable of being crushed or diverted from its ends as the rising tide.

Contemplating the teeming life of the shore, we have an uneasy sense of the communication of some universal truth that lies just beyond our grasp. What is the message signaled by the hordes of diatoms, flashing their microscopic lights in the night sea? What truth is expressed by the legions of the barnacles, whitening the rocks with their habitations, each small creature within finding the necessities of its existence in the sweep of the surf? And what is the meaning of so tiny a being as the transparent wisp of protoplasm that is a sea lace, existing for some reason inscrutable to us — a reason that demands its presence by the trillion amid the rocks and weeds of the shore? The meaning haunts and ever eludes us, and in its very pursuit we approach the ultimate mystery of Life itself.

SOURCES

CHAPTER 1: THE WRITER AND HIS SUBJECT

CHAPTER 2: TWO CURRENTS MEET

page
14 Mrs. L. L. King to Paul Brooks, July 16, 1971
15 RC to Dorothy Freeman, undated
16 RC, speech to Theta Sigma Phi (the national fraternity for women in journalism), April 21, 1954
16 Ibid.
16 RC to Elizabeth Pilant, July 8, 1956
16 RC to Curtis Bok, July 12, 1956
17 RC to Mrs. ——— McBride, for Pennsylvania College *Reporter*, Spring 1954
17 RC to Dorothy Freeman, November 8, 1954
20 RC, speech to Theta Sigma Phi, April 21, 1954
20 Philip Sterling, *Sea and Earth: The Life of Rachel Carson*, New York, 1970, p. 91
20 RC, speech to Theta Sigma Phi, April 21, 1954

CHAPTER 4: FIRSTBORN

30 RC, speech to Theta Sigma Phi, April 21, 1954
30 RC to Gerard Willem van Loon, July 13, 1962
32 Mrs. Glenn H. Algire to PB, February 15, 1970
33 RC to Dorothy Freeman, undated
34 Foreword, *Under the Sea-Wind*
35 RC to Curtis Bok, May 7, 1956

CHAPTER 6: WASHINGTON: WAR AND POSTWAR

69 RC, speech to Theta Sigma Phi, April 21, 1954
69 RC to Ada C. Govan, February 15, 1947
70 RC to Sonia Bleeker (Mrs. Herbert Zim), March 31, 1942
70 RC to Maria Lieper, February 8, 1942
70 Ibid., April 9, 1942
71 RC to Sonia Bleeker, March 15, 1942
71 Bob Hines to PB
71 RC to Maria Lieper, March 15, 1942
75 RC to Sonia Bleeker, March 17, 1944
75 RC to Marie Rodell, August 8, 1948
75 RC to Sonia Bleeker, December 29, 1944
75 Ibid., November 28, 1944
75 Ibid., January 8, 1945
76 Ibid., March 5, 1945
76 RC to William Beebe, October 26, 1945

page
124 Ibid., December 16, 1950
124 RC to Catherine Scott, January 21, 1951
125 RC to Marie Rodell, June 14, 1951
125 Ibid., June 10, 1951
125 Ibid., June 1951
127 RC to Nada Kramer, September 3, 1951
127n RC to Philip Vaudrin, June 1 and July 24, 1950
129 RC to Fon Boardman, February 20, 1952
131 Ibid., February 15, 1952
131 RC to Marie Rodell, September 18, 1952
131 RC, speech to Theta Sigma Phi, April 21, 1954
133 RC to Marie Rodell, January 30, 1951
134 RC to Marie Rodell, July 20, 1950

CHAPTER 12: THE EVOLUTION OF AN IDEA

151 Acceptance speech, American Association of University Women Achievement Award, June 22, 1956
151 Houghton Mifflin sales conference, May 1955
152 Ibid.
152 Footnote: RC to Marie Rodell, August 30, 1950
153 RC to PB, October 14, 1950
153 Application for Guggenheim Fellowship
154 RC to Marie Rodell, July 24, 1950
154 Ibid., September 10, 1950
154 RC to Fon Boardman, May 14, 1952
154 *Reader's Digest*, August 1953
156 Bob Hines to PB, July 10, 1951
156 Houghton Mifflin sales conference, May 1955
156 RC to Fon Boardman, May 14, 1952
157 RC to PB, April 26, 1952
157 Ibid., July 6, 1952
157 Audubon Society lecture, December 13, 1954
157 RC to PB, October 1, 1952
158 Ibid., March 3, 1953
158 Ibid., March 11, 1953
158 Ibid., June 24, 1953
159 Gold Medal Award speech, January 1953
159 Audubon Society lecture, December 13, 1954
160 RC to Marie Rodell, August 28, 1953
160 Ibid., September 27, 1953
160 Ibid., September 30, 1953
160 RC to PB, October 13, 1953
161 RC to Dorothy Freeman, October 18, 1953
161 RC to Henry Beston, May 14, 1954
162n Mrs. Glenn H. Algire to PB, February 15, 1970
163 RC to PB, April 27, 1955

page
163 Houghton Mifflin sales conference, May 1955
163 Edwin Way Teale to RC, April 22, 1955

CHAPTER 14: SKY, A CHILD'S WORLD AND A DREAM

198 RC to Marie Rodell, November 29, 1955
198 "Something About the Sky," *Omnibus* television program, March 11, 1956
199 RC to the author, March 14, 1956
199 RC to Vincent Schaefer, October 14, 1956
200 RC: "Memo of Motion Picture Possibilities of *The Edge of the Sea*," November 29, 1956
200 RC to Curtis Bok, March 12, 1956
201 RC to PB, March 14, 1956
201 RC to Bob Hines, August 13, 1956
201 *The Sense of Wonder*, Harper and Brothers, 1965, pp. 42–45
202 Curtis Bok to RC, November 22, 1955
202 RC to Curtis Bok
203 Ibid., January 11, 1956
204 Curtis Bok to RC, January 24, 1956
204 Ibid., April 11, 1956
205 RC to Curtis and Nellie Lee Bok, May 1956
206 RC to Curtis Bok, July 12, 1956
206 Curtis Bok to RC, June 16, 1956
206 RC to Marie Rodell, August 29, 1956
207 RC to Dorothy and Stanley Freeman, August 5, 1956
208 Footnote: E. Newton Harvey to RC, August 16, 1956
209 RC to Dorothy and Stanley Freeman, October 7, 1956
210 RC to Curtis and Nellie Lee Bok, December 12, 1956
211 RC to Marie Rodell, October 4, 1956
212 RC to Dorothy Freeman, December 8, 1956
213 RC to PB, April 8, 1957
213 Ibid., May 31, 1957
214 RC to Dorothy Freeman, November 12, 1957
214 RC to Marie Rodell, October 26, 1957
215 Curtis Bok to RC, June 14, 1958

CHAPTER 16: THE GENESIS OF SILENT SPRING

228 RC to Dorothy Freeman, June 1958
228 RC, speech to Women's National Book Association, February 15, 1963
229 RC to Harold Lynch, *Reader's Digest*, July 15, 1945
230 *Wolson Bulletin*, March 1945
230 Gove Hambridge, *Harper's* Magazine, February 1945
230 *The New Yorker*, May 26, 1945

CHAPTER 17: MARSHALING THE EXPERTS

CHAPTER 18: THE END AND THE BEGINNING

page
258 RC to Marjorie Spock, December 30, 1959
258 Ibid., March 14, 1960
259 Ibid., June 19, 1959
259 Mrs. Thomas Duff to PB, February 24, 1969
260 RC to Dorothy Freeman, October 1959
260 Ibid., November 1959
262 RC to PB, March 16, 1960
263 RC to George C. Wallace, September 1, 1960
263 RC to Mrs. F. L. Larkin, June 1, 1960
263 RC to PB, September 27, 1960
264 RC to C. Girard Davidson, June 8, 1960
264 RC to Marie Rodell, April 23, 1959
264 RC to Whitney Blake, February 17, 1960
264 RC to Fon Boardman, March 14, 1961
265 RC to PB, December 27, 1960
266 RC to Marjorie Spock and Mary Richards, February 6, 1961
266 RC to PB, March 1961
266 RC to Dorothy Freeman, March 13, 1961
268 RC to PB, June 26, 1961
269 RC to Lois Crisler, August 19, 1961
269 RC to Dorothy Freeman (?), September (?) 1961
270 Ibid., January 1962
271 RC to Lois Crisler, January 23, 1962
271 RC to Dorothy Freeman, January 23, 1962

CHAPTER 20: THE STORM

294n New York *Times*, January 16, 1965
295 *Chemical and Engineering News*, July 2, 1962
295 Gordon Conklin in *American Agriculturalist*, January 1963
295 *County Agent and Vo-Ag Teacher*, November 1962
296 Paul Knight, "A Case Study in Environmental Contamination" (unpublished)
297 William J. Darby, M.D., in *Nutrition Reviews*, January 1963
297 Frederick T. Stare, M.D., in *Chemical and Engineering News*, October 1962
297 *Time*, September 28, 1962
298 *Croplife*, February 1963
299 Robert White-Stevens in "CBS Reports," "The Silent Spring of Rachel Carson," April 3, 1963
299 RC to Dorothy Freeman, June 1962
299 RC to Paul Knight, July 10, 1962
299 Charles Simmons to RC, June 18, 1962
300 RC, speech to the National Parks Association, October 2, 1962
301 RC, speech to National Council of Women of the United States
302 RC, speech to the Women's National Press Club, December 5, 1962

page
306   *Science*, May 24, 1963
306   RC in New York *Herald Tribune*, May 19, 1963

CHAPTER 21: THE CLOSING JOURNEY

308   RC, Statement before the Senate Committee on Environmental
        Hazards ("Ribicoff Committee"), July 4, 1963
310   RC, Statement before the Senate Committee on Commerce, Hear-
        ing on S.1250 and S.1251, June 6, 1963
310   Paul Knight to PB, October 12, 1970
310   *New York Times Book Review*, Christmas 1962
311   *Times Literary Supplement* (London), February 22, 1963
311   *The Observer* (London), February 17, 1963
312   *House of Lords Debates*, March 20, 1963, p. 1134
313   RC to Arthur H. Carhart, January 16, 1963
313   Clarence Cottam to RC, January 13, 1964
313   RC to Clarence Cottam, January 7, 1964
313   *The Daily Mail* (London), January 31, 1964
314   RC to Dorothy Freeman, March 2, 1963
314   RC to Lois Crisler, March 19, 1963
314   RC to George Crile, Jr., M.D., February 17, 1963
315   RC, acceptance of the Schweitzer Medal, Animal Welfare Insti-
        tute, January 7, 1963
316   Ann Cottrell Free in *Defenders of Wildlife News Bulletin*, May–
        July 1964
317   RC, speech at annual meeting of the New England Wildflower
        Preservation Society, January, 1963
318   Thomas Merton to RC, January 12, 1963
318   RC to Dorothy Freeman, April 1, 1963
319   "CBS Reports," "The Silent Spring of Rachel Carson"
319   Ibid., March 12, 1963
319   Ibid., March 19, 1963
320   Ibid., March 11, 1963
320   Ibid., December 12, 1962
320   Dorothy Freeman Rand to PB, November 18, 1970
321   RC to PB, October 1963
321   RC to Lois Crisler, September 24, 1958
322   Ibid., November 28, 1963
323   RC to Dorothy Freeman, January 1964
323   New York *Herald Tribune*, March 23, 1964
323   RC to Dorothy Freeman, March 1963
324   RC, speech to Theta Sigma Phi, April 21, 1954
326   RC to Dorothy Freeman, September 10, 1963
327   *The Sea Around Us*, p. 216
327   *The Edge of the Sea*, pp. 249–250

RACHEL CARSON BIBLIOGRAPHY

BOOKS BY RACHEL CARSON

Under the Sea-Wind

Simon and Schuster, New York, 1941
Buchergilde, Gutenberg, Switzerland, 1945
Oxford University Press, New York, 1952
Staples Press, London, 1952
Amiot-Dumont, Paris, 1952
Garden City Books, New York 1953
Uitgeverij Born, Assen, The Netherlands, 1953
J. H. Schultz Forlag, Copenhagen, 1953
Tidens förlag, Stockholm, 1953
Edizione Casini, Florence, 1954
New American Library, New York, 1955
New Asia Trading Company, Colombo, Ceylon, 1956
Albert Bonniers, Stockholm, 1963
Panther Books, London, 1966
Vuk Karadzic, Belgrade, Yugoslavia, 1966

The Sea Around Us

Oxford University Press, New York, 1951
Staples Press, London, 1952
Tidens förlag, Stockholm, 1952
Editions Stock, Paris, 1952
J. H. Schultz Forlag, Copenhagen, 1952

The Sea Around Us (cont.)
Editorial Atlante, Mexico City, 1952
H. Aschehoug and Company, Oslo, 1952
Edizioni Casini, Rome, 1952
Uitgeverij Born, Assen, The Netherlands, 1952
Bungai Shunju Shinsha, Tokyo, 1952
Biederstein Verlag, Munich, 1952
Biederstein Verlag, (Illustrated Edition), Munich, 1953
Tammi, Helsinki, 1953
Mal og Menning, Reykjavik, 1953
Technichka Kniga, Belgrade, Yugoslavia, 1953
Lipa, Koper, Yugoslavia, 1953
New American Library, New York, 1954
Tauchnitz Verlag, Stuttgart, 1954
Ikaros, Athens, 1954
Shumawa Publishing House, Rangoon, Burma, 1954
Udom Publishing Company, Bangkok, Thailand, 1954
New Asia Trading Company, Colombo, Ceylon, 1955
Penguin Books, London, 1956
N. Tversky and Company, Tel Aviv, 1956
Editora Nacional, São Paulo, 1956
Kuo Publishing Company, Taipei, Taiwan, 1956
Ulyu Moonhwa Sa, Seoul, Korea, 1956
Sahitya, Prevartaka Co-op Society, Madras, India, 1956
Franklin Publications, Lahore, West Pakistan, 1956
Harsha Printing and Publications, Puttur, Madras, 1957
Egyptian Ministry of Education, Cairo, 1957
Allied Publishers, New Delhi, India, 1958
Rajpal and Sons, Delhi, India, 1959
Franklin Publications, Tehran, Iran, 1959
Oxford University Press (Revised Edition), New York, 1961
Prisma, Stockholm, 1962
Editions Stock (Abridged for Africa and Indo-China), Paris, 1962
Wydawniczy, Warsaw, 1962
Em. Quirido Utgeverij, Amsterdam, 1963
Hayakawa Shabo, Tokyo, 1964
Current Books, Madras, India, 1965
Higginbothams, Tamil, India, 1966
Gon-Yaung Press, Rangoon, Burma, 1967
Panther Books, London, 1969
J. H. Schultz Forlag, Copenhagen, 1969
Guilio Einaudi Editore, Turin, 1971

The Sea Around Us
Junior Editions

Golden Press, New York, 1958
William Collins & Sons, London, 1959
Folket I Bild, Stockholm, 1959
Casa Editrice Giuseppe Principato, Milan, 1960
Cocorico, Paris, 1961
Forleget Fremad, Copenhagen, 1961
Zuid-Nederlandse, Antwerp, 1963
Editorial Novaro S.A., México D.F., 1966
Otto Maier Verlag, Ravensburg, Germany, 1968

The Edge of the Sea
with illustrations by Robert Hines

Houghton Mifflin Company, Boston, 1955
Staples Press, London, 1956
Amiot-Dumont, Paris, 1956
Biederstein Verlag, Munich, 1957
New American Library, New York, 1959
Cadmus Books, Eau Claire, Wisconsin, 1965
Panther Books, London, 1965
New American Library, New York, 1971

The Rocky Coast

from The Edge of the Sea, *with photographs by Charles Pratt and drawings by Robert Hines*
McCall Publishing Company, New York, 1971

The Sea

(the three sea books in one volume)
McGibbon and Kee, London, 1964
Panther Books, London, 1967
McGibbon and Kee, London, 1968

Silent Spring

Houghton Mifflin Company, Boston, 1962
Hamish Hamilton, Ltd., London, 1963
Penguin Books, London, 1963
Plon, Paris, 1963
Biederstein Verlag, Munich, 1963
Feltrinelli Editore, Milan, 1963
Gyldendalske Boghandel, Copenhagen, 1963
Tidens förlag, Stockholm, 1963
Tiden Norsk Forlag, Norway, 1963
Tammi, Helsinki, 1963
H. J. W. Becht's Uitgeversmaatschappij N. V., Amsterdam, 1963
Fawcett Publications, New York, 1964
Luis de Caralt, Barcelona, 1964
Companhia Melhoramentos, São Paulo, 1964
Shincho Sha, Tokyo, 1964
Bokforidget Prisma, Stockholm, 1965
Almenna Bokafelagid, Reykjavik, 1965
Tiden Norsk Forlag, Norway, 1966
Editorial Portico, Lisbon, 1966
Teva-Ubriuth, Petah Tikvah, Israel, 1966
Livre de Poche, Paris, 1967
Tammi [reprint], Helsinki, 1970
Drzavna Zalozba Slovenije, Ljubljana, Yugoslavia, 1971

The Sense of Wonder
with photographs by Charles Pratt and others

Harper and Row, New York, 1965
Harper and Row, New York, 1967

MAGAZINE ARTICLES BY RACHEL CARSON

"Undersea" in The Atlantic Monthly, September 1937
"How About Citizen Papers for the Starling?" in Nature Magazine, June–
July 1939
"The Bat Knew It First" in Collier's, November 18, 1944
"Ocean Wonderland" in Transatlantic, April 1945
"The Bat Knew It First" [Condensation] in Reader's Digest, August 1945
"The Great Red Tide Mystery" in Field and Stream, February 1948

"Lost Worlds: The Challenge of the Islands" in *The Wood Thrush*, May–June, 1949

"Birth of an Island" in *Yale Review*, September 1950

"Wealth from the Salt Seas" in *Science Digest*, October 1950

"The Shape of Ancient Seas" in *Nature Magazine*, May 1951

"The Sea" in "Profiles," *The New Yorker*, June 2, 9, 16, 1951

"Why Our Winters Are Getting Warmer" [Excerpt from *The Sea Around Us*] in *Popular Science*, November 1951

"The Edge of the Sea" [Excerpt from *Under the Sea-Wind*] in *Life*, April 14, 1952

The Edge of the Sea [Excerpt] in "Profiles," *The New Yorker*, August 20 and 27, 1955

"The Mystery of Life at the Seashore," [Condensation of *The Edge of the Sea*] in *Reader's Digest*, February 1956

"Help Your Child to Wonder" in *Woman's Home Companion*, July 1956

"Help Your Child to Wonder" [Condensation] in *Reader's Digest*, September 1956

"Our Ever-Changing Shore" in *Holiday*, July 1958

Silent Spring [Excerpts] in "Reporter at Large," *The New Yorker*, June 16, 23, 30, 1962

"Poisoned Waters Kill Our Fish and Wildlife" [Excerpt from *Silent Spring*] in *Audubon Magazine*, September 1962

Beyond the Dreams of the Borgias" [Excerpt from *Silent Spring*] in *National Parks Magazine*, October 1962

"Beetle Scare, Spray Planes and Dead Wildlife" [Excerpt from *Silent Spring*] in *Audubon Magazine*, November 1962

"Moving Tides" [Excerpt from *The Sea Around Us*] in *Motor Boating*, July 1963

"Rachel Carson Answers Her Critics" in *Audubon Magazine*, September 1963

"Miss Carson Goes to Congress" in *American Forests*, October 1963

INDEX